ISLAM
BELIEFS AND TEACHINGS

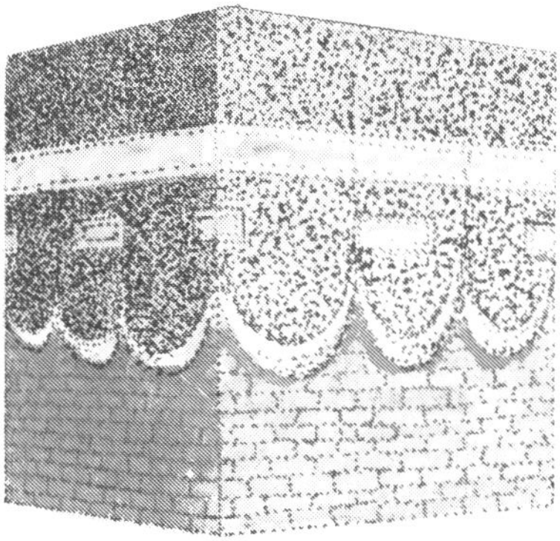

Ghulam Sarwar

The Muslim Educational Trust

1st Edition, October 1980. (10,000)
2nd Edition, August 1982. (12,000)
3rd Edition, December 1984. (20,000)

ISBN 0-907261-03-5

Published by
The Muslim Educational Trust
130 Stroud Green Road
London N4 3RZ, UK
Tel. 01-272 8502

British Library Cataloguing in Publication Data :
Sarwar, Ghulam
Islam : beliefs and teachings — 3rd Ed.
1. Islam
I. Title
297 BP161.2

ISBN 0-907261-03-5

Printed and bound in Great Britain by
Edwin Packer & Johnson Ltd.
Nottingham.

Contents

بِسْمِ اللّٰهِ الرَّحْمٰنِ الرَّحِيْمِ

Foreword

THE *Muslim Educational Trust* from its inception in 1966 has been striving for the Islamic education of the young generation of Muslims in Britain. The preservation of their religious and moral heritage is important as well as complex. To impart Islamic education to the children and to enable them to grow as Muslims in this society offers a great challenge to the British Muslims. A very important aspect of the problem is the need for suitable reading material. It gives me pleasure to say that the book *Islam : Beliefs and Teachings* published by the Trust goes a long way to fulfil this need.

The practical experience of the Trust in the field of Islamic education of Muslim children over many years, has led the Director of the Trust to produce this book. He is himself a seasoned educationist with a long personal experience of teaching. There are quite a few books about the introduction of Islam in western society, but the author of this book laboured hard to make it unique. He has used language which is simple and a style which is appealing to young minds. Starting from the fundamentals of the faith and practice of the Islamic religion, the book projects the key aspects of the life of Muḥammad, the prophet of Islam (may Peace and Blessings of Allah be upon him). There are short and simple Quranic stories of some famous prophets, short sketches of the rightly guided Caliphs, and three great Muslim women. Important information about Islamic morals, festivals and Muslim Ummah included. All the necessary facts about the religion and the followers of Islam have been laid down in small units.

The author has narrated the facts in such a way that there is a moral lesson for the young readers in each unit and through every lesson he motivates the readers to imbibe the spirit of Islam and transform it into practical living.

I hope that this book will be useful for all those who are interested and involved in Islamic education — children, teachers and parents. I thank Allah Almighty who enabled the Muslim Educational Trust to publish this book.

10 *Ramaḍān*, 1400 AH
22 July, 1980 CE

Ḥabībur Raḥmān
CHAIRMAN

بِسْمِ اللّٰهِ الرَّحْمٰنِ الرَّحِيْمِ

Author's preface to the 1st edition

PRAISE be to Allah, the Almighty who by His infinite mercy enabled me to write a much needed book on Islam.

For a long time, I felt the need for a standard text book on Islam suitable for use in secondary schools by the teachers, pupils and parents. I have gone through almost all the available material so far published in English for children. It appeared to me that an attempt should be made to incorporate major aspects of Islam in one book.

The outcome is *Islam : Beliefs and Teachings*. I do not claim it to be the best, but it is the product of very sincere and laborious efforts. How far I have succeeded in my attempt is for the readers to judge.

Books do provide a basis for education and it is the teachers who make them really useful and meaningful. Books on their own can do no miracle for young people unless they are properly geared to use them. I hope the Islamic teachers will remain conscious of this.

Islam : Beliefs and Teachings includes most of the contents of the syllabus which has been published recently by the Muslim Educational Trust. Although my main aim has been to produce a book for eleven plus school pupils, I hope it would benefit adults also. I have included a select bibliography of the sources which I have consulted and benefited from. I am responsible for any mistakes and I would welcome any suggestions for improvements to the book.

I am greatly indebted to *Mr David Browne*, a former school teacher and now a journalist and script writer, who has edited the draft and made very useful improvements in its language and style.

I am also grateful to *Maulāna Ḥabībur Raḥmān*, Chairman of the Muslim Educational Trust, for writing the foreword and going through the manuscript and making useful suggestions. I also thank *Dr G. M. Khan, Sayyid Ḥasan Muṭahar, Maulāna Ṣuhaib Ḥasan, Mr S.A. Ṣiddīqī* and *Mr Sulṭānul Ḥasan Fārūqī* for their suggestions and comments. Brother *Helāluddīn* and *Mr Abul Ḥusain* deserve my thanks for neatly typing the manuscript.

I am glad to mention my daughters *Parveen, Yasmeen* and *Nasreen* who are all at junior school yet took great interest in reading my drafts and helped me simplify many difficult expressions.

I will deem my efforts well rewarded if it inspires the young people to understand and practise Islam in a non-Muslim society.

May Allah accept my humble effort and make it a source of my salvation in the Hereafter. Āmīn.

13 *Ramaḍān*, 1400 AH
25 July, 1980 CE

Ghulam Sarwar

بِسْمِ اللهِ الرَّحْمٰنِ الرَّحِيْمِ

Author's preface to the 2nd edition

ALḤAMDU *Lillāh* (Praise be to Allah), the first edition of my book *Islam : Beliefs and Teachings* was sold out within *fifteen months* of its publication. I feel humbled by the mercy of Allah. I must thank the teachers, parents and pupils for their quick acceptance and appreciation.

Orders have been steadily pouring in, since the stock ran out in January, 1982. A quick reprint might have been the answer. But, I wanted to make some additions and corrections. The layout also needed improvements. So I opted for a revised second edition.

In this edition, I have included *Ṣalātul Witr, Ṣalātul Jum'ah, Ṣalātul Janāzah*, some *Du'ā'* and eleven *Sūrahs* of the *Qur'ān*. All other topics have been thoroughly revised. Suggestions on how to use the book have been added at the end of the book for the benefit of teachers and parents. There are also exercises for class room practice and home work at the end of each chapter. Some of the exercises in the later part of the book will require the use of extra material, the list of which can be found in the select bibliography. These improvements will, I hope make the book more useful.

I express my deep gratitude to those brothers and sisters who have been kind enough to suggest improvements and point out some mistakes. I must express frankly that I was unable to accept suggestions which were without supporting authentic references. By the same token, I have not included different opinions as I thought it might confuse young people for whom the book is mainly intended. When they are mature enough, they will be able to discuss different sources and make their own conclusions, but at this stage, my objective is to provide a simple, uncomplicated foundation.

I am grateful to Brother *Musṭafā Aksay* for drawing most of the illustrations.

I hope and pray that this second revised edition of the book will continue to receive support from the teachers, parents and pupils. Finally, I beg to my Lord, the Almighty to accept my humble effort and make it a source of my salvation in *Ākhirah*.

Whatever we have is from Allah.

"And my success in my task can only come from Allah. In Him I trust and unto Him I turn" (11:88).

London,
Ramaḍān, 1402 AH
July, 1982 CE

Ghulam Sarwar

Transliteration

Correct pronunciation of Arabic words is very important. Care and attention are needed in training young people to pronounce Arabic correctly.

Transliteration marks have been shown below on this page as a guide to correct pronunciation. These marks help to show how the words should sound. But it is not possible to show on a printed page exactly how to pronounce words.

For example, the word *Allāh* cannot be pronounced correctly unless the two *Ls* are sounded distinctly, and the last *A* is a long sound. The name *Muḥammad* (pbuh) should be pronounced with a glottal sound of *H* rather than the normal *H* sound.

It is better to listen to an Arabic-speaking person, or someone who has learned how to say Arabic words correctly. A tape-recording or record can help also.

Arabic letter	*Transliteration sign*	*Example*	*Arabic letter*	*Transliteration sign*	*Example*
ء	'	Malā'ikah	ط	ṭ	Lūṭ
ـَا ا	ā	Dāwūd	ظ	ẓ	Ẓuhr
ـُو و	ū	Dāwūd	ع	'	'Īsā
ـِي ي	ī	Khadījah	غ	gh	Maghrib
ب	b	Bilāl	ف	f	Fāṭimah
ت	t	Tirmidhī	ق	q	Fārūq
ث	th	'Uthmān	ك	k	Mikā'īl
ج	J	Jannah	ل	l	Allāh
ح	ḥ	Muḥammad	م	m	Mūsā
خ	kh	Khalīfah	ن	n	Nūḥ
د	d	Dāwūd	و	w	Ṣawm
ذ	dh	Tirmidhī	ه ة	h	Ibrāhīm
ر	r	Raḥmān	ة (silent)	h	Ṣalāh
ز	z	Zakāh	ي	y	Yāsīn
س	s	'Īsā	ـَوْ	aw	Yawmuddīn
ش	sh	Shahādah	ـَيْ	ai	Sulaimān
ص	ṣ	Ṣawm	ـِيّ	iyy	Zakariyyā
ض	ḍ	Ramaḍān	ـَوّ	aww	Awwāl

* We have avoided the transliteration of the words *Allah* and *Islam* as they occur too frequently in the book. In both the words *a* should be prolonged a bit to give the right pronunciation.

Abbreviations

pbuh stands for peace be upon him

RA stands for Raḍiyallāhu 'Anhu or 'Anhā (in singular) 'anhum or 'anhunna (plural)

Bin means son of *('Alī bin Abū Ṭālib)*

Bint means daughter of *(Khadījah bint Khuwailid)*

AH stands for After Hijrah

CE stands for Christian Era

Formula to change *AH* to *CE*

$$CE = \frac{32}{33}(AH) + 622$$

Example : 256 *AH* $= \frac{32}{33}(256) + 622 = 870$ (approx.)

Formula to change *CE* to *AH*

$$\mathrm{AH} = \frac{33}{32}(CE - 622)$$

Example : 870 *CE* $= \frac{33}{32}(870 - 622)$

$$= \frac{33}{32}\,248 = 256\ AH \text{ (approx.)}$$

Note : The Quranic quotations and references have been followed by the number of the *Sūrah* (Chapter) and then the number of the verse. Example : (2:177) means second *Sūrah*, verse no. 177.

1
Introduction and Basic Beliefs

In the name of Allah, the most Merciful, the most Kind.

Islam: Introduction

ISLAM is a complete way of life. It is the guidance provided by Allah, the Creator of the Universe, for all mankind. It covers all the things people do in their lifetime. Islam tells us the purpose of our creation, our final destiny and our place among other creatures. It shows us the best way to conduct our private, social, political, economic, moral and spiritual affairs of life.

Islam is an Arabic word which means submission and obedience. Submission is acceptance of Allah's commands. Allah, another Arabic word, is the proper name of God. Muslims should use the word Allah rather than the word God. Obedience means putting Allah's commands into practice. Submission and obedience to Allah bring peace. That is why Islam also means peace. A person who accepts the Islamic way of life and acts upon it is a Muslim.

Islam is the way of peace and harmony. If we look around, we see that everything including the sun, the moon and the stars, the high hills and the mighty oceans are obeying a Law — *the Law of Allah*. We find no disorder or chaos in them. A superb harmony and perfect order is evident in the system of Nature. The sun rises in the East and sets in the West and there has been no change to this rule. The moon and the stars shine at night. Day passes and night comes, so the process goes on. Flowers blossom and the trees have green leaves in the spring.

Everything has a set course and nothing can violate it. Have we ever noticed any violation of the Law of Allah by these objects of Nature? No, of course not. Why? Simply because they are made to obey Allah. They have no choice but to obey. This is why we find eternal peace in the system of Nature. But, in the case of human beings, it is different. Allah has given us the knowledge and will to choose between *right* and *wrong*. Not only this, He has also sent messengers and books for our guidance.

Yet, He does not force us to obey Him. He has given us the will to either obey or disobey Him. Why is this so? It is because He wants to test us. After this test there will be a day of reward and punishment. This is the *Day of Judgment*. Those of us who have passed the test will be rewarded with permanent happiness and peace in *Paradise* and those who have failed will suffer a terrible punishment in *Hell*. We can get this reward and escape punishment by obeying and worshipping Allah.

We already know that there is peace and harmony among other objects of Nature, because those things never disobey Allah. So, if we follow the guidance given to us through prophets and messengers, we are sure to have peace in the world we live in.

All human beings, by their very nature, like good things and dislike bad ones. For instance, everyone of us approves and likes truthfulness and hates falsehood. Even a liar does not like to be called a liar. Why? Because telling lies is a bad thing. In the same way, helping others, showing kindness, politeness, respect for parents and teachers, honesty and all other forms of good conduct are always liked and appreciated; but rudeness, cruelty, falsehood, hurting someone, disobedience to parents and teachers, using bad names and other bad conduct are despised and disliked by everyone. So, we can say that human nature likes the *Right* and dislikes the *Wrong*. Right is *Ma'rūf* and wrong is *Munkar* in the language of the *Qur'ān*.

Human nature also loves peace and hates disorder. Peace is the result of obedience to Allah's Law and disorder is the outcome of disobedience. Islam establishes this peace which is part of man's nature and hence, Islam is called the *Religion of Nature* which in Arabic is *Dīnul Fiṭrah*.

In order to achieve peace in society, Islam urges Muslims to work together towards what is right and away from what is evil. This

Innad dīna 'Indal lāhil Islām
"Surely, the way of life acceptable to Allah is Islam." (3:19).

united effort to root out evil and establish the truth is called *Jihād* which means to try one's utmost to see *Truth* prevail and *Falsehood* vanish from the society. The aim of *Jihād* is to achieve the pleasure of Allah. You will learn more about *Jihād* later in this book.

Purpose of Human Creation

Allah, the Almighty, created human beings to do his bidding and to obey his commands. Allah says in the *Qur'ān* :

"I have not created Jinn and mankind (for any other purpose) except to worship me" (51:56).

'Worship' in this verse means total obedience to Allah's commands. The Quranic word for worship is *'Ibādah*. Everything we do comes under *'Ibādah*, if we do them for Allah's sake. Our purpose in life is to please Allah through *'Ibādah*.

'Ibādah is the way to reach success and happiness in the life after death.

'Mohammedanism' is a misnomer

Islam is sometimes incorrectly called 'Mohammedanism' and the Muslims as 'Mohammedans'. Other religions have been named after their founder or after the community in which the religion prospered. For example, *Christianity* has been named after *Christ*, *Buddhism* after *Buddha* and *Judaism* after the tribe of *Judah*. But Islam has not been named after Muḥammad *(peace be upon him)*. It is the name of Allah's Guidance for mankind revealed through all the prophets, the last of whom was Muḥammad *(pbuh)*. So, it is wrong to call Islam 'Mohammedanism' and Muslims 'Mohammedans'.

Islam and *Muslim* are the words of the *Qur'ān*. The *Qur'ān* says, *"Surely, the way of life acceptable to Allah is Islam." (3:19). "He named you Muslims before and in this" (22:78)*. The message of all the prophets and messengers from Ādam *(peace be upon him)* down to Muḥammad *(pbuh)* is the same. They asked people to obey Allah and none other. This message, sent through prophets was completed at the time of Muḥammad *(pbuh)* who was the last of the chain of prophethood. This completion is mentioned in the *Qur'ān* : *"This day I have perfected your religion for you, completed my favour upon you and have chosen for you Islam as your way of life". (5:3).*

Exercise : 1

1st Form

1. Answer the following :
   a. What is *Islam?*
   b. What does *Islam* show us?
   c. Why does *Islam* mean peace?
   c. Why does *Allah* not force us to obey Him?
2. Fill in the blanks :
   Allah says in the ________, "I have not ________ *jinn* and ________ (for any other purpose) but to ________ me." (51:56).
3. Write the meanings of :
   a. *Islam*, b. *'Ibādah*, c. *Ma'ruf*, d. *Munkar*.

2nd and 3rd Forms

1. Read the first four paragraphs under the heading *Islam* and answer the following :
   a. What is *Islam?*
   b. Who is a *Muslim?*
   c. Why do we not notice any change in the *Law of Nature?*
   d. Why did *Allah* create us?
2. Read the paragraphs under the heading *Purpose of human creation* and write in your own words about *'Ibādah.*
3. Fill in the gaps :
   ________ and ________ are the words of the ________. The ________ says "________, the way of ________ acceptable to ________ is ________." (3:19). "He named ________ ________ before and in ________ (22:78). The ________ of all the ________ and ________ from ________ (peace be upon him) down to ________ (peace be upon him) is the ________.

4th, 5th and 6th Forms

1. Describe in your own words the *Islamic way of life.*
2. Explain what we should do to achieve peace in society.
3. Why is *Mohammedanism* a misnomer?
4. Explain in your words the purpose of the creation of mankind.

Basic Beliefs

The basic beliefs of Islam are :

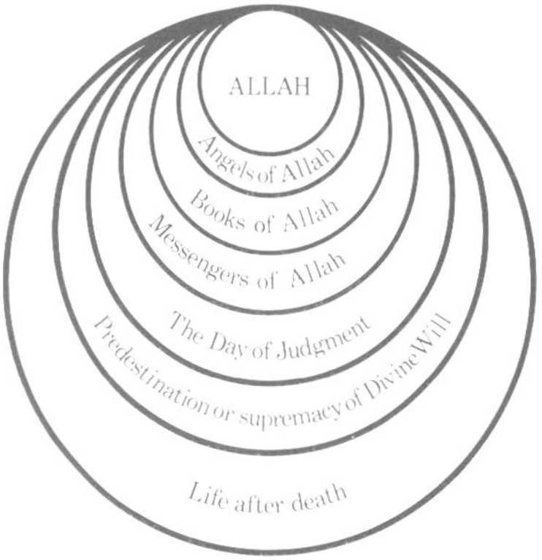

1 **Allah**
2 **Angels of Allah** *(Malā'ikah)*
3 **Books of Allah** *(Kutubullāh)*
4 **Messengers of Allah** *(Rusulullāh)*
5 **The Day of Judgment** *(Yawmuddīn)*
6 **Predestination or supremacy of Divine Will** *(Al-Qadr)*
7 **Life after death** *(Ākhirah)*

These beliefs have been stated precisely in **Al-Īmānul Mufaṣṣal**, the Faith in detail :

اٰمَنْتُ بِاللّٰهِ وَمَلٰٓئِكَتِهٖ وَكُتُبِهٖ وَرُسُلِهٖ وَالْيَوْمِ الْاٰخِرِ وَالْقَدْرِ
خَيْرِهٖ وَشَرِّهٖ مِنَ اللّٰهِ تَعَالٰى وَالْبَعْثِ بَعْدَ الْمَوْتِ ط

"Āmantu Billāhi, wa Malā'ikatihī, wa Kutubihī, wa Rusulihī, wal Yawmil Akhiri, wal Qadri, Khairihī wa Sharrihī minal Lahi Ta'ālā, wal Ba'thi Ba'dal Mawt."

This means :

"I believe in Allah, in His angels, in His books, in His messengers, in the Last Day *(Day of Judgment)* and in the fact that everything good or bad is decided by Allah, the Almighty, and in the Life after Death".

The seven beliefs can be grouped into three :

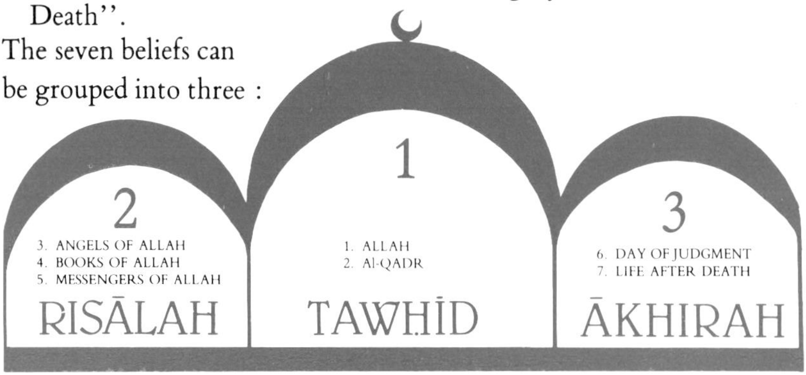

Tawḥīd (oneness of Allah)
Risālah (prophethood)
Ākhirah (life after death)

Tawḥīd, Risālah and *Ākhirah* summarise the whole of the Islamic system of life. So, we must understand them.

Tawḥīd

Allāh

ALLAH

Tawḥīd means the oneness of Allah. It is the main part of *Īmān* (Faith) and is beautifully expressed in the *Sūratul-Ikhlāṣ* of the *Qur'ān* :

"Say, He is Allah, the One. Allah is Eternal and Absolute. None is born of Him, nor is He born. And there is none like Him." (Sūrah 112).

Tawḥīd is the most important Islamic belief. It implies that everything on this earth is from the One and Only Creator, Allah, who is also the Sustainer of the universe and the Sole Source of its Guidance.

Tawḥīd is the belief in Allah with all His powers. Allah is All-knowing, All-wise and All-powerful. He is the Merciful and the Kind. He is with us all the time. He sees us, but we do not see Him. He is, was and always will be. He is the First and the Last. He has no partner or son. He gives us life and takes it away. We must return to Him after death.

The first duty of a Muslim is to declare his faith that "there is no god but Allah; Muḥammad is Allah's messenger". To make this declaration of faith a person must say in words and believe in his heart - *Lā ilāha illal Lāhu Muḥammadur rasūlullāh* - (there is no god but Allah; Muḥammad is Allah's messenger). The saying of these Arabic words is called *Ash-Shahādah* (Declaration of Faith). There are two parts of this declaration : (1) *Lā ilāha illal Lāh*, (2) *Muḥammadur Rasūlullāh.*

The first part of the declaration of faith is : *Lā ilāha illal Lāh*. It has two aspects : **i Negative ii Positive**. *Lā ilāha* is the negative aspect, while *Illal Lāh* is the positive one.

A believer must first cleanse his heart of any other god or any other object of worship, and only then can the faith in the Oneness of Allah take root in his heart.

Let us try to understand it with an example. Suppose we have a piece of land full of weeds and bushes where we want to produce wheat. Now, if we sow very good wheat seeds in the land without first cleaning it fully, we cannot hope to get a wheat crop out of the weeds and bushes. So, what must we do? We must cultivate the land, clear the weeds and bushes, prepare the soil before we sow the seeds. This time, we can expect good crops.

Let us compare the land with our heart. If our heart is full of belief in false gods, we cannot expect *Tawḥīd* to take root in our heart. So we must cleanse our heart of any other god or object of worship and only then will *Tawḥīd* take root in our heart and the light of faith will flow out of it.

Tawḥīd shapes and regulates the entire course of our life. This is why we must understand the meaning of *Tawḥīd*.

The vast and majestic universe with its flawless system clearly indicates that there is one Creator and one Supreme Controller.

When we think about the unique system and perfect order of the universe, we find there is no conflict. The sun, the moon, and the galaxy obey the same supreme Authority. The whole universe obeys the Laws of this Supreme Power. There is complete co-operation and harmony in the system. Everything is nicely set in its place. No improvement can be suggested and no flaw detected. This superb and perfect combination of order and beauty is clear proof of the presence of an All-wise and All-powerful Creator and Regulator.

Had there been more than one Creator and Controller of the planets, for example, there would have been conflict and chaos. We notice no such disorder in the universe. The efficient running of a school, the steering of a car or a ship, calls for one headmaster, one driver and one captain. No single institution can be run without problems and conflict with more than one leader, just as no vehicle can be driven by more than one person at the same time.

The universe, made up of many planets and stars is a unit. All its components have a common origin, a common purpose, because the universe was deliberately created by one Absolute Power. Everything in the universe works in harmony and co-operation, like various parts of the human body. The limbs of the human body seem to have different functions, but they all serve the same purpose - keeping the body fit and functioning properly.

Effect of Tawḥīd on Human Life

The belief in *Lā ilāha illal Lāh* or *Tawḥīd* has far-reaching effect on our life :

a A believer in *Tawḥīd* surrenders himself completely to the will of Allah and becomes His true servant and subject. Allah has created all that is in the earth and the heavens for the service of mankind. When a person surrenders himself to Allah's commands, he gains control over all other creations of the universe.

The *Qur'ān* confirms this when it says, *"Have you not seen how Allah has made all that is in the earth subservient to you?"* (22:65). *"See you not, how Allah has made serviceable unto you, whatever is in the sky and whatever is in the earth and has made His bounties flow to you in exceeding measure (both) seen and unseen" (31:20).*

These two verses clearly indicate that Allah has created everything on the earth and in the heavens for the service and comfort of humans. We can hope to get the services from other objects and creatures only when we believe and practise *Tawḥīd*. This means we must be totally obedient to Allah.

b It produces in the believer a high degree of self-respect and confidence. He knows that he depends on none but Allah for the fulfilment of His needs. He firmly believes that Allah alone has the power of providing all his requirements and no-one else has any power to do good or harm to him.

When can a believer be confident and develop self respect? He can be so only when he feels that he depends on none but his Creator for the fulfilment of his needs.

c This belief makes a believer humble and modest. He is never arrogant or haughty. He is fully aware that everything on earth belongs to Allah and he gains control over the rest of the creation only by being a subject of Allah. He also knows very well that whatever he has, is from Allah. So, there is no reason to be proud and boastful.

d Belief in *Tawḥīd* makes a believer dutiful and upright. The believer knows that he must carry out the commands of his Creator to succeed in this life and in the life hereafter. This awareness keeps him away from neglecting his duties and from other sins.

e It makes a believer contented. He does not become worried because he knows that Allah will take care of all his needs if he is truly obedient.

f It makes a person brave and courageous. It removes from his mind the fear of death or concern for safety. The believer knows that it is Allah who will cause death at the appointed time and none but He can harm the believer's safety. So, if he obeys Allah, he has nothing to worry about. He goes on doing his duty without any fear.

g A believer in *Tawḥīd* consciously feels himself to be part of the whole universe. He is the best of all creations of Allah - the Powerful Master of the whole universe. This belief enlarges his horizon and his outlook expands.

h It produces in a believer strong determination, patience and perseverance. The believer becomes single minded and dedicates himself to seeking the pleasure of his Creator.

Think of a boat. It has a rudder which guides the boat's movement : with the rudder under control, the boat moves forward proudly over the waves, but if the boat is not controlled by the rudder, it is tossed by every wave in the river or the sea.

So it is with a believer. When he surrenders himself to Allah alone, he can go forward in the affairs of life without fear. But if he does not obey Allah, he has to obey false gods like the fear of losing his job, fear of danger, fear of hunger and the like. When someone believes in Allah alone, his life is not ruled by such fears.

i The most important effect of the belief in — *Lā ilāha illal Lāh* — is that it makes a person obey and observe Allah's commands. A believer in *Tawḥīd* is sure that Allah knows and sees everything and he cannot escape Allah's ever-watchful eye for a single moment. In fact, Allah is nearer to him than his own jugular vein. So, a true believer does not commit a sin either secretly or in the darkness of night because he has the firm conviction that Allah sees everything all the time.

A believer in *Tawḥīd* seeks the pleasure of Allah by making his belief and action go together. Belief without practice has no place in Islam.

We, Muslims are the believers in *Tawḥīd*. We are Allah's servants and subjects. Our faith and practice must be the same.

Al-Qadr

We, believe that Allah has created the universe and He is its Absolute Controller and Regulator. Everything in the universe has a pre-determined set course which we call *Al-Qadr*. Nothing can happen without the will and the knowledge of Allah. Allah knows the present, the past and the future of every creature. The destiny of every creature is already known to Allah. (25:2, 33:38).

But this does not mean that man has no freedom of will. We know that we are the *Khalīfah* (agent) of Allah on this earth. We also know that Allah does not force us to do anything. It is up to us to obey or disobey Him. Whether we will obey or disobey is known to Him. But, the fact that Allah knows what we are going to do, does not affect our freedom of will. Man does not know what his destiny is. He has the free will to choose the course he will take.

We will be judged on the basis of our intentions on the *Day of Judgment*. If we follow Allah's guidance, we will be rewarded and if not, we will be punished.

By believing in *Al-Qadr* we testify that Allah is the Absolute Controller of all the affairs of His universe. It is He who decides what is good and what is bad.

Allah knows already the fate of all human beings. This does not mean that we can do whatever we like as if it made no difference to what happens to us. We must pay attention to the Divine Guidance provided by Allah the Almighty. He gave human beings free will. We can choose between right and wrong. We will be judged on our actions on earth on the day of *Ākhirah*.

Allah knows everything. He is the only one who can judge his subjects. He asks mankind to follow the Divine Guidance he has provided for man's fulfilment in the life after death. But it is entirely on the mercy of Allah who will be rewarded and who will not.

Allah knows what will happen to each one, but we do not know. This fore-knowledge of Allah is his divine quality — Ṣifat.

Sometimes things happen that do not seem to make sense to us. Why do earthquakes happen? Why do people starve in some countries around the world? Why do people suffer? What makes one man good and another a thief?

We do not know all the answers to these problems. We have only a little knowledge of the universe, but Allah knows everything. We would be wasting time if we blame Allah for the problems or the bad things that happen, simply because we do not seem to see the reasons behind them.

We should have firm faith in the wisdom of our All-knowing Creator and help people in distress as much as we can.

We are unable to understand and interpret many of Allah's actions. It is meaningless to argue that human beings act without freedom, and that we are forced to act the way we do. We decide for ourselves what we will do, and what we will not, and we are responsible for our own actions. This freedom of action does not clash with the fore-knowledge of Allah.

Exercise : 2

1st Form

1. Copy the diagram of the basic beliefs in your writing book.
2. Write the meaning of :
   a. *malā'ikah,* b. *Kutubullāh,* c. *Risālah,* d. *Ākhirah.*
3. Write the meaning of *Sūratul Ikhlāṣ*.
4. Answer the following :
   a. What does the word *Tawḥīd* mean?
   b. Who is the Controller of the Universe?
   c. Who is our Sustainer?
   d. Where is *Allah?*

2nd and 3rd Forms

1. Fill in the blanks :
   I believe in __________, in His __________, in His __________, in His __________ , in the _____ _____*(Day of Judgment)* and in the fact that everything__________or __________ is decided by __________ , the Almighty, and in the ______ ______ ______.
2. Write ten sentences about *Tawḥīd.*
3. Draw the design of *Allah* as given in the book.
4. Write the Arabic words for :
   a. Faith, b. Prophethood, c. The One, d. declaration of faith, e. angels, f. books of Allah, g. Oneness of Allah.

4th, 5th and 6th Forms

1. Group the seven basic beliefs into three basic concepts and draw your own diagram.
2. Explain the positive and negative aspect of *Tawḥīd.*
3. Explain in your words *Al-Qadr.*

Risālah (Prophethood)

Risālah is the channel of communication between Allah and mankind. Allah, in His infinite mercy has provided man with guidance to follow the right course and so make this world a happy and peaceful place to live in. There will be a great reward in the life after death for those who follow this guidance.

Since the beginning of the Creation, Allah has sent His guidance for mankind through His selected people. These chosen people are called prophets or messengers. They asked the people of their time to obey and worship Allah alone. They taught, guided and trained the people to follow the way of Allah.

Prophets and messengers were human beings. We should never refer to them as the sons of Allah. Allah is one and He has no partner or son. It is a sin to say that Allah has a son or a partner.

The message of all the prophets and messengers is one and the same. As Allah is One, so is His message. This message is : *"Worship Allah and there is no god for you but He"*. In other words, all the prophets preached the message of :

LĀ ILĀHA ILLAL LĀH

(There is no god but Allah).

You may ask, why do we need guidance from Allah? The answer is simple; we human beings are weak and frail; we have no knowledge of the future and the knowledge we do have is limited. Also we are not perfect. You can guess that with so many weaknesses, we are unable to make any guidance for ourselves which can hold good for all times and all conditions. This is the reason why Allah has blessed us with guidance through prophets and messengers.

Not only this, Allah has also sent books of guidance through the prophets and messengers (2:213, 7 :52). The *Qur'ān* is the last book of Allah's guidance. We will learn about it later.

Allah sent prophets and messengers to every nation at different times (10:47, 13:7, 35:24). It was necessary to send prophets at different times to bring forgetful human beings back to the **right path** *(Ṣirātul-Mustaqīm).*

PROPHETS OF ALLAH

According to a saying of *Muḥammad* (pbuh) the number of prophets is one hundred and twenty four thousand. The *Qur'ān* mentions only the twenty-five most prominent by name :

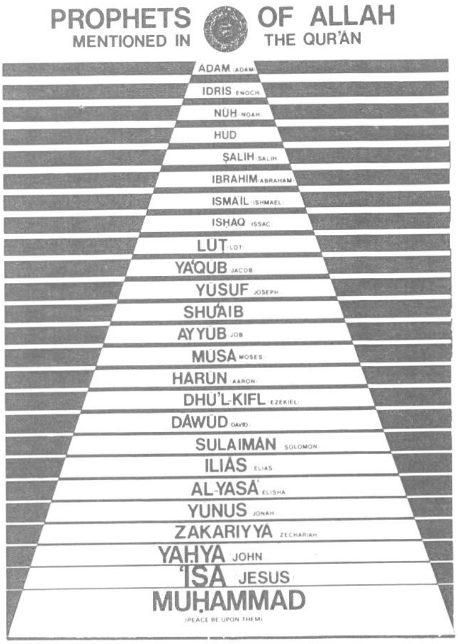

As Muslims, we must believe in all the prophets and messengers (2:285). Allah's guidance to mankind which began with *Ādam* (pbuh) was completed with *Muḥammad* (pbuh).

	Quranic name	*Biblical name*
1	Ādam	*Adam*
2	Idrīs	*Enoch*
3	Nūḥ	*Noah*
4	Hūd	—
5	Ṣāliḥ	*Salih*
6	Ibrāhīm	*Abraham*
7	Ismā'īl	*Ishmael*
8	Isḥāq	*Isaac*
9	Lūṭ	*Lot*
10	Ya'qūb	*Jacob*
11	Yūsuf	*Joseph*
12	Shu'aīb	—
13	Ayyūb	*Job*
14	Mūsā	*Moses*
15	Hārūn	*Aaron*
16	Dhū'l-kifl	*Ezekiel*
17	Dāwūd	*David*
18	Sulaimān	*Solomon*
19	Iliās	*Elias*
20	Al-Yasā'	*Elisha*
21	Yūnus	*Jonah*
22	Zakariyyā	*Zechariah*
23	Yaḥyā	*John*
24	'Īsā	*Jesus*
25	Muḥammad	—

Angels

We have already mentioned belief in Angels *(Malā'ikah)* in the *Īmān-ul-Mufaṣṣal*. Who are the angels? What do they do? Can we see them? How are they different from man?

Angels are a special creation of Allah. They have been created from divine light *(Nūr)* to perform specific functions. By comparison, *Ādam*, the first man was created from clay, and *Jinn* from fire. *'Iblīs*, the devil is from the *jinn*. Some people think *'Iblīs* was the leader of the angels. This is not true according to the *Qur'ān* (18:50).

Angels have been given the necessary qualities and powers to carry out their duties, but they do not have free will. They always obey Allah and can never disobey Him. Man, on the other hand, has been given free will and can choose between right and wrong; this is why man will have to face the test on the day of judgment.

Angels do what Allah commands them. They are the innocent servants of Allah's will. They help men in the use of free will. Man decides what to do and angels help him to carry out the decision.

The duty of Angels is to glorify and praise Allah. They never get tired. They are always ready to obey Allah. They do not need sleep, nor do they require the things a human being would need.

We cannot see the angels unless they appear in human form. Angel *Jibrā'īl* once appeared before a gathering of the companions of the Prophet in order to teach them about Islam. Angels can take any suitable form to do their duties.

There is a host of angels in the kingdom of Allah. Prominent among them are :

Jibrā'īl *(Gabriel)*
Mikā'īl *(Michael)*
'Izrā'īl *(Azrail)*
Isrāfīl *(Israfil)*

Jibrā'īl brought the revelation from Allah to the prophet Muḥammad *(pbuh)* and to all other prophets. *'Izrā'īl* — also called 'the angel of death' *(Malakul mawt)* — is responsible for ending our life. *Isrāfīl* will blow the trumpet at the time of the end of the world and on the day of judgment.

Some angels are busy recording all that we do. They are called the respected recorders *(Kirāman Kātibīn)*. Not a single word we say goes unrecorded. (50:18).

Allah maintains His kingdom in the most superb way, and angels are His most obedient and loyal servants. Angels will welcome in *Heaven* those of us who always obey Allah's commands and will throw the wrong-doer into *Hell*. (39:71-74).

The Books of Allah

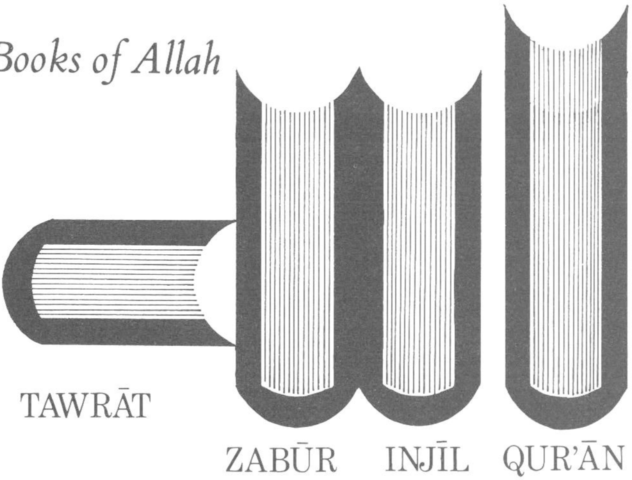

So far we have learned that we human beings are the servants of Allah and His agents on earth. But we need guidance to carry out our duties as Allah's agents. We are unable to guide ourselves, because we have many weaknesses within us and we are frail and short-sighted. Only Allah is above all these shortcomings and He alone has the power to give us guidance that is valid for all times and places. We know that Allah has not left us without guidance and that He has sent prophets and messengers to show us the right path in life. In addition to this, He also sent books of guidance through them.

Allah's favours and blessings are countless. He has provided us with all that we need. Just imagine how wonderfully He arranged our growth in the tender and affectionate care of our parents from birth to youth. We can also ask who provided us with food when we were in our mother's womb? Who filled our mother's breasts with milk to suckle as soon as we were born? It is Allah, the Merciful, of course.

Allah's greatest favour to mankind is His guidance contained in the books of revelation. The pure, perfect and most useful knowledge comes only from Allah, the Wisest and the Greatest. (2:146-147, 4:163, 53:1-6).

A Muslim believes in all the revealed books which are mentioned in the *Qur'ān*. They are : **Tawrāt** *(Torah)* of Mūsā (Moses), **Zabūr** *(Psalms)* of Dāwūd (David), **Injīl** *(Gospel)* of 'Īsā (Jesus) and the **Qur'ān** revealed to Muḥammad *(pbuh)*. The Qur'ān also mentions *Suḥuf-i-Ibrāhīm* (Scrolls of Abraham).

Of the divine books, only the *Qur'ān* exists in its original form, unchanged and unmixed. *Zabūr, Tawrāt*[1] and *Injīl*[2] are not available in their original language and form. Even their original texts do not exist. These books were compiled by their followers after many years of the death[3] of the Prophets to whom they were revealed. Their compilers have modified, changed and distorted Allah's words. They have mixed divine words with those of human beings.

The Bible which is a combination of the *Old Testament* and the *New Testament* has been translated into English from available Greek manuscripts. Any careful reader can easily find out the additions and alterations made to them.

The Bible, as it is available today, has many incorrect things in it[4]. Its authenticity and divinity are doubtful. It contains misleading and false stories about Prophets. The message of Allah sent through them was either lost or distorted through neglect and folly of their followers. As against this, the *Qur'ān* contains Allah's guidance for mankind in its original language, unchanged and undistorted. It restates in clear and unambiguous language the message of Allah which the followers of earlier Prophets have lost. The message of the *Qur'ān* is valid for all times and conditions.

Note :

1 *The Tawrāt* was revealed in Hebrew and the *Injīl*, most probably in the Aramaic (Syriac) language.

2 *The Bible* consists of : the *Old Testament* and the *New Testament. The Old Testament* includes five books of the *Pentateuch (Genesis, Exodus, Leviticus, Numbers* and *Deuteronomy)*, Book of *Ezra, Psalms* and others.

The New Testament includes four gospels : *Matthew, Mark, Luke* and *John*. The *Gospel of Barnabas* which appears to be the most authentic version of Prophet *'Īsā's* life is not included in it.

3 *The Injīl* (Gospel) has been compiled after the prophet *'Īsā* (Jesus) was taken up by Allah. According to Christians, *'Īsā* was crucified and died as a result. The *Qur'ān* refutes it and states that Jesus was taken up by Allah (4:157—158).

4 a *Prophet Nūḥ* (Noah), is described as drunk and naked in the book of *Genesis* (Ch. 9 verses 20-22).

b Falsehood attributed to *Prophet Ibrāhīm* (Abraham) (*Genesis*, Ch. 12 verses 9-21).

c Incest ascribed to *Lūṭ* (Lot) in *Genesis* (Ch. 19 verses 31-37).

d Falsehood attributed to *Isḥāq* (Isaac) in *Genesis* (Ch. 26 verses 7-11).

e A comparison of verses 16, 17 of Ch. 19 in *Gospel of Matthew* with the verses 17, 18 of Ch. 10 of the *Gospel of Mark* will show the method of distortion by individual compilers.

Source : The New English Bible, Oxford University Press, 1970.

Exercise : 3

1st Form

1. Fill in thc blanks :

   ______ was the ______ of communication ______ *Allah* and ______ . *Allah*, in His infinite ______ has provided ______ with ______ to follow the ______ course and so ______ this ______ a happy and ______ place to ______ in. There will be a ______ ______ in the life ______ ______ for those who ______ this ______.
2. Write the names of four great *angels.*
3. Draw the diagram of the *books of Allah* in your writing book.

2nd and 3rd Forms

1. Answer the following :
   a. What is *Risālah?*
   b. Who was the first *Prophet of Allah?*
   c. Who was the last *Prophet of Allah?*
   d. What is *Ṣiratul Mustaqīm?*
2. Write ten sentences about the *angels of Allah.*
3. Fill in the blanks :

   Allah's ______ and ______ are countless. He has ______ us with ______ that we ______ . Just ______ how wonderfully He ______ our growth in the ______ and ______ care of ______ parents from birth to ______. We can also ______ who ______ us with ______ when we ______ in our ______ womb?

4th, 5th and 6th Forms

1. Define *Risālah* and explain its significance.
2. Explain in your own words the status and duties of the *angels of Allah.*
3. Write an account of the need for *Revealed Books by Allah.*

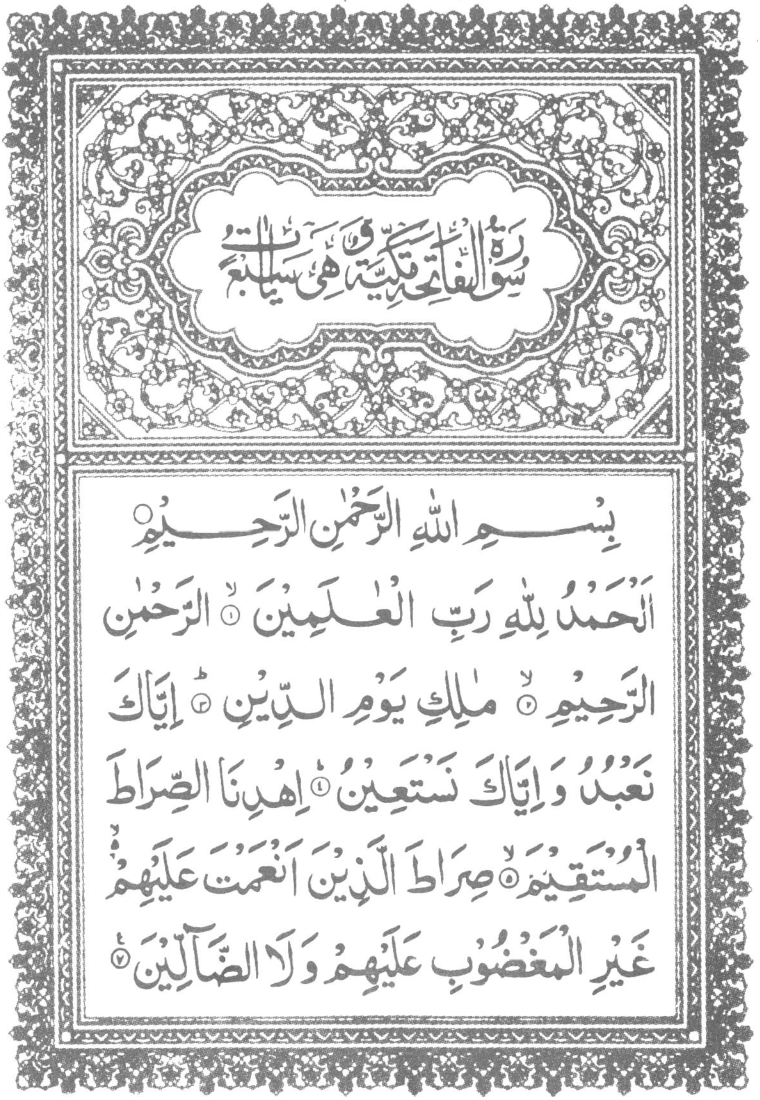

Sūrat ul-Fātiḥah

The Qur'ān

The *Qur'ān* is the complete book of guidance for mankind. It is the sacred book of the Muslims and the main source of Law in Islam. The whole of the *Qur'ān* is from Allah. Each word of it is a revealed word.

It was sent down to *Muḥammad* (pbuh) through the angel *Jibrā'īl*. The *Qur'ān* is in the *Arabic* language. It was revealed piecemeal and completed over a period of twenty three years.

No other book in the world can match the *Qur'ān* in respect of its recording and preservation. The astonishing fact about this book of Allah is that it has remained unchanged even to a dot over the last fourteen hundred years. The *Qur'ān* was recorded as soon as it was revealed under the personal supervision of *Prophet Muḥammad* (pbuh). The *Qur'ān* exists today in its original form unaltered and undistorted. It is a living miracle in the sense that it has survived so many centuries without suffering any change. The Quranic message goes beyond time and space. Every word of it — even the smallest particles and signs are intact in the hearts of thousands of Muslims who continue to memorise and recite it every day. No variation of text can be found in it. You can check this for yourself by listening to the recitation of Muslims from different parts of the world.

Allah the Almighty has Himself taken the responsibility of preserving the *Qur'ān* and He says, *"Surely, we have revealed this reminder (Dhikr) and Lo, We verily are its Guardian"* (15:9). This verse clearly mentions that Allah revealed the *Qur'ān* and He will protect it.

The *Qur'ān* is a living proof of the existence of Allah, the All-powerful. It is also a testimony of the validity of the Islamic way of life for all times. *Arabic*, the language of the *Qur'ān*, unlike the languages of other revealed books, is a living, dynamic and a very rich language. Millions of people all over the world speak and use *Arabic* in their daily life. This is a further testimony to the unchanging character of the *Qur'ān*.

The subject matter of the Qur'ān is man and his ultimate goal in life. Its teachings cover all areas of this life and the life after death. It contains principles, doctrines and directions for every sphere of human activity. The theme of the *Qur'ān* consists broadly of three fundamental beliefs — *Tawḥīd, Risālah* and *Ākhirah*. Tawḥīd is the basic theme of the *Qur'ān*. All the prophets and messengers of Allah called people towards Tawḥīd. The *Qur'ān* gives a picturesque description of the Paradise which will be awarded to the truly obedient servants of Allah. The severe punishment to be meted out to the evildoers has also been depicted vividly in the *Qur'ān*.

The *Qur'ān* urges people to follow its guidance and teachings. The success of human beings on this earth and in life after death depends on obedience to the Quranic teachings. We cannot perform our duties as the servants of Allah and His agents if we do not follow the *Qur'ān*. The *Qur'ān* urges us to work for the supremacy of Allah and for the removal of all evils.

The superb style of the *Qur'ān* has a tremendous effect on its readers. It totally changes the pattern of life of those who believe and practise its teachings. It leaves a soothing effect on the mind of the reader, even if he does not fully understand its meaning.

The *Qur'ān* has thirty parts *(Ajzā')* and *114* chapters *(Sūrahs)* and 6236 verses *(Āyāhs)*. Chapters revealed when the Prophet was living in *Makkah* are known as *Makkī* and those revealed in *Madīnah* are called *Madanī*.

The collection and compilation of the Qur'ān

Each and every word of the *Qur'ān* was recorded as soon as it was revealed by Allah to the prophet through angel *Jibrā'īl*. The Prophet's Secretary, *Zaid Bin Thābit*, used to record them exactly as the Prophet told him. He would read back to the Prophet what he had recorded.

Many of the early muslims memorised the *Qur'ān* immediately after the verses were revealed. Some of the famous *Ḥuffāẓ* (plural : persons who memorised the *Qur'ān*/singular : *Ḥāfiẓ)* were : *Mu'adh Ibn Jabal, 'Ubādah Ibn Ṣāmit, Abud Dardā', Abū Ayyūb* and *'Ubayy Ibn Ka'b* (may Allah be pleased with them).

Shortly after the death of the Prophet in *632 CE., 'Umar (RA)* suggested to *Khalīfah Abū Bakr (RA)* that the *Qur'ān* should be compiled in one volume. Up to then, the *Qur'ān* was written down in pieces in order as they were revealed. A committee was formed under *Zaid Bin Thābit* to gather the scattered material of the *Qur'ān* into one volume.

Great care was taken to compile the *Qur'ān* exactly as it had been recorded during the time of the Prophet *(pbuh)*. After careful checking and rechecking the work was completed. During the *Khilāfah* of *'Umar (RA)*, the copy was kept with *Ḥafṣah (RA)* one of the widows of the Prophet *(pbuh)*.

Later, many schools were established for the teaching of the *Qur'ān* throughout the muslim territories. During *'Umar's (RA)* time, one such school in *Damascus* had sixteen hundred pupils under *Abud Dardā' (RA)* one of the famous *Ḥuffāẓ*.

As the Islamic State expanded, people in various places recited the *Qur'ān* in their local dialect and there arose a possibility of confusion and misunderstanding. To avoid this, *Khalīfah 'Uthmān (RA)* ordered the preparation of one standard version of the *Qur'ān* to be written in the dialect of the tribe of the *Quraish*. The Prophet *Muḥammad* (pbuh) was from the *Quraish* tribe and it was felt that this was the right dialect for the recitation of the *Qur'ān. Zaid Bin Thābit (RA), 'Abdullāh Ibn Az-Zubair (RA), Sa'īd Ibnul 'Āṣ* and *'Abdur Raḥmān Bin Al-Ḥārith (RA)* were asked to prepare copies from the copy of *Ḥafṣah (RA)*.

Copies were prepared and they were checked with the original. Standard copies were then sent to different parts of the Islamic State. Not only were the copies sent, but a teacher was sent with them, to teach how to recite the *Qur'ān* properly and correctly.

This far-sighted action by *Khalīfah 'Uthmān (RA)* made the uniform recitation of the *Qur'ān* possible. Two original copies from *Khalīfah 'Uthmān's (RA)* time still exist today — one at *Topkapi* in Istanbul *(Turkey)* and the other at *Tashkent* (USSR). The National Library of *Karachi*, Pakistan has a photocopy of the *Tashkent* original.

The revelation of the *Qur'ān* began in *610 CE.* at *Ḥirā'*.

The first verses are :

سُورَةُ الْعَلَقِ

بِسْمِ اللَّهِ الرَّحْمَٰنِ الرَّحِيمِ ○

اقْرَأْ بِاسْمِ رَبِّكَ الَّذِي خَلَقَ ۝ خَلَقَ الْإِنسَانَ مِنْ عَلَقٍ ۝

اقْرَأْ وَرَبُّكَ الْأَكْرَمُ ۝ الَّذِي عَلَّمَ بِالْقَلَمِ ۝ عَلَّمَ الْإِنسَانَ مَا لَمْ يَعْلَمْ ۝

"Iqra'bi-ismi Rabbikal Ladhī Khalaq,
Khalaqal insāna min 'alaq
Iqra' wa rabbukal Akram
Alladhī 'allama bil Qalam
'Allamal Insāna mā lam Ya'lam"
which means :
"Read in the name of your Lord who created.

Created man from a clot of blood.
Read, your Lord is most Generous.
Who taught by the pen.
Taught man what he did not know.'' (96:1-5).

The *Qur'ān* was revealed over a period of *22 years 5 months and 14 days*.

The longest chapter *(sūrah)* of the *Qur'ān* is *Sūratul-Baqarah* (The Cow) with *286 verses* and the shortest chapter *(sūrah)* is *Sūratul-Kawthar* (Abundance) which has three verses.

The last verse of the *Qur'ān* which was revealed shortly before Prophet's *(pbuh)* death is :

الْيَوْمَ أَكْمَلْتُ لَكُمْ دِينَكُمْ وَأَتْمَمْتُ عَلَيْكُمْ
نِعْمَتِي وَرَضِيتُ لَكُمُ الْإِسْلَامَ دِينًا

Al yawma akmaltu lakum dīnakum
Wa atmamtu 'alaikum ni'matī wa raḍitu lakumul islāma dīnan.
which means :
"This day I have perfected your religion for you, completed my favour upon you and have chosen for you Islam as your way of life." (5:3).

Death

Death is a natural event for all living things. It comes to everyone of us. We all will die. The *Qur'ān* says :

"Everyone shall have to die." (3:185).

Death brings an end to our temporary life on this earth. It is an occasion of sorrow and grief for the loved ones of the deceased. In Islam, people mourn by reciting the *Qur'ān* and prayers for the dead.

Islam asks us to keep in mind that death can arrive at any time. Only Allah knows when his servants will die. Death puts an end to our human body, but it does not destroy our soul. The soul is taken away by the angel, *Malakul Mawt* ('Izrā'īl or Azrail) to Allah.

A person is sure to behave well and to do as Allah commands if he remembers death and life after death.

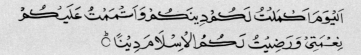

In Islam, a dead body is given a wash before it is buried. It is covered with white sheets and fragrance is spread all over the body. A funeral prayer is conducted before burial. This prayer is called *Janāzah*.

Ākhirah

We have already mentioned the three most important beliefs in Islam : *Tawḥīd* (oneness of Allah), *Risālah* (prophethood) and *Ākhirah* (life after death). Now we will look at : *Ākhirah*.

Belief in *Ākhirah* is very important and is vital for all Muslims. Our life on this earth is temporary and is meant to be a preparation for *Ākhirah* which is *never ending*. Life on this earth becomes meaningless if good actions are not rewarded and bad conduct punished. Regular attendance in school would be to no purpose without an examination after a period to decide the success of the pupils. In the same way, our life on earth is meaningless without a test after death on the Day of Judgment *(Yawmul Ākhirah* or *Yawmuddīn)* in the court of Justice of Almighty Allah.

To prepare ourselves for this day of test, we need to follow the guidance given through the prophets. Without life after death, there would have been no need for prophets and messengers.

There are people who do not care whether there is a life after death. Some even do not believe in it at all. These people will suffer terribly for their unbelief. A sensible person cannot possibly say there is no life after death. He can be doubtful but he would be always at a loss, if his doubt proves untrue.

So, the safe course to follow is to believe in all that the prophets and messengers told people to believe. Not to care about *Ākhirah* is a serious failing. We are certain that all human beings die, so it is quite reasonable to prepare for that eternal life which no doubt will follow death.

Doubts have been expressed by unbelievers about life after death. They cannot understand how Allah can raise men and women after death. But Allah can make human beings out of nothing. So it is not difficult for Him to raise them after death.

The *Qur'ān* says :

> *"Does man think that we shall not assemble his bones? Yes, surely, yes, we are able to restore the very shape of his fingers."* (75:3,4).

Life on this earth would be horrible if all people thought that there would be no life after death. There would be no restraint or control on what we do. Belief in *Ākhirah* has a tremendous influence on the life of a Muslim. He knows that Allah is watching all his actions and he will have to account for them on the Day of Judgment. His conduct and behaviour will therefore be responsible, controlled and careful. He will always try to do those things which Allah will favour and give up those actions which will incur His punishment.

A Muslim believes that he will be rewarded in the life after death for all his good actions. He will live in *Heaven*, a place of eternal happiness and peace.

Wrong-doers will be punished on the *Day of Judgment* and will be sent to *Hell*, a place of severe punishment and suffering.

To prepare for that day and to be rewarded by Allah the Merciful and the Kind, we need to do all that Allah demands of us and give up all bad habits and wrong actions. We can do this if we follow the guidance given to *Muḥammad* (pbuh) by Allah. This is the safest course for our success in the *Ākhirah*.

Exercise : 4

1st Form

1. Answer the following :
   a. What is the *Qur'ān?*
   b. How many parts are there in the *Qur'ān?*
   c. When were the first verses of the *Qur'ān* revealed?
   d. What does the *Qur'ān* say about death?
2. Fill in the blanks :
   Belief in __________ is very important and is __________ for all __________ . Our life on __________ is __________ is __________ and is __________ to be a __________ for __________ which is never __________ .
3. Write the names of three early *Ḥuffāẓ* of the *Qur'ān.*

2nd and 3rd Forms

1. Write ten sentences about the *Qur'ān.*
2. Answer the following :
   a. Who revealed the *Qur'ān?*
   b. Who suggested the compilation of the *Qur'ān?*
   c. How long did it take for the *Qur'ān* to be completed?
   d. What is the first verse of the *Qur'ān?*
3. Fill in the blanks :
   Life on this __________ would be __________ if all people __________ that there would be no __________ __________ __________. There would be no __________ or control on what ______ ______. Belief in __________ has a tremendous __________ on the __________ of a __________.

4th, 5th and 6th Forms

1. Answer the following :
   a. What is the subject-matter of the *Qur'ān?*
   b. What does the *Qur'ān* ask us to do?
   c. Who is the Guardian of the *Qur'ān?*
   d. Which *Khalīfah* ordered the compilation of the *Qur'ān?*
   e. Who ordered the preparation of a standard version of the *Qur'ān* in the dialect of the *Quraish* tribe?
2. Write down the meaning of the first five verses of the *Qur'ān.*
3. Explain the significance of the belief in *Ākhirah* — one of the three basic concepts of *Islam.*

2

Basic Duties of Islam

ISLAM has five basic duties which Muslims must perform. They are known as the five pillars of Islam *(Arkān ul Islam)*. These pillars are mentioned in the following *Ḥadīth* (a saying of prophet Muḥammad *(pbuh)* :

بُنِيَ الإِسْلَامُ عَلَى خَمْسٍ : شَهَادَةِ أَنْ لَا إِلٰهَ إِلَّا اللّٰهُ وَأَنَّ مُحَمَّدًا
رَسُولُ اللّٰهِ، وَإِقَامِ الصَّلَاةِ، وَإِيتَاءِ الزَّكَاةِ، وَالْحَجِّ وَصَوْمِ
رَمَضَانَ . (بُخَارِي)

"Buniyal Islāmu 'ālā khamsin; Shahādati 'an lā ilāha illal lāhu wa anna Muḥammadar rasūlul lāhi; wa iqāmis Ṣalāti, wa ītā'iz Zakāti, wal Ḥajji, wa Ṣawmi Ramaḍān" (Bukhārī).

The meaning of this *Ḥadīth* is :

"Islam is based on five things : declaring that there is no god but *Allah* and that Muḥammad is the messenger of Allah, the establishment of *Ṣalāh*, the payment of *Zakāh,* the *Ḥajj* and *Ṣawm* in the month of Ramaḍān."

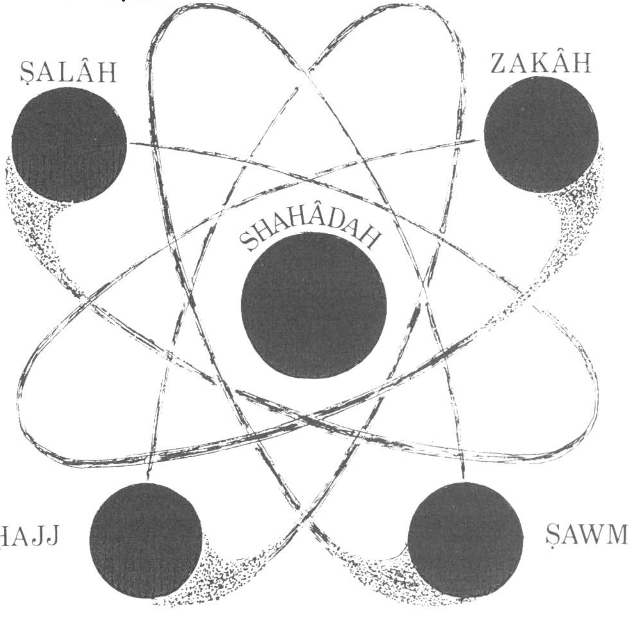

The five pillars as mentioned in the *Ḥadīth* are :

Shahādah *(declaration of faith)*
Ṣalāh *(five compulsory daily prayers)*
Zakāh *(welfare contribution)*
Ḥajj *(pilgrimage to Makkah)*
Ṣawm *(fasting during Ramaḍān)*

Shahādah

لا اله الا الله
محمد رسول الله

Declaration of faith

A Muslim declares his faith by reciting :

لَآ اِلٰهَ اِلَّا اللّٰهُ مُحَمَّدٌ رَّسُوْلُ اللّٰهِ

Lā ilāha illal lāhu muḥammadur rasūlul lāh.

These Arabic words mean : *"There is no god but Allah, Muḥammad is the messenger of Allah"*. This declaration is called *Kalimah Ṭayyibah*. It summarizes the whole of Islamic belief. The first part *(Lā Ilāha Illal Lāh)* is about the Oneness of Allah *(Tawḥīd in Arabic)* while the second part *(Muḥammadur Rasūlul Lāh)* concerns the prophethood *(Risālah)* of *Muḥammad* (peace be upon him). The four Arabic words of the frist part are : *Lā* which means no; *Ilāha* meaning god; *Illa* meaning but; and *Allah*. The second part has three words : *Muḥammad; Rasul* meaning messenger; and *Allah*.

The first pillar of Islam is Shahādah, which concerns belief in Tawḥīd and Risālah of Muḥammad (pbuh). The other four pillars make up 'Ibādah. 'Ibādah, an Arabic term, includes any activity which is done to gain Allah's favour. Ṣalāh, Zakāh, Ṣawm and Ḥajj are the main forms of worship or 'Ibādah. If we perform them regularly and correctly, we come closer to Allah, our Creator and Sustainer.

These four basic duties of *Ṣalāh, Zakāh, Ṣawm* and *Ḥajj* comprise the training programme which has been designed for us by Allah so that we can shape our life around *Shahādah*. We already know that we belong to Allah and He is our Master. So, in order to behave like the servant of our Creator, we must practise *Ṣalāh, Zakāh, Ṣawm* and *Ḥajj* faithfully.

Ṣalāh

Ṣalāh is the second pillar of Islam. It refers to the five compulsory daily prayers. *Ṣalāh* is offered five times a day individually or in congregation. We offer *Ṣalāh* to remember Allah. It brings us closer to Him. The *Qur'ān* says :

"Establish Ṣalāh to remember me (Allah)" (20:14).

Ṣalāh is the practical proof of our faith in Allah and Islam. It has been made compulsory at certain fixed times. Allah says in the *Qur'ān* :

"Ṣalāh at fixed times has been enjoined on the believers" (4:103).

The five daily prayers are :

Fajr *(from dawn until just before sunrise)*
Ẓuhr *(after mid-day until afternoon)*
'Aṣr *(from late afternoon until just before sunset)*
Maghrib *(after sunset until daylight ends)*
'Ishā' *(night until midnight or dawn)*

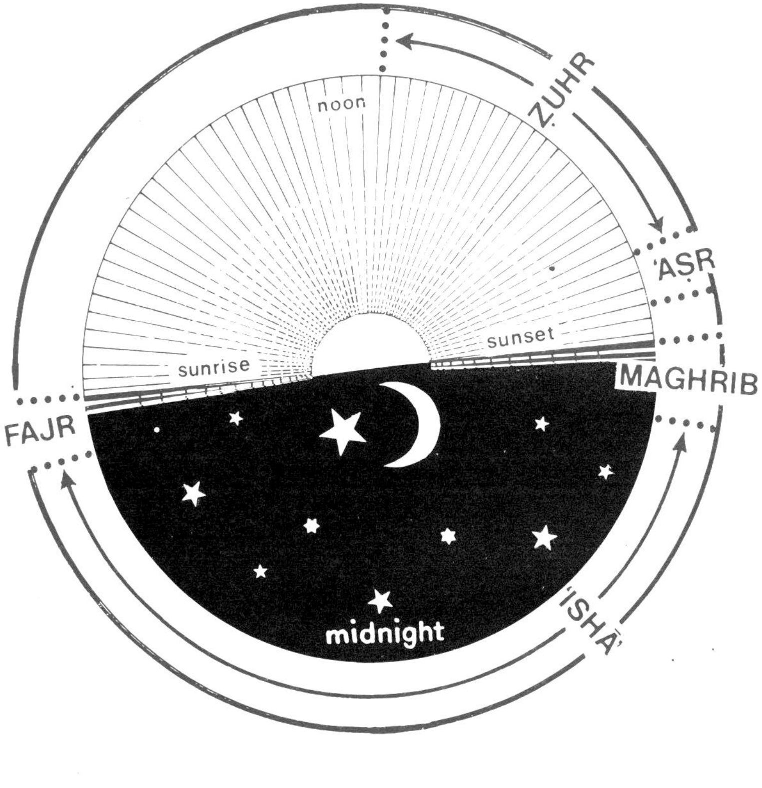

Timings of five daily Ṣalāh

You must know at this stage how to offer *Ṣalāh*. First, try to understand clearly why we need to offer *Ṣalāh*. We offer Ṣalāh to remember Allah our Creator and to be close to Him and to gain His favour.

To say your Ṣalāh you must be clean and pure. The *Qur'ān* says : *"Surely Allah loves those who turn to Him and those who care for cleanliness."* (2:222). Cleanliness of the body and clothes is called *Ṭahārah* or purification. You may be clean outwardly and still not be pure — it is especially important to remove all trace of urine or excrement from the clothes worn for *Ṣalāh*.

How can we have cleanliness? We can have a full wash of the whole body with pure water or we can have a part wash, cleaning only parts of the body. The full wash is called *Ghusl*, and the part wash is *Wuḍū* (ablution), in Arabic.

Keep in mind that Muslims are not allowed to have a shower in the nude in the presence of others.

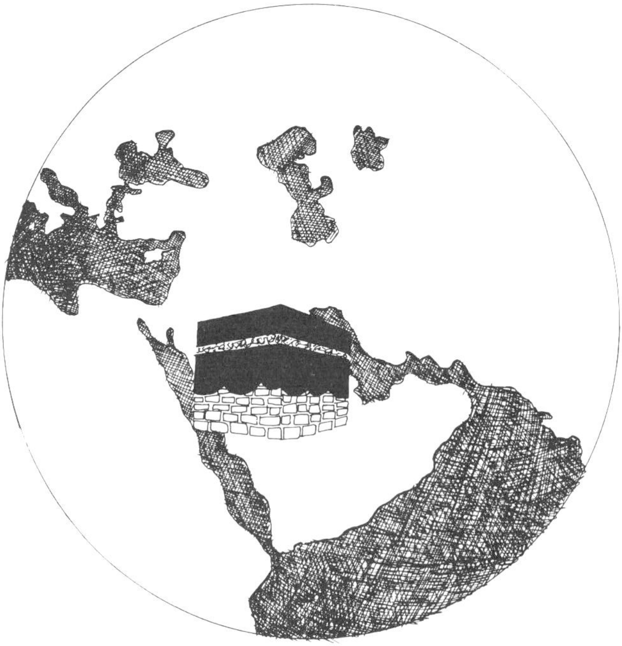

Wuḍū'

Before we can begin to say *Ṣalāh*, we must first prepare ourselves. This preparation includes making sure we are clean, and this is done by carrying out *Wuḍū'*.

Wuḍū' (Ablution) is essential for performing *Ṣalāh*, we cannot offer our *Ṣalāh* without first making *Wuḍū'*. These are the steps to take :

a First make *Niyyah* (intention) saying *Bismillāhir raḥmānir raḥīm*[1] (In the name of Allah the most Merciful, the most Kind); then wash both hands up to the wrists three times making sure that water has reached between the fingers.

b Next, put a handful of water into the mouth and rinse it thoroughly three times.

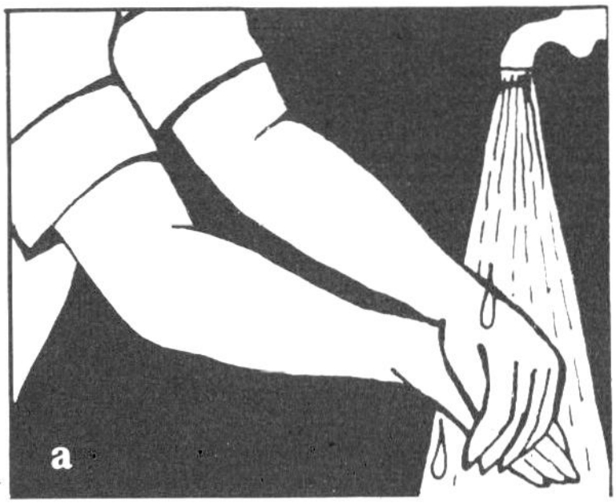

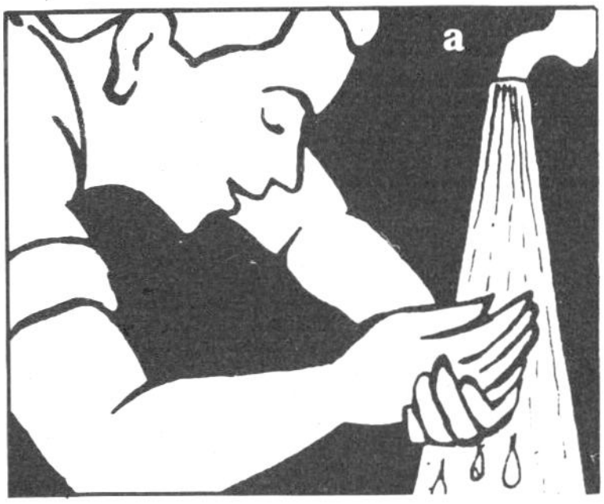

c After this sniff water into the nostrils three times to clean them and then wash the tip of the nose three times.

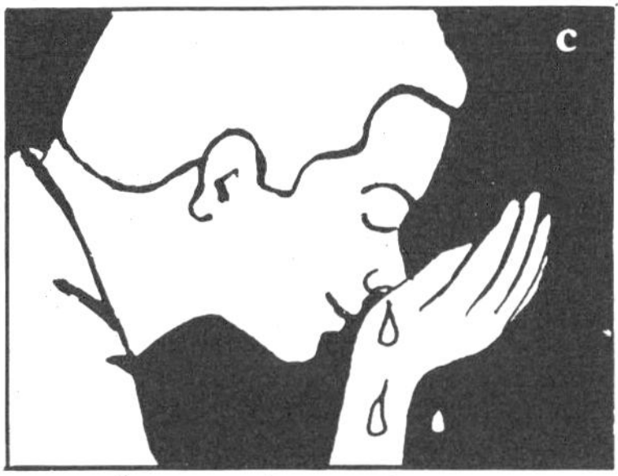

[1] بِسْمِ اللّٰهِ الرَّحْمٰنِ الرَّحِيْمِ

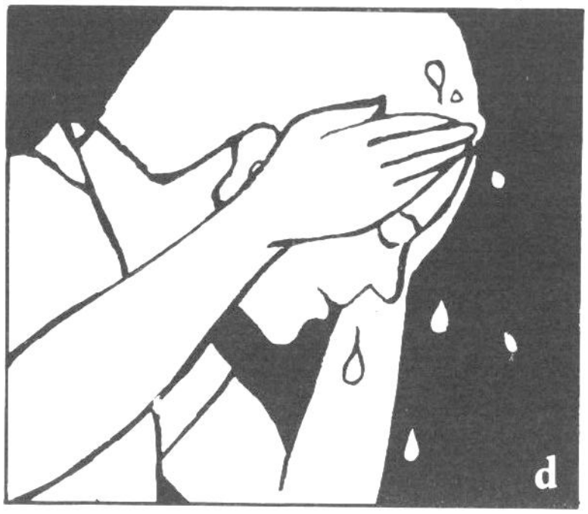

d Wash the face three times from right ear to left ear and from forehead to throat.

e Wash the right arm and then left arm thoroughly from wrist to elbow three times.

f Then move the palm of the wet hand over head, starting from the top of forehead to the back and pass both hands over the back of the head to the neck.

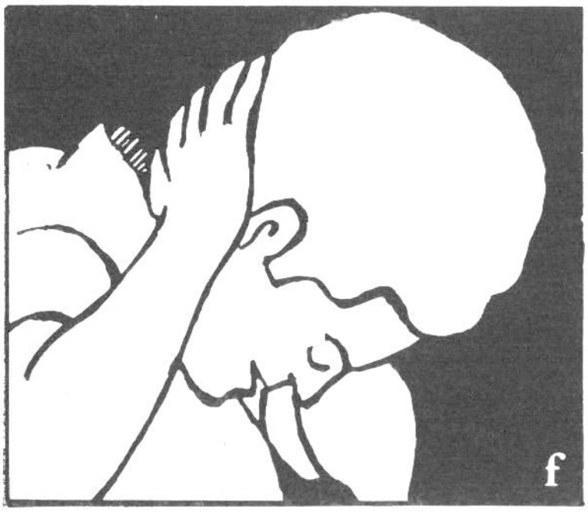

g Next, rub wet fingers into the grooves of both ears and holes and also pass the wet thumbs behind the ears.

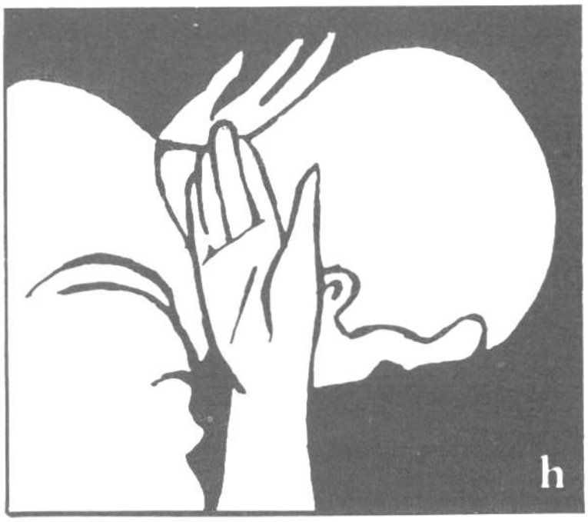

h Next pass the backs of wet hands over the nape.

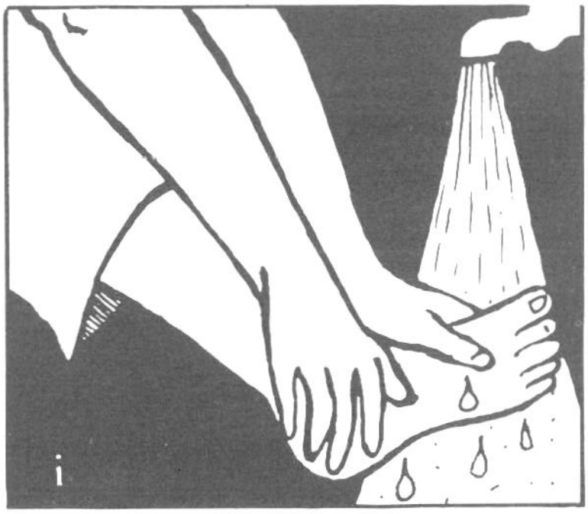

i Finally wash both feet to the ankles starting from the right and making sure that water has reached between the toes and all other parts of the feet.

If you did a complete *Wuḍū'* before putting on your socks, it is not necessary to take them off everytime you repeat *Wuḍū'*. It is enough to wipe the upper part of the socks with wet hands. Such *Wuḍū'* lasts for twenty four hours only (three days for a journey) but a fresh *Wuḍū'* must be made after socks are taken off.

At the end of the steps recite :

أَشْهَدُ أَنْ لَّا إِلٰهَ إِلَّا اللّٰهُ وَحْدَهُ لَا شَرِيْكَ لَهُ، وَأَشْهَدُ أَنَّ مُحَمَّدًا
عَبْدُهُ وَرَسُوْلُهُ -

"Ash hadu an lā ilāha illal lāhu wahdahu lā sharīkalahu wa ash hadu anna muḥammadan 'abduhu wa rasūluhu".

This means :

I bear witness that there is no god but Allah and He is one and has no partner and I bear witness that Muḥammad is His servant and messenger.

Fresh *Wuḍū'* is needed after :

- a Natural discharges : urine, stools, wind and the like.
- b Flow of blood or pus and the like from any part of the body.
- c Full mouth vomiting.
- d Falling asleep.

Tayammum (Dry Ablution)

You can perform your Ṣalāh by *Tayammum* when :

a You are sick and cannot use water.
b Water is not available.
c Use of water is harmful

In these cases, what you are required to do is :

1 Place both hands lightly on earth, sand, stone or any other object having dust on it.
2 Blow the dust off the hands and wipe the face with them once in the same way as done in Wuḍū.
3 Repeat as in (1) and wipe the right arm up to the elbow with the left hand and left arm with the right hand.

Adhān (Call to prayer)

It is strongly recommended that wherever possible Muslims should offer their compulsory *(farḍ)* prayers in the mosque. To call Muslims to prayer, the Prophet *Muḥammad* (pbuh) introduced the system of *Adhān*.

The person who gives the *Adhān* is called the *Mu'azzin* (Caller). While calling for prayer, he stands in the *Minaret* or in the courtyard of the mosque, facing the *Qiblah* and raises his hands to his ears and calls out :

اَللّٰهُ اَكْبَرُ ط	اَللّٰهُ اَكْبَرُ ط	اَللّٰهُ اَكْبَرُ ط	اَللّٰهُ اَكْبَرُ ط
Allāhu Akbar	*Allāhu Akbar*	*Allāhu Akbar*	*Allāhu Akbar*
(Allah is the Greatest)	(Allah is the Greatest)	(Allah is the Greatest)	(Allah is the Greatest)

اَشْهَدُ اَنْ لَّآ اِلٰهَ اِلَّا اللّٰهُ ط	اَشْهَدُ اَنْ لَّآ اِلٰهَ اِلَّا اللّٰهُ ط
Ashhadu an lā ilāha illallāh	*Ashhadu an lā ilāha illallāh*
(I bear witness that there is no god but Allah)	(I bear witness that there is no god but Allah)

أَشْهَدُ أَنَّ مُحَمَّدًا رَّسُوْلُ اللّٰهِ ط

Ashhadu anna muḥammadar rasūlullāh
(I bear witness that Muhammad is Allah's messenger)

أَشْهَدُ أَنَّ مُحَمَّدًا رَّسُوْلُ اللّٰهِ ط

Ashhadu anna muḥammadar rasūlullāh
(I bear witness that Muhammad is Allah's messenger)

حَيَّ عَلَى الصَّلٰوةِ ط

Ḥayya 'alaṣ ṣalāh
(Rush to prayer)

حَيَّ عَلَى الصَّلٰوةِ ط

Ḥayya 'alaṣ ṣalāh
(Rush to prayer)

حَيَّ عَلَى الْفَلَاحِ ط

Ḥayya 'alal falāḥ
(Rush to success)

حَيَّ عَلَى الْفَلَاحِ ط

Ḥayya 'alal falāḥ
(Rush to success)

اَللّٰهُ أَكْبَرُ ط

Allāhu Akbar
(Allah is the Greatest)

اَللّٰهُ أَكْبَرُ ط

Allāhu Akbar
(Allah is the Greatest)

لَآ إِلٰهَ إِلَّا اللّٰهُ ط

Lā ilāha illal lāh
(There is no god but Allah)

During the Adhān for Fajr Ṣalāh, the following is added after *'Ḥayya 'alal falāḥ'*.

اَلصَّلٰوةُ خَيْرٌ مِّنَ النَّوْمِ ط

Aṣṣalātu khairum minan naum
(Ṣalāh is better than sleep)

اَلصَّلٰوةُ خَيْرٌ مِّنَ النَّوْمِ ط

Aṣṣalātu khairum minan naum
(Ṣalāh is better than sleep)

IQĀMAH

Iqāmah is another call to prayer said inside the mosque, just before the actual start of *Ṣalāh* in congregation. When the Muslims stand in rows, the *Mua'dhdhin* recites *Iqāmah* which is exactly like *Adhān*, except that after *'Ḥayya 'alal falāḥ'* the following is added :

قَدْ قَامَتِ الصَّلٰوةُ ط

Qad Qāmatiṣ ṣalāh
(The prayer has begun)

قَدْ قَامَتِ الصَّلٰوةُ ط

Qad Qāmatiṣ ṣalāh
(The prayer has begun)

Iqāmah is said in a lower voice than *Adhān*.

Farḍ (Compulsory) Ṣalāh

A Muslim must pray five times a day. The compulsory prayers are called *Farḍ* in Arabic. Each unit of prayer is called a *Raka'h. Farḍ* prayers are :

Fajr	… … 2 Raka'hs
Ẓuhr	… … 4 Raka'hs
'Aṣr	… … 4 Raka'hs
Maghrib	… … 3 Raka'hs
'Ishā'	… … 4 Raka'hs
**Jumu'ah*	… … 2 Raka'hs

*(in place of Ẓuhr on Friday)

Sunnah Ṣalāh

Prophet Muḥammad *(pbuh)* prayed extra raka'hs in addition to *Farḍ* prayers. These prayers are called *Sunnah*. Prophet Muḥammad *(pbuh)* always prayed two raka'hs before the *Farḍ* of *Fajr* and three *raka'hs* after the *Farḍ* of *'Ishā'* even on a journey. The three raka'hs after *'Ishā'* are called *Witr* (odd number).

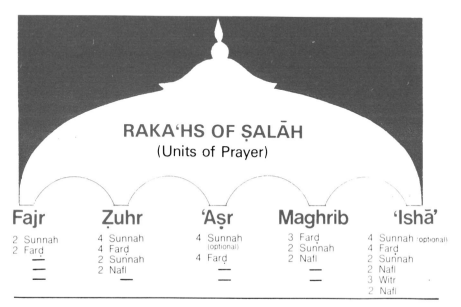

Fajr	Ẓuhr	'Aṣr	Maghrib	'Ishā'
2 Sunnah	4 Sunnah	4 Sunnah (optional)	3 Farḍ	4 Sunnah (optional)
2 Farḍ	4 Farḍ	4 Farḍ	2 Sunnah	4 Farḍ
	2 Sunnah		2 Nafl	2 Sunnah
	2 Nafl			2 Nafl
				3 Witr
				2 Nafl

Sunnah prayers are :

Fajr	… …	2 raka'hs before *Farḍ*
Ẓuhr	… …	4 before Farḍ and 2 after
'Aṣr	… …	4 (optional) before *Farḍ*
Maghrib	… …	2 raka'hs after *Farḍ*
'Ishā'	… …	4 optional before *Farḍ*, 2 raka'hs after *Farḍ* and 3 *Witr*.

Between *'Ishā'* and *Fajr*, a prayer called *Tahajjud* was regularly offered by the Prophet. It was obligatory for the Prophet. Devout Muslims try to follow the practice.

Muslims also pray additional raka'hs other than *Farḍ* and *Sunnah*. These are called *Nafillāh* (optional).

Times when you must not pray :

1 From the beginning of sunrise until after 15-20 minutes later.
2 When the sun is at its height *(Zenith* or *Meridian)*.
3 From the beginning of sunset until it is fully set.

How to perform Ṣalāh

Having cleansed yourselves by *Wuḍū*, now proceed to perform *Ṣalāh*. Wuḍū is a ritual cleansing, but before you begin your Ṣalāh, you must make sure that you have a clean body, a clean place and that you are wearing clean clothes.

The way to offer *Ṣalāh* is :

1 Stand upright on your prayer mat facing the direction of *Al-Ka'bah*. This standing is called *Qiyām* and the direction is called *Qiblah* in Arabic. *Qiblah* is in the South East from England.

2 Say *Niyyah* (intention) either verbally or in your mind. Niyyah is said with the words :

	*two**	*farḍ**		*Fajr**	
"I intend to say	*three*	*sunnah*		*Ẓuhr*	
	four	*raka'ahs*	of Ṣalātul	*'Aṣr*	for Allah facing *Ka'bah*"
				Maghrib	
				'Iṣhā	

3 Raise your hands up to your ears (women and girls up to their shoulders) and say *Allāhu Akbar*[1] (Allah is the Greatest). This is called *Takbīratul Iḥrām*.

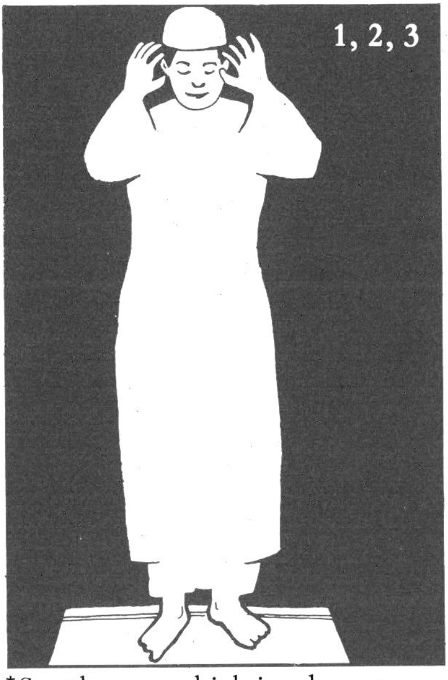

*Say the one which is relevant

[1] الله اكبر

4 Now place your right hand on your left hand just below the navel or on the chest (women and girls put their hands on chest) and recite :

سُبْحَانَكَ اللّٰهُمَّ وَبِحَمْدِكَ وَتَبَارَكَ اسْمُكَ وَتَعَالٰى جَدُّكَ وَلَا إِلٰهَ غَيْرُكَ

Subḥānaka allāhumma wa bi ḥamdika wa tabāra kasmuka wa ta'ālā jadduka wa lā ilāha ghairuka.

This means : O Allah, glory and praise are for You, and blessed is Your name, and exalted is Your Majesty; there is no god but You.

Then recite : أَعُوْذُ بِاللّٰهِ مِنَ الشَّيْطَانِ الرَّجِيْمِ ○

A'ūdhu billāhi minash shaiṭānir rajīm

which means : I seek shelter in Allah from the rejected satan.

بِسْمِ اللّٰهِ الرَّحْمٰنِ الرَّحِيْمِ ○

Bismillāhir raḥmānir raḥīm

which means : In the name of Allah, the most Merciful, the most Kind.

5 After this, recite *sūrat-ul-Fātiḥah* (opening chapter) of the *Qur'ān :*

سُوْرَةُ الْفَاتِحَة

بِسْمِ اللّٰهِ الرَّحْمٰنِ الرَّحِيْمِ ○

اَلْحَمْدُ لِلّٰهِ رَبِّ الْعٰلَمِيْنَ ○ الرَّحْمٰنِ الرَّحِيْمِ ○ مٰلِكِ يَوْمِ الدِّيْنِ ○

إِيَّاكَ نَعْبُدُ وَإِيَّاكَ نَسْتَعِيْنُ ○ اِهْدِنَا الصِّرَاطَ الْمُسْتَقِيْمَ ○

صِرَاطَ الَّذِيْنَ أَنْعَمْتَ عَلَيْهِمْ ۙ غَيْرِ الْمَغْضُوْبِ عَلَيْهِمْ

وَلَا الضَّآلِّيْنَ ○

Al ḥamdu lil lāhi rabbil 'ālamīn. Arrahmānir raḥīm. Māliki Yawmiddīn. Iyyāka na'budu wa iyyāka nasta'īn. Ihdinaṣ ṣirātal mustaqīm. Ṣirāṭal ladhīna an 'amta 'alaihim, ghairil maghḍūbi 'alaihim wa laḍ ḍāllīn. (Āmīn).

"All praise is for Allah, the Lord of the Universe, the most Merciful, the most Kind; Master of the day of judgment. You alone we worship, from You alone we seek help. Guide us along the straight path — the path of those whom You favoured, not of those who earned Your anger or went astray."

The recitation of *Al-Fātiḥah* is a must in all prayers.

6 Now recite any other passage from the *Qur'ān*. For example :

بِسْمِ اللَّهِ الرَّحْمَٰنِ الرَّحِيمِ ۝

Bismillāhir raḥmanir raḥīm

قُلْ هُوَ اللَّهُ أَحَدٌ ۝ اللَّهُ الصَّمَدُ ۝ لَمْ يَلِدْ ۝ وَلَمْ يُولَدْ ۝
وَلَمْ يَكُن لَّهُ كُفُوًا أَحَدٌ ۝

Qul hu wal lāhu aḥad, allāhuṣ ṣamad, lam yalid wa lam yūlad, wa lam ya kul lahu kufuwan aḥad.

In the name of Allah, the most Merciful, the most Kind.
"Say, He is Allah, the One. Allah is Eternal and Absolute. None is born of Him nor is He born and there is none like Him."

7 Now bow down saying : *Allāhu Akbar*[2] and place your hands on your knees and say : *Ṣubḥāna Rabbīyal 'Aẓīm*[3] (Glory to my Lord, the Great) three times. This position is called *Rukū'*.

8 Stand up from the bowing position saying: *'Sami' Allāhu Liman Ḥamidah*[4] (Allah hears those who praise Him). *Rabbanā Lakal Ḥamd*[5] (Our Lord, praise be to You). This standing is called *Qiyām* or 'Itidal in Arabic.

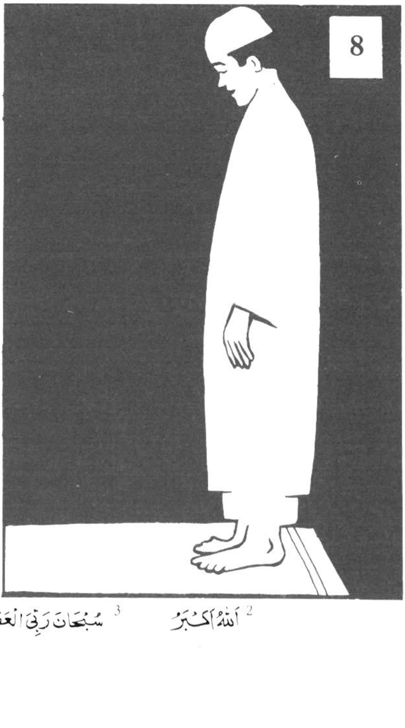

2 اللهُ أَكْبَرُ 3 سُبْحَانَ رَبِّيَ الْعَظِيمِ 4 سَمِعَ اللهُ لِمَنْ حَمِدَهُ 5 رَبَّنَا لَكَ الْحَمْدُ

9 Prostrate on the floor on your prayer mat saying *Allāhu Akbar*[6], with your forehead, nose, palms of both hands and your knees touching the floor. Recite *Ṣubḥāna Rabbīyal A'lā*[7] (Glory to my Lord, the Highest) three times. This position is called *Sajdah*. Your arms should not touch the floor.

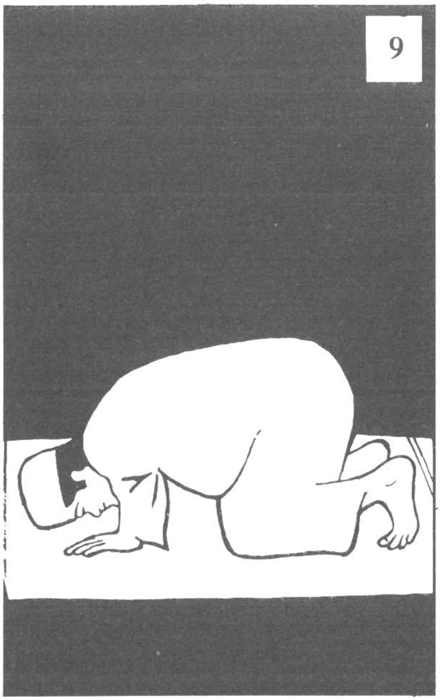

10 Get up from the floor saying *Allāhu Akbar*[8] and sit upright with your knees bent and palms placed on them. After a moment's rest* prostrate again on the floor saying : *Allāhu Akbar*[9] and recite *Ṣubḥāna Rabbīyal A'lā*[10] three times. Get up from this position saying *Allāhu Akbar*[11].

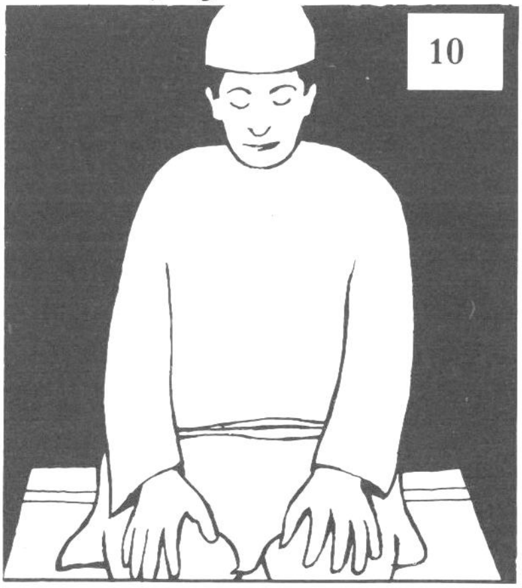

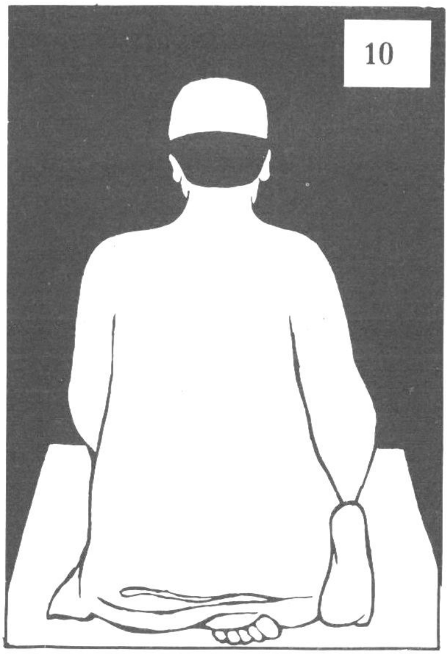

6 الله أكبر
7 سبحان ربي الأعلى
8 الله أكبر
9 الله أكبر
10 سبحان ربي الأعلى
11 الله أكبر

*Here you can say the *Du'ā'* : Rabbighfirlī wa arḥmanī warjuqnī.

This completes one Raka'h or one unit of *Ṣalāh*. The second raka'h is performed in the same way, except that you do not recite *Subhanaka, Ta'awwudh* and *Tasmiyah* and after the second prostration you sit upright and recite quietly *At-Tashahhud :*

اَلتَّحِيَّاتُ لِلّٰهِ وَالصَّلَوٰتُ وَالطَّيِّبَاتُ اَلسَّلَامُ عَلَيْكَ اَيُّهَا النَّبِىُّ

وَرَحْمَةُ اللّٰهِ وَبَرَكَاتُهٗ ۔ اَلسَّلَامُ عَلَيْنَا وَعَلٰى عِبَادِ اللّٰهِ الصّٰلِحِيْنَ ○

اَشْهَدُ اَنْ لَّآ اِلٰهَ اِلَّا اللّٰهُ وَاَشْهَدُ اَنَّ مُحَمَّدًا عَبْدُهٗ وَرَسُوْلُهٗ ○

At-Taḥiyyātu Lillāhi	— *All prayer is for Allah*
Waṣ Ṣalawātu Waṭ Ṭayyibātu	— *and worship and goodness*
As-Salāmu 'Alaika Ayyuhannabīyyu	— *Peace be on you, O prophet*
Wa Raḥmatullāhi Wa Barakātuhu	— *and the mercy of Allah and His blessings*
Assālamu 'Alainā	— *Peace be on us* ·
Wa 'Alā 'Ibadillahiṣ Ṣāliḥīn	— *and on the righteous servants of Allah*
Ash Hādu An Lāilāha Illal Lāhu	— *I bear witness that there is no god but Allah*
Wa Ash Hādu Anna Muḥammadan 'Abduhu Wa Rasūluhu	— *and bear witness that Muḥammad is His servant and messenger*

In a three raka'h *ṣalāh* (as in *Maghrib*) or a four raka'h *ṣalāh (Ẓuhr, 'Aṣr* and *'Īshā')* you stand up for the remaining raka'h after *Tashahhud.* But for a two raka'h ṣalāh you remain seated after the second raka'h and recite *As-Ṣalāh 'alan nabiyy* (blessings for the Prophet) or *Darūd :*

اَللّٰهُمَّ صَلِّ عَلٰى مُحَمَّدٍ وَّعَلٰٓى اٰلِ مُحَمَّدٍ كَمَا صَلَّيْتَ عَلٰٓى اِبْرٰهِيْمَ

وَعَلٰٓى اٰلِ اِبْرٰهِيْمَ اِنَّكَ حَمِيْدٌ مَّجِيْدٌ ○

Allāhumma Ṣalli 'Alā Muḥammadin	— *O Allah, let Your blessing come upon Muḥammad*
Wa 'Alā Āli Muḥammadin	— *and the family of Muḥammad*
Kamā Ṣallaita 'Alā Ibrāhīma Wa 'Alā Āli Ibrāhīma	— *as You blessed Ibrāhīm and his family*
Innaka Ḥamīdun Majīd	— *truly You are the Praiseworthy and Glorious.*

اَللّٰهُمَّ بَارِكْ عَلٰى مُحَمَّدٍ وَّعَلٰى اٰلِ مُحَمَّدٍ كَمَا بَارَكْتَ عَلٰى
اِبْرَاهِيْمَ وَعَلٰى اٰلِ اِبْرَاهِيْمَ اِنَّكَ حَمِيْدٌ مَّجِيْدٌ ۝

Allāhumma Bārik 'Alā Muḥammadin Wa 'Alā Āli Muḥammadin	— *O Allah, bless Muḥammad and the family of Muḥammad*
Kamā Bārakta 'Alā Ibrāhīma Wa 'Alā Ali Ibrāhīma	— *as You blessed Ibrāhīm and his family*
Innaka Ḥamīdun Majīd	— *truly You are the Praiseworthy and Glorious.*

After this, say any of the following *Du'ā* (supplication) :

اَللّٰهُمَّ اِنِّيْ ظَلَمْتُ نَفْسِيْ ظُلْمًا كَثِيْرًا وَّلَا يَغْفِرُ الذُّنُوْبَ اِلَّا اَنْتَ
فَاغْفِرْ لِيْ مَغْفِرَةً مِّنْ عِنْدِكَ وَارْحَمْنِيْ اِنَّكَ اَنْتَ الْغَفُوْرُ الرَّحِيْمُ ۝

Allāhumma innī ẓalamtu nafsī ẓulman kathīran wa lā yaghfirudh dhunūba illā anta faghfirlī maghfiratan min 'indika wa arḥamnī innaka antal ghafūrur raḥīm.

This means :

"O Allah, I have been unjust to myself and no-one grants pardon for sins except You, therefore, forgive me with Your forgiveness and have mercy on me. Surely, You are the Forgiver, the Merciful."

رَبِّ اجْعَلْنِيْ مُقِيْمَ الصَّلٰوةِ وَمِنْ ذُرِّيَّتِيْ رَبَّنَا وَتَقَبَّلْ دُعَآءِ ۝
رَبَّنَا اغْفِرْ لِيْ وَلِوَالِدَيَّ وَلِلْمُؤْمِنِيْنَ يَوْمَ يَقُوْمُ الْحِسَابُ -

Rabbi ja'alnī muqīmaṣ ṣalāta wa min dhurriyyatī rabbanā wa taqabbal du'ā'. Rabbanāghfirlī waliwālidaiyya wa lil mu'minīna yawma yaqūmul ḥisāb.

Meaning :

"O Lord, make me and my children steadfast in Ṣalāh. Our Lord, accept the prayer. Our Lord forgive me and my parents and the believers on the day of judgment."

11 Now turn your face to the right saying : *Assālamu 'Alaikum Wa Raḥmatullāh*[12] (peace and the mercy of Allah be on you) and then to the left repeating the words.

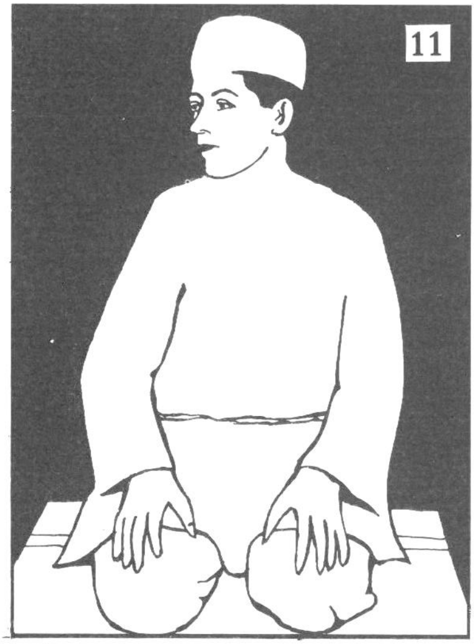

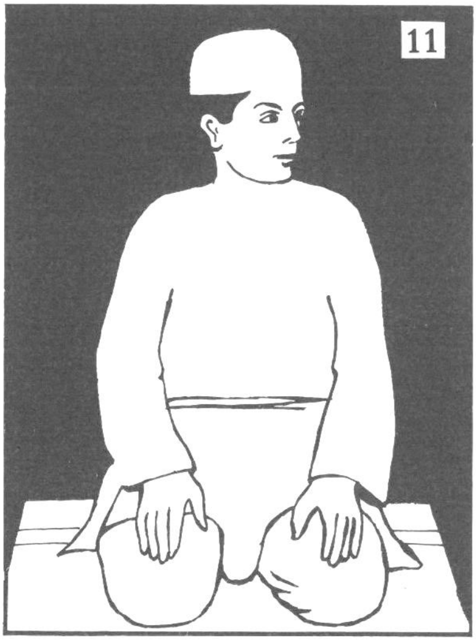

12 اَلسَّلَامُ عَلَيْكُمْ وَرَحْمَةُ اللهِ

This completes the two raka'h Ṣalāh. In the four raka'h *Ṣalāh* of *Ẓuhr, 'Aṣr* and *'Īshā'*, the whole procedure is repeated except that when you get up to complete the remaining two raka'h (one raka'h in *Maghrib* and *Witr*) after *Tashahhud*, you only recite *Al-Fātiḥah* in Farḍ prayers and no other *sūrah*.

In the Farḍ prayer of *Fajr, Maghrib* and *'Ishā'* the *Qur'ān* is recited aloud while in *Ẓuhr* and *'Aṣr* it is recited silently. In all prayers, Tasbīḥ *(Ṣubbḥāna Rabbīyal 'Aẓīm* and *Ṣubhāna Rabbīyal a'lā), Tashahhud* and *Darūd* are said quietly. When the Fajr, Maghrib and 'Ishā' prayers are said in congregation, the *Imām* (one who leads the prayer), recites the *Qur'ān* aloud. This applies also to *Jumu'ah* prayer *(Friday prayer in place of Ẓuhr).*

ṢALĀTUL WITR

Witr (odd number) prayer has three Raka'hs. The first two Raka'hs are said like the first two Raka'hs of the Maghrib prayer and after *Tashahhud* in the second Raka'h, stand up saying *Allāhu Akbar* for the third Raka'h. Recite Sūratul Fātiḥah and some other verses from the Qur'ān and before going to Ruku' raise your hands up to the ears saying *Allāhu Akbar* and recite the following du'ā after placing your hands below your navel or on the chest. This du'ā is called *Du'ā al-Qunūt.*

اَللّٰهُمَّ إِنَّا نَسْتَعِينُكَ وَنَسْتَغْفِرُكَ وَنُؤْمِنُ بِكَ وَنَتَوَكَّلُ عَلَيْكَ وَنُثْنِي
عَلَيْكَ الْخَيْرَ وَنَشْكُرُكَ وَلَا نَكْفُرُكَ وَنَخْلَعُ وَنَتْرُكُ مَنْ يَفْجُرُكَ.
اَللّٰهُمَّ إِيَّاكَ نَعْبُدُ وَلَكَ نُصَلِّي وَنَسْجُدُ وَإِلَيْكَ نَسْعَى وَنَحْفِدُ
وَنَرْجُو رَحْمَتَكَ وَنَخْشَى عَذَابَكَ إِنَّ عَذَابَكَ بِالْكُفَّارِ مُلْحِقٌ.

Allāhumma innā nasta'īnuka wa nastaghfiruka, wa nu'minu bika wa natawakkalu 'alaika wa nuthnī 'alaikal khair, wa nashkuruka wa lā nakfuruka wa nakhla'u wa natruku manyyafjuruka, allāhumma iyyāka na'budu, wa laka nuṣallī wa nasjudu wa ilaika nas'ā wa naḥfidu wa narjū raḥmataka wa nakshā 'adhābaka inna 'adhābaka bil kuffāri mulḥiq.

This means : "O Allah, we seek Your help and ask Your forgiveness and we believe in You and trust in You. We praise You in the best way and we thank You and we are not ungrateful and we cast off and forsake him who disobeys You. O Allah, You alone we worship and to You we pray and before you we prostrate, to You we turn in haste, and hope for Your mercy and fear Your punishment."

After this, say *Allāhu Akbar* and bow down in Ruku' and complete the rest of the prayer like the Maghrib prayer.

SAJDATUS SAHW

(Prostration of forgetfulness)

Since we are human beings, we are not above mistakes and errors. If we forget to do something in our *ṣalāh*, we can make up for it by making two extra *sajdah* as we do in any rak'ah of ṣalāh. This is called *Sajdatus Sahw.* This is done at the end of the last rak'ah of *ṣalāh.* What you have to do is to say Tashahhud and then turn your face to the right saying *Assalāmu 'alaikum wa raḥmatullāh* and make two extra sajdah with tasbīḥ *(Ṣubḥāna Rabbīyal 'alā)* and then recite *Tashahhud* again with *ṣalāh 'alan Nabiyy* (Darūd) and du'ā. Now you turn your face first to the right and then to the left saying *Assalāmu 'alaikum wa raḥmatullāh.*

The *Sajdatus Sahw* is necessary if you forget to do any essentials of ṣalāh, for example, forgetting to recite parts of the *Qur'ān* after *Al-Fātiḥah*, forgetting to say the first *Tashahhud* in a four rak'ah *ṣalāh*, or saying *salām* after two rak'ahs in a four rak'ah ṣalāh.

Your ṣalāh will not be valid, if you do any of the following :

1 *Miss out Niyyah (intention).*
2 *Miss out Takbīraṭul Iḥrām.*
3 *Forget to recite Al-Fātiḥah.*
4 *Forget or do not make ruku' or sajdah.*
5 *Do not face Qiblah.*
6 *Do not have Wuḍū'.*
7 *Talk during ṣalāh.*
8 *Eat or drink during ṣalāh.*
9 *Do not sit for Tashahhud.*

Under these circumstances, you must repeat your *ṣalāh. Sajdatus Sahw* will not be enough.

ṢALĀTUL JUMU'AH (Friday Prayer)

Ṣalātul Jumu'ah or Friday Prayer is offered in congregation. All adult Muslims must take part. It is offered on *Friday* during *Ẓuhr* time. It is not a must for women, but they can join this prayer if it does not upset their household duties.

People assemble for this *Ṣalāh* immediately after noon. On arriving at the mosque or the prayer hall, they offer 2 or 4 or 6 or more Rak'ahs *Sunnah* prayer and then the *Imām* (prayer leader) delivers a *khutbah* (sermon). After khutbah, the *Imām* leads a two rak'ah farḍ prayer. After the farḍ prayer, 2, 4 or 6 or more rak'ahs of *sunnah* or *nafillah* prayers are offered privately by each person.

Muslims are a community. *Ṣalātul Jumu'ah* is a community prayer. Each week on *Friday*, Muslims living in an area get together to offer this prayer.

Mosques used to be the Centre of all Islamic activities during our Prophet's time, but not so, now-a-days.

Friday prayer is an occasion for the assembly of the Muslims of an area. It gives them an opportunity to meet, discuss and solve their community problems. It develops unity, co-operation and cohesiveness.

In an Islamic state, the Head of state or his representative is supposed to lead the five daily prayers and the *Friday Prayer* at the central mosque of the Capital as was used to be done by the Prophet Muḥammad *(pbuh)* — the first head of Islamic State in *Madīnah.*

How wonderful it would be to live in a country where the Head of the state or his representative would lead the prayer in the central mosque of the Capital! This practice of the prophet must be revived in all Islamic states.

ṢALĀTUL JANĀZAH (Funeral Prayer)

Earlier we discussed death briefly. It is sure to come in everyone's life. When a Muslim dies, his body is given a wash and then a funeral prayer called *Ṣalātul Janāzah* is offered in congregation. This *ṣalāh*, unlike other *ṣalāh* has neither any *ruku'* (bowing) nor any *sajdah* (prostration) and you don't have to recite *Tashahhud*.

It is a collective obligation *(Farḍ Kifāyah)* on all the Muslims of the locality of the dead person. But if a number of them join in the obligation is discharged on behalf of all. But if no-one joins in, everyone of the locality will be considered sinful before Allah. This is how the prayer is offered :

1 Make *niyyah* (intention) that you are saying this prayer to Allah for the dead person.

2 Stand in rows for the performance of the funeral prayer facing Qiblah. The coffin is placed in front of the congregation in a bier.

3 Say *Allāhu Akbar* after the *Imām*, (this takbīr is *Takbīratul Iḥrām* and there will be three more takbīrāt after this) and raise your hands up to your ears and bring them down again and place them on or below your chest, putting the right hand on the left and recite the following :

سُبْحَانَكَ اللّٰهُمَّ وَبِحَمْدِكَ وَتَبَارَكَ اسْمُكَ وَتَعَالٰى جَدُّكَ
وَجَلَّ ثَنَاؤُكَ وَلَا إِلٰهَ غَيْرُكَ

Subḥānaka ạllāhumma wa biḥamdika wa tabārkasmuka wa ta'lā jadduka wa jalla thanāu'ka wa lā ilāha ghairuka.

Meaning :

"O Allah, Glory and Praise are for You and blessed is Your name, and exalted is Your Majesty and Glorious is Your Praise and there is no god but You."

Then the *Imām* will say *'Allāhu Akbar'* loudly and you have to follow him repeating the words quietly. There is no need to raise your hands up to your ears this time. Now, recite the following *Darūd :*

اَللّٰهُمَّ صَلِّ عَلٰى مُحَمَّدٍ وَّعَلٰٓى اٰلِ مُحَمَّدٍ كَمَا صَلَّيْتَ عَلٰٓى اِبْرَاهِيْمَ
وَعَلٰٓى اٰلِ اِبْرَاهِيْمَ اِنَّكَ حَمِيْدٌ مَّجِيْدٌ ○

Allāhumma ṣalli 'alā Muḥammadin wa 'alā āli Muḥammadin kamā ṣallaita 'alā Ibrāhīma wa 'alā āli Ibrāhīma innaka ḥamīdun majīd.

Meaning :

"O Allah, let Your blessing come upon Muḥammad and the family of Muḥammad as You blessed Ibrahim and his family. Truly You are the Praiseworthy and Glorious."

اَللّٰهُمَّ بَارِكْ عَلٰى مُحَمَّدٍ وَّعَلٰٓى اٰلِ مُحَمَّدٍ كَمَا بَارَكْتَ عَلٰى
اِبْرَاهِيْمَ وَعَلٰٓى اٰلِ اِبْرَاهِيْمَ اِنَّكَ حَمِيْدٌ مَّجِيْدٌ ○

Allāhumma bārik 'alā Muḥammadin wa 'alā āli Muḥammadin kamā bārakta 'alā Ibrāhīma wa 'alā āli Ibrāhīma innaka ḥamīdun majīd.

Meaning :

"O Allah, bless Muḥammad and the family of Muḥammad as You blessed Ibrahim and his family. Truly You are the Praiseworthy and Glorious."

After this, the second *Takbīr* will be said loudly by the *Imām* and those in the congregation will repeat it quietly. Then if the dead person is an adult male Muslim, recite the following *Du'ā :*

اَللّٰهُمَّ اغْفِرْ لِحَيِّنَا وَمَيِّتِنَا وَشَاهِدِنَا وَغَائِبِنَا وَصَغِيْرِنَا
وَكَبِيْرِنَا وَذَكَرِنَا وَاُنْثَانَا اَللّٰهُمَّ مَنْ اَحْيَيْتَهٗ مِنَّا
فَاَحْيِهٖ عَلَى الْاِسْلَامِ وَمَنْ تَوَفَّيْتَهٗ مِنَّا فَتَوَفَّهٗ عَلَى الْاِيْمَانِ

Allāhummaghfir liḥayyinā wa mayyitinā wa shāhidinā wa ghā'ibinā wa ṣaghirinā wa kabirinā wa dhakarinā wa unthānā allāhumma man aḥyaitahu minnā fāaḥyihi 'alal Islām wa man tawaffaitahu minnā fatawaffahu 'alal ıman.

Meaning :

"O Allah, forgive those of us who are still alive and those who have passed away, those present and those absent and our young and the elderly, the males and the females. O Allah, the one whom You wish to keep alive from among us make him live according to Islam and anyone whom You wish to die from among us, let him die in the state of *īmān* (faith).

If the dead is an adult woman, then the last two lines of this *Du'ā* are replaced by :

اَللّٰهُمَّ مَنْ اَحْيَيْتَهَا مِنَّا فَاَحْيِهَا عَلَى الْاِسْلَامِ
وَمَنْ تَوَفَّيْتَهَا مِنَّا فَتَوَفَّهَا عَلَى الْاِيْمَانِ

Allāhumma man aḥyaitahā minnā fa aḥyihā 'alāl Islām, wa man tawaffaitahā minnā fatawaffahā 'alāl īmān.

Meaning :

"O Allah, she to whom You wish to keep alive from us, make her live according to Islam and she to whom You wish to die from among us, let her die in the state of īmān.

If the dead is a boy, then recite the following :

اَللّٰهُمَّ اجْعَلْهُ لَنَا فَرَطًا وَّاجْعَلْهُ لَنَا اَجْرًا وَّذُخْرًا وَّاجْعَلْهُ لَنَا
شَافِعًا وَّمُشَفَّعًا ۔

Allāhumma aj'alhulanā farṭān wa aja'lhu lanā ajrān wa dhukhrān wa aj'alhu lanā shāfi'ān wa mushfa'ān.

Meaning :

"O Allah, make him our forerunner and make him for us a reward and a treasure; make him one who will plead for us, and accept his pleading."

If the deceased is a girl, then recite the following :

اَللّٰهُمَّ اجْعَلْهَا لَنَا فَرَطًا وَّاجْعَلْهَا لَنَا اَجْرًا وَّذُخْرًا وَّاجْعَلْهَا
لَنَا شَافِعَةً وَّمُشَفَّعَةً ۔

Allāhumma aja'lhā lanā farṭān wa aja'lhā lanā ajrān wa dhukhrān wa aja'lhā lanā shāfi'atan wa mushfa'ah.

Meaning :

"O Allah, make her our forerunner and make her for us a reward and a treasure; make her one who will plead for us and accept her pleading."

After reciting any of the above *du'ās* according to the status of the dead person, the *Imām* says *Allāhu Akbar* loudly and you have to repeat the words *Allāhu Akbar* quietly.

Then the *Imām* turns his face first to the right saying *Assalāmu 'alaikum wa Raḥmatullāh* and then to the left repeating the same words. Follow the *Imām*, repeating the Arabic words quietly.

This completes *Ṣalātul Janāzah.*

Some Du'ās After Prayer

It is good practice to ask the forgiveness and mercy of Allah at the end of your *ṣalāh*. You can say this in your own words and in your own language. But it is better for you to memorise some Du'ā's in Arabic.

رَبَّنَآ اٰتِنَا فِى الدُّنْيَا حَسَنَةً وَّفِى الْاٰخِرَةِ حَسَنَةً وَّقِنَا عَذَابَ النَّارِ ○

Rabbanā ātinā fiddunıā ḥasanah wa fil ākhirati ḥasanah wa qinā 'adhābannār.

Meaning :

''O Our Lord, grant us good in this world and good in the hereafter and save us from the punishment of Hell-fire.

اَللّٰهُمَّ اَنْتَ السَّلَامُ وَمِنْكَ السَّلَامُ تَبَارَكْتَ يَاذَا الْجَلَالِ وَالْاِكْرَامِ

Allāhumma antas salāmu wa minkas salāmu tabārakata yā dhāljalāli wal ikrām.

Meaning :

''O Allah, You are the source of peace and from You comes peace, exalted You are, O Lord of Majesty and Honour.

اَللّٰهُمَّ اغْفِرْلِىْ وَلِوَالِدَىَّ وَلِاُسْتَاذِىْ وَلِجَمِيْعِ الْمُؤْمِنِيْنَ وَالْمُؤْمِنَاتِ
وَالْمُسْلِمِيْنَ وَالْمُسْلِمَاتِ بِرَحْمَتِكَ يَآ اَرْحَمَ الرَّاحِمِيْنَ ○

Allāhummaghfirlī waliwālidaiyya waliustādhī wali jamī'il mu'minīna, Walmu'minati wal muslimīna wal muslimāti biraḥmatika yā 'arḥamurrāhimīn.

Meaning :

''O Allah, forgive me and my parents and my teachers and all the believing men and women and all muslim-men and women with your mercy. O Most Merciful of all who have mercy.''

رَبَّنَا ظَلَمْنَآ اَنْفُسَنَا وَاِنْ لَّمْ تَغْفِرْلَنَا وَتَرْحَمْنَا لَنَكُوْنَنَّ مِنَ الْخٰسِرِيْنَ ○

Rabbanā ẓalamnā anfusinā wa inlam taghfirlanā wa tarḥamnā lana kunanna minal khāsirīn.

Meaning :

''Our Lord, we have wronged ourselves and if You do not forgive us and have no mercy on us, surely we will be of the losers.''

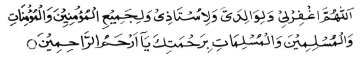

Exercise : 5

1st Form

1. Answer the following :
   a. What are the five basic duties of *Islam?*
   b. What is the *declaration of faith?*
   c. What are the five daily prayers?
   d. How many *Farḍ raka'hs* are there in the five daily prayers?
2. Fill in the blanks :
   To say your __________ , you must be __________ and pure. The *Qur'ān* says "Surely, *Allah* __________ those who __________ to Him and those who care for __________ . (2:222).
3. Draw the calligraphy of the declaration of faith as on Page 41.

2nd and 3rd Forms

1. Fill in the gaps :
   Islam is based on __________ things : declaring that there is _____ god but ______________ and that __________ is the messenger of __________ , the establishment of __________ , the payment of __________ , the __________ and __________ in the month of __________ .
2. Draw the illustration about the timings of prayer in your writing book.
3. Write the meaning of *Sūratul Fātiḥah.*

4th, 5th and 6th Forms

1. Describe in your own words the importance of *Ṣalāh* and list its lessons.
2. Write down the meaning in English of *Tashahhud.*
3. Under what conditions must you repeat your *Ṣalāh?*

Exercise : 5(a)

1st Form

1. Write the names of five daily prayers with their timings.
2. What do you recite after you finish your *Wuḍū'*? Write down its English meaning.
3. What makes you repeat your *Wuḍū'*?

Exercise : 5(b)

1st Form

1. How do you make your *Niyyah* for prayer?
2. Answer the following :
   a. What is *Qiblah?*
   b. What is the direction of *Qiblah* from England?
   c. What is *Qiyām?*
   d. What is *Ruku'?*
   e. What is *Sajdah?*
3. Write the meaning of :
   a. *Bismillāhir raḥmānir Raḥīm*
   b. *A'udhu billāhi minash shaiṭānir rajīm.*

Exercise : 5(c)

1st Form

1. What is the meaning of the *Tasbīḥ* which is recited in *Ruku'?*
2. What do we recite in *Sajdah?*
3. What is *Sajdatus Sahw?*
4. Draw a table of the *raka'hs of Ṣalāh.*
5. What is the purpose of *Ṣalāh?*

Exercise : 5(d)

1st Form

1. Write the meaning in English of *Du'ā' Al-Qunūt.*
2. Write one *Du'ā* in Arabic and in English.
3. What is the importance of *Ṣalātul Jumu'ah?*
4. When are you not allowed to say your *Ṣalāh?*
5. What is *Ṣalātul Janāzah?* When would you be guilty if you did not join it?

Eleven Surahs of the Qur'ān

1. Al-Fātiḥah

سُوْرَةُ الْفَاتِحَة

بِسْمِ اللّٰهِ الرَّحْمٰنِ الرَّحِيْمِ ○
اَلْحَمْدُ لِلّٰهِ رَبِّ الْعٰلَمِيْنَ ○ الرَّحْمٰنِ الرَّحِيْمِ ○ مٰلِكِ يَوْمِ الدِّيْنِ ○
اِيَّاكَ نَعْبُدُ وَاِيَّاكَ نَسْتَعِيْنُ ○ اِهْدِنَا الصِّرَاطَ الْمُسْتَقِيْمَ ○
صِرَاطَ الَّذِيْنَ اَنْعَمْتَ عَلَيْهِمْ ۙ غَيْرِ الْمَغْضُوْبِ عَلَيْهِمْ
وَلَا الضَّآلِّيْنَ ○

Bismillāhir raḥmānir raḥīm
Alḥamdu lillāhi rabbil 'ālamīn.
Arrahmānir raḥīm.
Māliki yawmiddīn.
Iyyāka na'budu wa iyyāka nasta'īn.
Ihdinaṣ ṣirāṭal Mustaqīm.
Ṣirāṭalladhīna an'amta 'alaihim,
Ghairil maghdūbi 'alaihim wa lāddāllīn. (Āmīn).
Meaning :
In the name of Allah, the most Merciful, the most Kind.
All praise is for Allah, the Lord of the Worlds,
The most Merciful, the most Kind;
Master of the day of Judgment.
You alone we worship; and You alone we ask for help.
Guide us along the straight way —
The way of those whom You have favoured
and not of those who earn Your anger
nor of those who go astray.

2. An Nas (114)

سُوْرَةُ النَّاس

بِسْمِ اللّٰهِ الرَّحْمٰنِ الرَّحِيْمِ ○
قُلْ اَعُوْذُ بِرَبِّ النَّاسِ ○ مَلِكِ النَّاسِ ○ اِلٰهِ النَّاسِ ○ مِنْ شَرِّ الْوَسْوَاسِ ۙ
الْخَنَّاسِ ○ الَّذِىْ يُوَسْوِسُ فِىْ صُدُوْرِ النَّاسِ ○ مِنَ الْجِنَّةِ وَالنَّاسِ ○

Bismillāhir raḥmānir raḥīm.
Qul a'ūdhu birabbin nās.
Malikin nās. Ilāhin nās.
Min sharril waswāsil khannās.
Alladhī yuwaswisu fi ṣudūrinnās
Minal jinnati wannās.
Meaning :
In the name of Allah, the most Merciful, the most Kind.
Say, I seek refuge in the Lord of mankind,
the King of mankind,
the God of mankind,
from the mischief of the sneaking whisperer,
Who whispers in the hearts of mankind,
from among jinn and mankind.

3. **Al-Falaq (113)** سُورَةُ الْفَلَقِ

بِسْمِ اللهِ الرَّحْمٰنِ الرَّحِيْمِ ○
قُلْ اَعُوْذُ بِرَبِّ الْفَلَقِ ○ مِنْ شَرِّ مَا خَلَقَ ○ وَمِنْ شَرِّ غَاسِقٍ اِذَا
وَقَبَ ○ وَمِنْ شَرِّ النَّفّٰثٰتِ فِى الْعُقَدِ ○ وَمِنْ شَرِّ حَاسِدٍ اِذَا حَسَدَ ○

Bismillāhir raḥmānir raḥīm.
Qul a'ūdhu bi rabbil falaq.
Min sharri mā khalaq.
Wa min sharri ghāsiqin idhā waqab.
Wa min sharrin naffāthāti fill 'uqad.
Wa min sharri ḥāsidin idhā ḥasad.
Meaning :
In the name of Allah, the most Merciful, the most Kind.
Say, I seek refuge in the Lord of the Daybreak;
from the evil of what He has created;
from the evil of the darkness when it is intense;
from the evil of those who seek to promote discord
(malignant witchcraft);
from the evil of the envier when he envies.

4. **Al-Ikhlāṣ (112)**

سُوْرَةُ الْاِخْلَاص

بِسْمِ اللهِ الرَّحْمٰنِ الرَّحِيْمِ ○

قُلْ هُوَ اللهُ اَحَدٌ ○ اَللهُ الصَّمَدُ ○ لَمْ يَلِدْ ○ وَلَمْ يُوْلَدْ ○

وَلَمْ يَكُنْ لَّهٗ كُفُوًا اَحَدٌ ○

Bismillāhir raḥmānir raḥīm
Qul huwāllāhu aḥad.
Allāhuṣ ṣamad.
Lam yalid wa lam yūlad.
Wa lam yakul lahu kufuwān aḥad.

Meaning :

In the name of Allah, the most Merciful, the most Kind.
Say, He is Allah, the One.
Allah is Eternal and Absolute.
None is born of Him nor is He born.
And there is none like Him.

5. **Al-Lahab (111)**

سُوْرَةُ اللَّهَبِ

بِسْمِ اللهِ الرَّحْمٰنِ الرَّحِيْمِ ○

تَبَّتْ يَدَآ اَبِيْ لَهَبٍ وَّتَبَّ ○ مَآ اَغْنٰى عَنْهُ مَالُهٗ وَمَا كَسَبَ ○

سَيَصْلٰى نَارًا ذَاتَ لَهَبٍ ○ وَّامْرَاَتُهٗ ۗ حَمَّالَةَ الْحَطَبِ ○

فِيْ جِيْدِهَا حَبْلٌ مِّنْ مَّسَدٍ ○

Bismillāhir raḥmānir raḥīim.
Tabbat yadā abī Lahabin wa tabb.
Mā agnā 'anhu māluhu wa mā kasab.
Sayaṣlā nāran dhāta lahab.
Wāmrātuhu ḥammā latal haṭab.
Fī jīdihā ḥablum mim masad.

Meaning :

In the name of Allah, the most Merciful, the most Kind.
May the hands of Abu Lahab perish; doomed he is.
His wealth and his gains shall not avail him.
He shall enter a blazing fire,
and his wife, the carrier of firewood,
shall have a rope of palm fibre round her neck.

6. **An-Naṣr (110)** سُوْرَةُ النَّصْر

بِسْمِ اللّٰهِ الرَّحْمٰنِ الرَّحِيْمِ ○

إِذَا جَآءَ نَصْرُ اللّٰهِ وَالْفَتْحُ ○ وَرَأَيْتَ النَّاسَ يَدْخُلُوْنَ فِيْ دِيْنِ اللّٰهِ
أَفْوَاجًا ○ فَسَبِّحْ بِحَمْدِ رَبِّكَ وَاسْتَغْفِرْهُ إِنَّهُ كَانَ تَوَّابًا ○

Bismillāhir raḥmānir raḥīm.
Idhā Jāā' naṣrullāhi walfatḥu.
Wa ra aitannāsa yad khulūna fi dīnillāhi afwājā..
Fasabbiḥ biḥamdi rabbika wastaghfirhu,
Innahu kāna tawwāba.

Meaning :

In the name of Allah, the most Merciful, the most Kind.
When the victory granted by Allah and the conquest come;
and you see people embracing the religion of Allah in large numbers
then celebrate the praises of your Lord, and seek His forgiveness.
He is ever ready to show mercy.

7. **Al-Kāfirūn (109)** سُوْرَةُ الْكٰفِرُوْن

بِسْمِ اللّٰهِ الرَّحْمٰنِ الرَّحِيْمِ ○

قُلْ يٰٓأَيُّهَا الْكٰفِرُوْنَ ○ لَآ أَعْبُدُ مَا تَعْبُدُوْنَ ○ وَلَآ أَنْتُمْ
عٰبِدُوْنَ مَآ أَعْبُدُ ○ وَلَآ أَنَا عَابِدٌ مَّا عَبَدْتُّمْ ○ وَلَآ أَنْتُمْ
عٰبِدُوْنَ مَآ أَعْبُدُ ○ لَكُمْ دِيْنُكُمْ وَلِيَ دِيْنِ ○

Bismillāhir raḥmānir raḥīm.
Qul yā ayyuhāl kāfirūn.
Lā a'budu mā ta'budūn.
Wa lā antum 'ābidūna mā a'bud.
Wa lā anā 'ābidum mā'abadtum.
Wa lā antum 'ābidūna mā a'bud.
La kum dīnukum walia dīn.

Meaning :

In the name of Allah, the most Merciful, the most Kind.
Say, O disbelievers!
I do not worship what you worship;
nor do you worship what I worship.
I shall never worship what you worship.
Neither you worship what I worship.
You have your own religion and I have mine.

8. Al-Kawthar (108) سُوْرَةُ الْكَوْثَرِ

بِسْمِ اللّٰهِ الرَّحْمٰنِ الرَّحِيْمِ ○

إِنَّا أَعْطَيْنٰكَ الْكَوْثَرَ ○ فَصَلِّ لِرَبِّكَ وَانْحَرْ ○ إِنَّ شَانِئَكَ هُوَ الْأَبْتَرُ ○

Bismillāhir raḥmānir raḥīm.
Innā a'ṭainakal kawthar.
Fa ṣalli lirabbika wanḥar.
Inna shāni'aka huwāl abtar.
Meaning :
In the name of Allah, the most Merciful, the most Kind.
Indeed we have given you the Kawthar (Abundance or fountain);
So pray to your Lord and make sacrifice.
Surely your hater is the one cut off.

9. Al-Mā'ūn (107) سُوْرَةُ الْمَاعُوْنِ

بِسْمِ اللّٰهِ الرَّحْمٰنِ الرَّحِيْمِ ○

أَرَءَيْتَ الَّذِيْ يُكَذِّبُ بِالدِّيْنِ ○ فَذٰلِكَ الَّذِيْ يَدُعُّ الْيَتِيْمَ ○
وَلَا يَحُضُّ عَلٰى طَعَامِ الْمِسْكِيْنِ ○ فَوَيْلٌ لِّلْمُصَلِّيْنَ ○
الَّذِيْنَ هُمْ عَنْ صَلَاتِهِمْ سَاهُوْنَ ○ الَّذِيْنَ هُمْ يُرَآءُوْنَ ○
وَيَمْنَعُوْنَ الْمَاعُوْنَ ○

Bismillāhir raḥmānir raḥīm.
Ara'ital ladhī yukadhdhibu biddīn.
Fadhālikal ladhī yadu'ul yatīm.
Wa lāyaḥuḍḍu 'alā ta'āmil miskīn.
Fawailul lil muṣallīn.
Alladhīna hum 'an ṣalātihim sāhūn.
Alladhīna hum yurā'wūn.
wayamna'ūnal mā'ūn.
Meaning :
In the name of Allah, the most Merciful, the most Kind.
Have you seen him who denies our religion?
It is he who harshly repels the orphan
and does not urge others to feed the needy.
Woe to those who pray
but are heedless of their prayers;
who put on a show of piety
but refuse to give even the smallest help to others.

10. **Quraish (106)** سُوْرَةُ قُرَيْشٍ

بِسْمِ اللّٰهِ الرَّحْمٰنِ الرَّحِيْمِ ۝

لِاِيْلٰفِ قُرَيْشٍ ۝ اٖلٰفِهِمْ رِحْلَةَ الشِّتَآءِ وَالصَّيْفِ ۝ فَلْيَعْبُدُوْا

رَبَّ هٰذَا الْبَيْتِ ۝ الَّذِيْٓ اَطْعَمَهُمْ مِّنْ جُوْعٍ ۙ وَّاٰمَنَهُمْ مِّنْ خَوْفٍ ۝

Bismillāhir raḥmānir raḥīm
Li īlāfi quraishin.
Īlāfi him riḥlatashitā'i waṣ ṣaif.
Falya'budū rabba hādhāl bait.
Alladhī 'aṭ'amahum min ju'in,
Wa āmanahum min khawf.

Meaning :

In the name of Allah, the most Merciful, the most Kind.
For the tradition of the Quraish :
their tradition of travelling in winter and summer.
Let them worship the Lord of this house,
Who provides them with food lest they
should go hungry, and with security
lest they should live in fear.

11. **Al-Fil (105)** سُوْرَةُ الْفِيْلِ

بِسْمِ اللّٰهِ الرَّحْمٰنِ الرَّحِيْمِ ۝

اَلَمْ تَرَ كَيْفَ فَعَلَ رَبُّكَ بِاَصْحٰبِ الْفِيْلِ ۝ اَلَمْ يَجْعَلْ كَيْدَهُمْ

فِيْ تَضْلِيْلٍ ۝ وَّاَرْسَلَ عَلَيْهِمْ طَيْرًا اَبَابِيْلَ ۝ تَرْمِيْهِمْ بِحِجَارَةٍ

مِّنْ سِجِّيْلٍ ۝ فَجَعَلَهُمْ كَعَصْفٍ مَّاْكُوْلٍ ۝

Bismillāhir raḥmānir raḥīm.
Alam tara kaifa fa'ala rabbuka bi aṣḥābil fīl.
Alam yaj'al kaidahum fī taḍlīl.
Wa arsala 'alaihim ṭairān abābīl.
Tarmīhim biḥijāratin min sijjīl
Fa ja'alahum ka'aṣfin ma'kūl.

Meaning :

In the name of Allah, the most Merciful, the most Kind.
Have you not seen how your Lord has
dealt with the people of the elephant?
Did he not cause their treacherous plan to be futile,
and send against them flights of birds,
which pelted them with stones of sand and clay?
Thus He made them like devoured dry leaves.

Lessons of Ṣalāh

Ṣalāh is the most important of the five basic duties of Islam. We come closer to Allah, by performing it regularly, correctly and with full awareness of its significance and meaning. At this stage, refresh your memory about the purpose of our creation and the need for performing Islamic duties. Allah has created us to worship Him. He says in the *Qur'ān : "I have not created jinn and human beings (for any other purpose) except to worship me"* (51:56). So, whatever duty we carry out, we must bear in mind that we are doing it for Allah's sake. Only then, can we expect to gain the desired benefits of the performance of *Ṣalāh.*

The lessons of *Ṣalāh* are :

1 *It brings men and women closer to Allah.*
2 *It keeps human beings away from indecent, shameful and forbidden activities.*
3 *It is a training programme designed to control evil desires and passions.*
4 *It purifies the heart, develops the mind and comforts the soul.*
5 *It is a constant reminder of Allah and His greatness.*
6 *It develops discipline and will power.*
7 *It is a guide to the most upright way of life.*
8 *It is a proof of true equality, solid unity and universal brotherhood.*
9 *It is the source of patience, courage, hope and confidence.*
10 *It is a means of cleanliness, purity and punctuality.*
11 *It develops gratitude, humility and refinement.*
12 *It is the demonstration of our obedience to our Creator.*
13 *It is the solid programme of preparing oneself for Jihād — Striving one's utmost to please Allah.*

If your Ṣalāh does not improve your conduct you must think seriously and find out where you are going wrong.

Zakāh

Zakāh (welfare contribution) is the third pillar of Islam. The Arabic word *Zakāh* means to purify or cleanse. *Zakāh* is to be paid once a year on savings at the rate of two and a half per cent. This rate applies to cash, bank savings and gold and silver jewellery. The rate for cattle and agricultural produce is different.

Payment of *Zakāh* is a means of keeping our wealth clear of greed

SCHEDULE OF ZAKAH

	Wealth on which Zakāh is payable	Amount which determines the payment of *Zakāh* *(NIṢĀB)*	Rate of Zakāh
1	Agricultural produce	*5 Awsuq (653kg)* per harvest ★	*5* per cent produce in case of irrigated land; *10* per cent of produce from rain fed land.
2	Gold, Silver, ornaments of gold and silver	*85* grams of gold or *595* grams of silver ★	*2.5* per cent of value
3	Cash in hand or at Bank	Value of *595* grams of silver ★	*2.5* per cent of amount
4	Trading goods	Value of *595* grams of silver ★	*2.5* per cent value of goods
5	Cows and buffaloes	*30* in number	For every *30*, one *1*-year-old; for every *40*, one *2*-year-old
6	Goats and sheep	*40* in number	One for first *40*; two for *120*; three for *300*; one more for every *100*
7	Produce of mines	Any quantities	*20* per cent of value of produce
8	Camels	*5* in number	a Up to *24*, one sheep or goat for each five camels b *25-35*, one *1*-year-old she-camel c *36-45*, one *2*-year-old she-camel d *46-60*, one *3*-year-old she-camel e *61-75*, one *4*-year-old she-camel f *76-90*, two *2*-year-old she-camels g *91-120*, two *3*-year-old she-camels h *121* or more, one *2*-year-old she-camel for each additional *40*, or one *3*-year-old she-camel for each additional *50*

★ *Fiqhuz Zakāh* — Yūsuf Qarḍāwī, Vol. I, Page 260, 273 (Beirut, 1977).

and selfishness. It also encourages us to be honest in our earnings and expenditure.

Zakāh is a compulsory payment and is neither charity nor a tax. Charity is optional and taxes can be used by the state for any purpose, but *Zakāh* has to be spent under fixed headings like helping the poor, the needy, payment of salaries to its collectors, to free captives and debtors, for travellers in need, to win over hearts and for the cause of Allah (9:60).

Zakāh is an act of *'Ibādah. 'Ibādah* is an Arabic term which means worship and obedience. It includes all activities of life, if we do them to please Allah. We pay *Zakāh* to gain Allah's favour.

Zakāh provides us with the opportunity of sharing our excess wealth with those less fortunate than ourselves. In fact we and our wealth belong to Allah. He is the real owner and we are merely the trustees of His wealth. We do our duty as trustees if we pay *Zakāh* as an obligatory part of *'Ibādah*.

We learned earlier that Islam is a complete code of life which includes among other things, the economic side of life. Islam has its own economic principles. *Zakāh* is one of the basic principles of the Islamic economy, based on social welfare and fair distribution of wealth. In addition to the compulsory payment of *Zakāh*, Muslims are encouraged in the Qur'ān to make voluntary contributions to help the poor and the needy, and for other social welfare purposes. This voluntary contribution is called *Ṣadaqah* (charity).

Through the payment of *Zakāh*, the rich share their wealth with the poor and thus the process of concentration of wealth is checked and fair distribution ensured.

Ṣawm

Ṣawm (fasting), the fourth pillar of Islam, is another act of *'Ibādah*. All adult Muslims must fast from dawn to sunset every day of *Ramaḍān*, the ninth month of the Islamic calendar. This means abstaining from eating, drinking, smoking and conjugal relations during the hours of fasting. Travellers and the sick can defer fasting during Ramaḍān and make up for it later.

Ṣawm develops self-control and helps us to overcome selfishness, greed, laziness and other faults. It is an annual training programme to refresh us for carrying out our duties towards Allah, the Creator and Sustainer. *Ṣawm* gives us the feeling of hunger and thirst. We experience for ourselves what it is like to have an empty stomach. This develops our feeling for the poor and hungry people. Fasting teaches us to control the love of comfort. It also helps us to keep our sexual desires within control. Hunger, comfort and sex are three factors which must be kept under control to behave as Allah's servants.

It helps us to remain truly obedient to Allah's commands. That is why the *Qur'ān* says : *"O you who believe; Fasting is prescribed for you as it was prescribed for those before you that you are expected to be truly obedient".* (2:183). A truly obedient Muslim is called a *Muttaqī* and his true obedience or piety — developed through ṣawm — is known as *TAQWĀ* in Islam. *Taqwā* keeps a person away from sin.

The month of *Ramaḍān* is a month of forgiveness, mercy and a means of avoiding the punishment of Hell.

The duty of fasting is only for Allah's sake and there is a very pleasing and attractive reward for this in the life after death.

The following acts will break the fast :

a Deliberate eating or drinking during fasting hours.
b If anything enters the body through the nose or mouth; this includes smoking or sniffing any powdered substance.
c Having any conjugal relations during fasting hours.

An injection in the muscle is allowed during fasting but not an intraveneous nutritional injection. Unintentional eating or drinking due to forgetfulness or rinsing out the mouth or bathing and putting drops in the eye do not make the fast invalid.

A Muslim is expected to remain away from all bad actions during his fast. He should not tell a lie, break a promise or do any deceitful act.

The very purpose of fasting is to make a Muslim able to control his passions, so that he becomes a person of good deeds and intentions. Anger — a common human weakness — can also be brought under control by fasting.

In addition to the compulsory fasting in *Ramaḍān*, a Muslim may fast during other times of the year. These facts will be treated as *Sunnah.*

Fasting is not allowed during menstruation of women. They are required to make up the days lost during this period at some other time. A Muslim must not fast :

a on the day of *'Īdul Fiṭr*

b on the day of *'Īdul Aḍḥā*

The Qur'ān was revealed in the month of Ramaḍān. There is a night in the month which is "better than a thousand months" (97:3). This night is called *LAILATUL QADR* (night of power). According to *Ḥadīth*, this night occurs during the last ten days of Ramaḍān (most probably the odd numbered nights). It is a night of great importance; we should worship as much as we can on this night.

An additional prayer known as *TARĀWĪḤ* (20 raka'h or 8 raka'h) is offered during *Ramaḍān* after *'Ishā'*. This is a sunnah prayer in which efforts are made to recite as much of the *Qur'ān* as possible. In many mosques, the whole *Qur'ān* is recited in *Tarāwīḥ* prayer. This prayer is generally offered in congregation. Those who cannot join a congregation should offer *Tarāwīḥ* at home. A pre-dawn meal known as *Suḥūr* is taken in *Ramaḍān*.

At the end of Ramaḍān Muslims celebrate *'ĪDUL FIṬR*, a day of thanksgiving and happiness. It is one of the great occasions for the Muslim community. On this day, Muslims offer special prayers in congregation and thank Allah for His blessings and mercy.

Ḥajj

Ḥajj is the fifth pillar of Islam. It is a visit to *Al-Ka'bah*, the house of Allah in Makkah, once in a lifetime by those Muslims who can afford to make the journey. It is performed during the period from the 8th to 13th *Dhū'l Ḥijjah*, the twelfth month of the Islamic calendar.

Al-Ka'bah, known as *Baitullāh* (House of Allah), is a cube-like one-storey building which was built originally by *Ādam* and later rebuilt by Prophet *Ibrāhīm* (Abraham) and his son *Ismā'īl* (Ishmael). It is the first house ever built for the sole purpose of the worship of Allah. Allah has blessed this *Al-Ka'bah*. Muslims who can afford to make the journey and are physically fit come here every year from all over the world.

The occasion may rightly be called the *Annual International Muslim Assembly*. During *Ḥajj*, the Islamic brotherhood becomes particularly evident and can be experienced in a special way by everyone who takes

Al-Ka'bah — The 'House of Allah' at Makkah

part. Barriers of language, territory, colour and race disappear and the bond of faith is uppermost. Everyone has the same status in the house of Allah — the status of His servant.

Ḥajj has a number of important rituals associated with it, including :

1 *Putting on Iḥrām.*
2 *Going round Al-Ka'bah seven times.*
3 *A fast walk between Aṣ-Ṣafā and Al-Marwah near Al-Ka'bah.*
4 *Visiting and staying at MINĀ, 'ARAFAH and MUZDALIFAH.*
5 *Throwing pebbles at three fixed places in Minā..*
6 *Cutting or shortening hair.*
7 *Sacrifice of an animal (sheep, goat, cow or camel).*

At the time of *Ḥajj*, while approaching *Makkah*, a pilgrim must put on *Iḥrām* before reaching a point called *MĪQĀT* (station). Iḥrām is two sheets of unsewn white cloth for men. This is a very simple form of dress a pilgrim must wear in place of his normal everyday clothes. For a woman, *Iḥrām* is her ordinary dress.

This change is very significant. It reminds the pilgrim of his position in relation to Allah. He is a humble servant of his creator. It also reminds him that after death he will be wrapped in white sheets and his favourite or expensive clothes will be left behind.

When he puts on *Iḥrām*, the pilgrim expresses his intention *(Niyyah)* by saying "I intend to put on *Iḥrām* for *Ḥajj*".

There are then some restrictions on the pilgrim while in the state of *Iḥrām*. He or she *must not* :

a	*use perfume*	*— to help forget enjoyment of ordinary daily life*
b	*kill or harm animals, even insects*	*— to feel that everything belongs to Allah*
c	*break or uproot plants*	*— to kill one's urge for aggression and feel a love for nature*
d	*hunt*	*— to develop mercy*
e	*marry or take part in a wedding*	*— to forget normal life and think of the Creator*
f	*anything dishonest or arrogant*	*— to behave like a servant of Allah*
g	*carry arms*	*— to give up aggressive attitude*
h	*cover the head (males)*	*— to express humbleness*
i	*cover the face (females)*	*— to feel a pure atmosphere*
j	*wear shoes covering ankles*	*— to express simplicity*
k	*cut hair*	*— to express non-interference with nature*
l	*clip nails*	
m	*conjugal relations*	*— to forget worldly pleasure*

All these restrictions make a pilgrim think of Allah and his ultimate goal in life — success in the life after death — and nothing else. While in *Iḥrām* the pilgrim recites *Talbīyah* as follows :

لَبَّيْكَ اللّٰهُمَّ لَبَّيْكَ ، لَبَّيْكَ لَا شَرِيْكَ لَكَ لَبَّيْكَ ،
اِنَّ الْحَمْدَ وَالنِّعْمَتَ لَكَ وَالْمُلْكَ ، لَا شَرِيْكَ لَكَ

Labbaika allāhumma labbaik, labbaika lā sharīka laka labbaik, innal ḥamda wanni'mata laka wal mulk, lā sharīka lak.

"Here I am O Lord, here I am, here I am, You have no partner, here I am, surely praise, blessings and the kingdom are for You. You have no partner."

Ḥajj has in it all the lessons of ṣalāh, zakāh and ṣawm. Do you remember why we offer Ṣalāh, pay Zakāh and fast? We offer Ṣalāh to remember Allah, pay Zakāh to please Him and fast only for His sake. During Ṣalāh, we present ourselves to Allah five times a day, but during Ḥajj we have to think of Allah all the time. At the time of Ṣalāh, we face towards Al-Kab'ah, but during Ḥajj we actually go there in person. Zakāh teaches us to pay part of our savings for welfare and other good causes for Allah's sake; but during Ḥajj we must sacrifice much more of our money for the pleasure of Allah.

Ṣawm teaches us to control ourselves during daylight hours from eating, drinking or smoking or having conjugal relations. But in the state of Iḥrām there are many more restrictions. Eating and drinking are not prohibited in the state of Iḥrām.

What do we learn from all these exercises during Ḥajj? We learn that we belong to Allah, we will return to Him and we must do as He commands us.

Jihād

Jihād is the use of all our energies and resources to establish the Islamic system of life, in order to gain Allah's favour. *Jihād* is an Arabic word which means to try one's utmost. It is a continuous process. In its first phase a Muslim learns to control his own bad desires and intentions. We need to strive hard to achieve this. This is *Jihād* within ourselves and is the basis for the comprehensive Jihād which is concerned with establishing *Ma'rūf* (right) and removing *Munkar* (evil) from our lives and from society. It demands the use of all our material and mental resources. Eventually we may be required to give our life for the cause of Islam.

The aim of *Jihād* is to seek pleasure of Allah. This must not be forgotten because this purpose is the basis of all Islamic endeavours.

Earlier, we learned about the basic duties of *Shahādah, Ṣalāh, Zakāh,*

Ṣawm and *Ḥajj*. All these duties teach us to obey Allah and gain his favour so that we pass the test on the day of judgment, and receive the reward of entering the Paradise — the place of permanent happiness, joy and peace.

Regular and conscious performance of the four basic duties will inspire us to live and die for the cause of Islam, which we believe to be the only right course for the success in life here and hereafter. In other words, all Islamic duties should prepare us to engage in Jihād. Jihād is the end result of our efforts in *Ṣalāh, Zakāh, Ṣawm* and *Ḥajj*. We cannot think of Islam without *Jihād*.

We would like to see truth prevail and untruth vanish, but we are aware that this cannot happen on its own; we have to do our utmost to achieve it. The performance of other Islamic duties will be meaningless if they do not lead us towards the target of *Jihād*.

The method of *Jihād* is the one practised by the prophet *Muḥammad* (pbuh). His life is the perfect example for us and we will learn about it later.

Our duties as Muslims is to carry out Allah's commands and to urge others to do the same. This duty has been given to us by Allah in his own words in the *Qur'ān* :

"You are the best of Ummah (community) you have been raised for mankind so that you command what is right and forbid what is evil, and you believe in Allah." (3:110).

We should ask others to be obedient to Allah in an appealing and convincing way. Our own life-style will count for much here. It is most important that we try hard to practise what we say. Allah does not like those whose words and deeds are not the same. The *Qur'ān* says, *"Why do you ask of others the right conduct and you yourselves forget?"* (2:44). In another place in the Qur'ān Allah says, *"O you who believe! Why do you say that which you do not? It is most hateful to Allah that you say that which you do not"* (61:2, 3).

These verses clearly direct us to compare our own deeds with our words. To achieve this, we must carry out our duty to do good ourselves and urge others to do the same. This will enable us to remove our weaknesses and deficiencies. None of us is perfect, but our imperfections would gradually decrease if we do our very best to pursue our duty of *Jihād*.

Exercise : 6

1st Form

1. Write the meaning of *Sūratul Kawthar.*
2. Answer the following questions :
   a. What is the meaning of *Zakāh?*
   b. What is the rate of *Zakāh* on your cash savings?
   c. What is the time of *Ṣawm* in *Ramaḍān?*
   d. What is *Lailatul Qadr?*
3. Write a story about *'Īdul Fiṭr.*
4. Write in your own words about *Ḥajj?*

2nd and 3rd Forms

1. How do you make *Niyyah* for your *Ṣalāh?*
2. Write down the meaning in English of *Sūratul Lahab.*
3. Answer the following questions :
   a. What lesson do we get from the payment of *Zakāh?*
   b. What does *Ṣawm* develop in us?
   c. What makes our fasting invalid?
   d. Where is *Al-Ka'bah?*
   e. What is *Jihād?*
4. Fill in the blanks :
   Ḥajj has in it all the __________ of __________, __________, __________. Do you __________ why we __________ *Ṣalāh*, pay __________, and __________? We offer __________ to remember __________, pay __________ to __________ Him and __________ only for His __________.

4th, 5th and 6th Forms

1. Explain the importance of *Zakāh* in the context of social welfare in an Islamic society.
2. What are the moral and social lesson of *Ṣawm?*
3. What is the significance of putting an *iḥrām* during *Ḥajj?*
4. Discuss the importance of *Jihād* in a Muslim's life.

3

Life of Muḥammad (pbuh)

Muḥammad (pbuh)

Introduction

"Indeed, in the Messenger of Allah, you have for you, the best example." (33:21).

"We sent you (Muḥammad) not but as a blessing for the Universe." (21:107).

"He it is who has sent His messenger with the guidance and the religion of truth, that He may make it conqueror of all religion, however much idolaters may be averse." (61:9).

SO far you have been learning the basic things about Islam. Now it is time to learn about our great and dear Prophet, Muḥammad *(peace be upon him)*. It is through Muḥammad *(pbuh)* that Allah has completed the Islamic way of life.

No other person in the history of mankind has left so deep an impact on the life of his followers as Muḥammad *(pbuh)*, the last messenger of Allah. His life is the best example *(Uswatun-Ḥasanah)* for us to follow. He has shown us how to obey Allah, the Lord of the Universe. Allah says in the *Qur'ān :*

"Say (O Muḥammad), if you love Allah, follow me; Allah will love you and forgive your sins, Allah is Forgiving and Merciful." (3:31).

It means that Allah will be pleased with us only if we practise Islam as practised by Muḥammad *(pbuh)*. He has been described in the *Qur'ān* as 'the blessing for the Universe' *(Raḥmatul lil 'ālamīn)*.

Muḥammad's *(pbuh)* duty, according to the *Qur'ān* was to make Islam supreme over all other systems of life (61:9, 48:28, 7:33).

In other words, you can say that Muḥammad *(pbuh)* was made the messenger of Allah to see that truth prevails and falsehood vanishes. As Muslims, we must also work towards the establishment of the supremacy of Allah's Law and the removal of evil from society. This is Jihād, which we learned about earlier.

The difference between Muḥammad *(pbuh)* and us is that he received guidance direct from Allah through revelation, but we did not. Muḥammad *(pbuh)* was not only a messenger but a man as well. He was not a super human being, but a mortal man and the last of the messengers of Allah. (18:110).

Birth and Childhood

Muḥammad *(pbuh)* was born in the noble tribe of the *Quraish* in Makkah in Saudi Arabia in 571 CE (Christian Era). His father, *'Abdullāh*, died before his birth and *Āminah*, his mother died when he was only six. A few days after his birth he was given to the care of *Ḥalīmah*, his foster-mother who suckled him and took care of him for about two years. It was the custom of the tribe of *Quraish* to give their new born babies to foster-mothers for breast-feeding.

After the death of his mother, his grandfather, *'Abdul Muṭṭalib*, looked after him. From early childhood, then, Muḥammad *(pbuh)* suffered one shock after another. His grandfather died when he was only eight years old, so Muḥammad *(pbuh)* was now looked after by his uncle, *Abū Ṭālib*, a leader of the *Quraish* and a merchant.

The name *Muḥammad* means *praiseworthy*.

A Business Trip to Syria

Muḥammad *(pbuh)* was growing up in the affectionate care of his uncle, *Abū Ṭālib*, when at the age of twelve he accompanied him on a business trip to Syria. When their caravan reached *Buṣrā* in Syria, a Christian priest called *Baḥīrā* invited them to a dinner. This was unusual. *Abū Ṭālib* and his caravan had passed this way before, several times, but was never before asked in by the priest. All the members of the caravan went to the dinner, except Muḥammad *(pbuh)*, who stayed behind, probably to look after the camels and the merchandise. *Baḥīrah* insisted on having Muḥammad *(pbuh)* join in the dinner. When he did, *Baḥīrah* asked him a few questions, and Muḥammad *(pbuh)* answered precisely and to the point.

When he heard the answers, *Baḥīrah* — a person well versed in Christianity and *the Bible* — could recognise from his reading that the boy Muḥammad *(pbuh)* was going to be a prophet in the future. He advised *Abū Ṭālib* to take special care of his nephew. When they finished their trading, *Abū Ṭālib* lost no time in returning to *Makkah* with Muḥammad *(pbuh)*.

Teenager and the Battle of Fujjār and Ḥilf-ul-Fuḍūl

When Muḥammad *(pbuh)* was fifteen, a local war broke out during the *Ḥajj* season between the tribes of *Quraish* and *Hawāzin*. According to Makkan tradition, war was forbidden in the pilgrimage season *(Ḥajj)*. Despite this, the war lasted four years with intervals, and caused tremendous hardship to people on both sides. Life was becoming intolerable because of the unnecessary bloodshed.

The reason for the war seemed silly to Muḥammad *(pbuh)*, and he felt quite disgusted at the senseless bloodshed. But it made people think. It inspired many of them to take steps to stop the war and make peace.

At the initiative of *Az-Zubair*, Muḥammad's *(pbuh)* uncle, a meeting was called at the house of *'Abdullāh Ibn Jud'ān*, who was an influential and wealthy person.

A society called *Ḥilf-ul-Fuḍūl* (Alliance for charity) was formed at this meeting, to help the oppressed, the poor and the needy. Muḥammad *(pbuh)* was present at the meeting and took the following oath :

"I uphold the pact concluded in my presence when Ibn Jud'ān gave us a great banquet. Should it ever be invoked, I shall immediately rise to answer the call".

The participation of Muḥammad *(pbuh)* in *Ḥilf-ul-Fuḍūl* is a proof of his concern and interest in the welfare activities, even in his youth.

A word of advice for you here. As young people, when you study the life of Muḥammad *(pbuh)*, you should decide to take part in the welfare of people in general and the welfare of your fellow youngsters in particular. You should study the life of Muḥammad *(pbuh)*, take lessons from it and put them into practice. If you look around you, you will find many unjust and wrong things are taking root in society. You should decide as a young person to do whatever you can to remedy the injustices and wrong-doing.

Young Shepherd

While still a boy, Muḥammad *(pbuh)* tended sheep and during this period had plenty of time to think and contemplate. He moved around with his flock in the vast expanse of the Arabian desert. It provided him with a unique opportunity to have a clear vision of nature, and to see the wonders of the creation of Allah.

Muḥammad *(pbuh)* was very proud of having spent his boyhood as a shepherd. He used to say, "Allah sent no prophet who was not a shepherd. *Mūsā* (Moses) was a shepherd, *Dāwūd* (David) was also a shepherd." The reason for this might be that Allah wanted His messengers to have experience of life as a shepherd, to help deal with human beings with rare patience, in preaching Allah's message. It is very difficult to control a flock of sheep, goats or camels which do not have any understanding or sense of right and wrong. It needs a lot of patience and care to handle animals. The experience was eventually very useful for the messengers in their task of propagating the message of Allah.

Marriage

As Muḥammad *(pbuh)* grew up, he helped in running the business of his uncle, who was managing his family with some difficulty. During this time, Muḥammad *(pbuh)* received an offer from a noble lady named *Khadījah*, to look after her business affairs. Muḥammad's *(pbuh)* fame as an honest and upright young man had now become well known in *Makkah*, which is why *Khadījah* made the proposal.

Muḥammad *(pbuh)* accepted the offer and set out for Syria with the goods of *Khadījah*, accompanied by another of her employees, called *Maysarah*. This was Muḥammad's *(pbuh)* second business trip to Syria.

He had sold the goods and bought what he was told to, before returning to *Makkah*. He made big profits for *Khadījah* on this trip because of his intelligence, skill and honesty. It was almost double what anyone else had earned for *Khadījah* in the past. During the journey, his companion *Maysarah*, noticed that Muḥammad *(pbuh)* was protected from the heat of the sun by clouds.

On their return, *Maysarah* hurried to *Khadījah* and told her about his experience of Muḥammad *(pbuh)* and about the big profits he made for her.

Khadījah, the daughter of *Khuwailid*, was a determined, intelligent and noble woman. She was deeply impressed by the ability, character and performance of Muḥammad *(pbuh)*.

Khadījah decided to send a proposal of marriage to Muḥammad *(pbuh)*. On the advice of his uncle, *Abū Ṭālib*, Muḥammad *(pbuh)* consented to the proposal and the wedding ceremony went ahead.

Now Muḥammad *(pbuh)* was a family man and the marriage marked the beginning of a new phase in his life. He was twenty five years of age when he married. *Khadījah* was forty and a widow.

They had six children — two boys, *Qāsim* and *'Abdullāh* (also known as *Ṭāhir* and *Ṭayyib*) and four girls, *Zainab, Ruqaiyyah, Umm Kulthūm* and *Fāṭimah*. All his sons died before prophethood and the daughters lived into Islam, embraced it and later migrated to *Madīnah*.

Physical Features

Muḥammad *(pbuh)* was a handsome man of medium build — neither very tall nor short. He had a large head, very black thick hair, a wide forehead, heavy eye brows and large dark eyes with long eye lashes. He had a fine nose, well placed teeth, a thick beard, a long handsome neck and a wide chest and shoulders. His skin was light coloured and he had thick palms and feet. He walked steadily with firm steps. His appearance had the mark of deep thought and contemplation. His eyes gave the feeling of the authority of a commander.

Rebuilding Al-Ka'bah

The *Ka'bah* needed repairs or rather rebuilding after a sudden flood had damaged it and cracked its walls. The task was divided among the four tribes of the Quraish. Muḥammad *(pbuh)* took an active part in the work. The rebuilding progressed and the walls were raised until it was time to place the Black Stone *(AL-ḤAJR UL-ASWAD)* on the East wall of the Ka'bah. The Black Stone was regarded as very sacred by the Makkans. This stone is still regarded as very sacred by the Muslims. At the time of Ḥajj, the pilgrims kiss this stone as a mark of respect.

But there were arguments about who should have the honour of placing this holy stone in its place. The situation became tense and there was almost a possibility of civil war over the issue. To avoid bloodshed, an idea put forward by the oldest man of *Makkah* — *Abū Umayyah* — was accepted. He proposed to all the people present : "Let the first man to enter the gate of the mosque next morning decide the matter in dispute among us."

What a pleasant surprise! The first man to enter the mosque was Muḥammad *(pbuh)*! All the people shouted in a chorus, "This is the trustworthy one" (*Al-Āmīn*, in Arabic). "This is Muḥammad *(pbuh)*."

When he came to them, he was asked to decide the matter and he agreed.

He said to them, "Give me a cloak." When they brought him a cloak, he spread it on the ground, placed the Black Stone over it and said, "Let the elders of each clan hold on to one edge of the cloak." They did so and carried the stone to its place. Muḥammad *(pbuh)* then picked up the stone and put it in its place on the wall of the Ka'bah. In this way he acted as a sort of umpire among his people and averted a bloody civil war. The rebuilding continued and was completed by the Quraish. Muḥammad *(pbuh)* was then thirty five years old.

This event shows beyond any doubt that even before his prophethood, Muḥammad *(pbuh)* was the judge and referee of the *Quraish* at the time of their disputes and crises. He earned the good names of *Al-Āmīn* (the trustworthy) and *Aṣ-Ṣādiq* (the truthful). The Irony was that after his prophethood, many of these same people turned against him because of their ignorance, and became too stone-hearted to listen to the call of the truth.

Search for the Truth

Muḥammad *(pbuh)* was a soft spoken, gentle person who loved to think and meditate. He was unusual, compared with others of his age, in that he had no interest in the temptations of worldly life, which was appropriate for the person who was destined to be the guide and the teacher for mankind.

Muḥammad *(pbuh)* used to retreat in seclusion and solitude to a cave, *Ḥirā'*, in the mount *Nūr* very often. There he passed his time in meditation and devotion. He used to pass the month of Ramaḍān in this cave. He sunk himself into deep thoughts about the mysteries of nature. It was an eager longing and serious search for the truth.

Why did he do this? He did it because he did not find the answers to the questions arising in his inquisitive mind about man, his creation and his ultimate goal.

He got quite fed up with existing social and political systems. The religions of the Jews and the Christians at that time were so corrupted by the rabbis and priests that they no longer had any appeal to reason and wisdom. He was unable to adjust himself to the senseless bloodshed, tribal disputes, oppression of the helpless by the powerful, idol worship and the degraded status of women.

The Makkans worshipped idols made by themselves. Muḥammad *(pbuh)* used to think about the stupidity of idol worship. The idols could not move, talk or do anything. How could they respond to the requests of human beings?

All these appeared nonsense to Muḥammad's *(pbuh)* thinking mind. The retreat in the cave *Ḥirā'* was to find answers to these deep-rooted feelings in his own self. It was a search for comfort, consolation, peace, tranquility and right guidance. Could it be anything else? Of course not. Muḥammad's *(pbuh)* mind was full of feelings, sympathy and concern for the welfare of the people of *Makkah*. How could his upright mind rest while turmoil, injustice, falsehood and exploitation were rampant in *Makkah*?

The idols, including the three biggest, *Al-Lāt, Al-'Uzzā, Al-Hobl*, were lifeless stones unable to help themselves if somebody happened to break them. But the Makkans worshipped them, asked their help, took oaths in their name, fought for them. Muḥammad's *(pbuh)* curious mind was striving for the truth, to get rid of the social misdeeds and change the existing social and political order.

It was during the days of his retreat in the month of *Ramaḍān* that Allah, the Lord of the Universe, favoured Muḥammad *(pbuh)* with His blessing — the first revelation of the *Qur'ān*.

Receiving the Truth

Muḥammad *(pbuh)* had reached the age of forty when one night, while meditating in his mountain retreat in the cave *Ḥirā'* in *Ramaḍān*, an angel appeared before him.

"Read!" said the angel.

"I am not a reader," replied Muḥammad *(pbuh)*. At this, the angel hugged him and squeezed him so hard that he thought he would die of suffocation. He was then released and the angel again said, *"Read!"* Muḥammad *(pbuh)* gave the same reply. The angel squeezed him harder and then released him. The angel asked him a third time, *"Read!"* Muḥammad *(pbuh)* repeated his reply, *"I am not a reader."* The angel hugged him again even harder for the third time and then released him saying :

اقْرَأْ بِاسْمِ رَبِّكَ الَّذِى خَلَقَ ۝ خَلَقَ الْإِنسَانَ مِنْ عَلَقٍ ۝
اقْرَأْ وَرَبُّكَ الْأَكْرَمُ ۝ الَّذِى عَلَّمَ بِالْقَلَمِ ۝ عَلَّمَ الْإِنسَانَ مَا لَمْ يَعْلَمْ ۝

"Read in the name of your Lord who created.
Created man from a clot of blood.
Read, your Lord is most Generous.
Who taught by the pen.
Taught man what he did not know." (96:1-5).

Muḥammad *(pbuh)* recited the verses and felt as though the words were written on his heart. These are the first revealed verses of the *Qur'ān*.

He became greatly troubled at this strange happening. He thought he might be possessed by evil spirits. He looked around and saw nothing. He was fearful and terrified. He stood motionless.

Muḥammad *(pbuh)* looked at the sky and was surprised to see the angel *Jibrā'īl* flying in the shape of a giant man. The angel said, "O Muḥammad *(pbuh)*, you are the messenger of Allah and I am *Jibrā'īl*." And wherever he looked, Muḥammad *(pbuh)* saw *Jibrā'īl* flying in the distance. He stood still until the angel disappeared.

Muḥammad *(pbuh)* rushed home in a panic and sat close to *Khadījah*. He told her all that happened. *Khadījah*, his noble, loving and caring wife, had faith in the character of her husband and comforted him, saying, *"Rejoice, O son of my uncle, and be of good heart. Surely by Him in whose hand is Khadījah's soul, I have hope that you will be the prophet of this people.*

"You have never done any wrong to anyone. You are kind to others and you help the poor. So Allah will not let you down." Muḥammad *(pbuh)*

asked *Khadījah* to wrap him up with blankets. He was wrapped up and he fell asleep.

When Muḥammad *(pbuh)* woke up, *Khadījah* took him to her cousin, *Waraqah Bin Nawfal*, who was a Christian and had knowledge of the scriptures of the Torah and the Gospel. *Waraqah* heard all that happened from Muḥammad *(pbuh)* and said, "This is the same one who keeps the secrets *(angel Gabriel)* whom Allah had sent to *Moses*. I wish I were young and could live up to the time when your people would turn you out."

Some months after the first revelation Muḥammad *(pbuh)* saw the angel *Jibrā'īl* again, flying in the sky seated in a floating chair. The Prophet became frightened and rushed home. He asked *Khadījah* to cover him up. She wrapped him with blankets and he fell asleep. After a few moments, *Khadījah* noticed that the Prophet was shivering, breathing deeply and sweating. The angel *Jibrā'īl* brought the second revelation to him which was *"O you who lie wrapped in your mantle, arise and warn! Glorify your Lord. Purify yourself. Give up uncleanliness. Give not in order to have more in return. For the sake of your Lord, endure patiently."* (74:1-7).

Seeing him in this position, *Khadījah* pleaded with Muḥammad *(pbuh)* to rest a little longer. But Muḥammad *(pbuh)* was now reassured

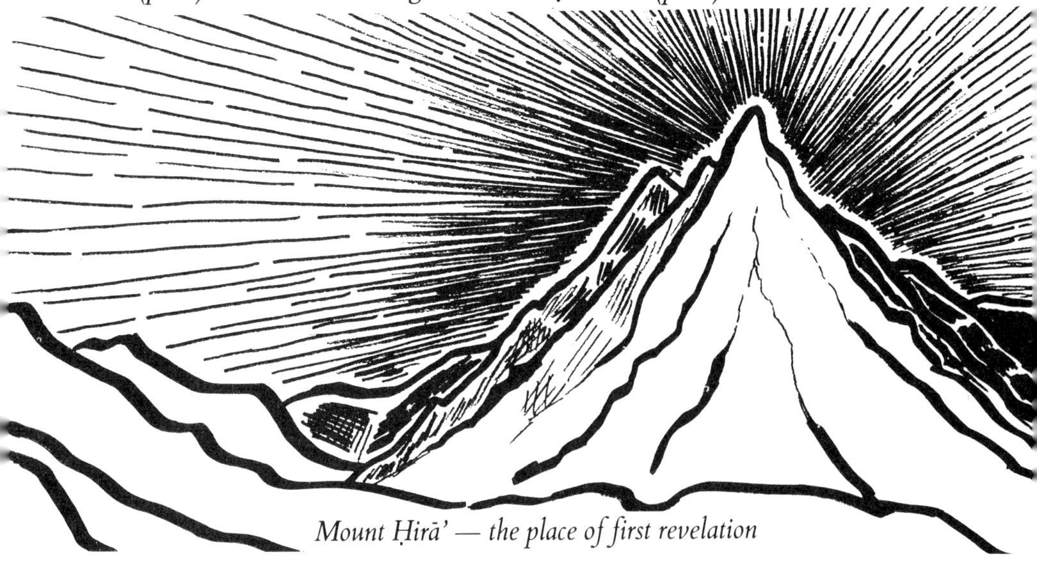

Mount Ḥirā' — the place of first revelation

and said in a firm voice, *"O Khadījah, the time of slumber and rest is past. Jibrā'īl has asked me to warn men and call them to Allah and to His worship. But whom shall I call? And who will listen to me?"*

Khadījah encouraged and assured Muḥammad *(pbuh)* about the success of his prophethood and declared her own acceptance of Islam. She thus became the first Muslim.

What a marvellous thing! *Khadījah* accepts her husband as the prophet of Allah! Who can better testify to the integrity of a person than his wife? She knew Muḥammad *(pbuh)* better than anyone else did, and could testify to his honesty and trustworthiness. No man can hide his weakness from his wife because she knows him so closely and intimately.

Islamic Movement begins

The revelation marked the beginning of Muḥammad's *(pbuh)* role as a messenger of Allah. It was also the starting point of the Islamic movement carried out by him during the rest of his life. The first phase of the movement lasted for three years, from *610 CE* (the year of revelation) to the end of *612 CE*.

To begin with Muḥammad *(pbuh)* preached the message of Allah only to his friends, his closest relatives and those whom he could trust. *'Alī,** his cousin, the son of *Abū Ṭālib*, was the second Muslim and the third was *Zaid** son of *Ḥārithah,* (Muḥammad's (pbuh) servant). *Abū Bakr** was the first from among Muḥammad's (pbuh) friends to become a Muslim. Notice here the composition of the early Muslims.

First — *Khadījah** Muḥammad's (pbuh) wife accepts Islam; second — *'Alī*, his cousin; third — *Zaid* his household servant. Outside the household, it was *Abū Bakr*. All of them were his near and dear ones.

Ten year old 'Alī accepts Islam

This briefly is how *'Alī*, the cousin of the prophet and then a boy of only ten, accepted the truth. Allah taught Muḥammad *(pbuh)* through angel *Jibrā'īl* (Gabriel) how to make ablution *(wuḍū)* and how to pray. Muḥammad *(pbuh)* in turn taught *Khadījah* and both of them used to offer *Ṣalāh* together.

'Alī saw the Prophet and his wife kneeling and prostrating and

---

*We should say Raḍiyallāhu 'anhu (RA) after the name of a male companion (Ṣaḥābī) of the Prophet and Raḍiyallāhu 'anhā after the name of a female companion (Ṣaḥābīyah).

reciting the *Qur'ān*. *'Alī* was amazed at this unusual scene and asked the Prophet after the prayer, "To whom did you prostrate yourselves?" The Prophet answered, "We have prostrated ourselves to Allah who has sent me as Prophet and has commanded me to call human beings unto Him."

The Prophet then invited *'Alī* to worship only Allah and to accept the message of Allah revealed to him.

He also recited to him something from the *Qur'ān*. *'Alī*, felt excited and thrilled but thought for a moment and said that he would consult his father *Abū Ṭālib* about this. He passed the night agitated and restless, thinking about the call of Muḥammad *(pbuh)*. Next morning, he rushed to the prophet and declared his faith in Islam. The young boy said, "Allah created me without consulting *Abū Ṭālib* my father. Why then should I consult him in order to worship Allah?"

Is it not exciting for you too to learn this? It should inspire you also to want to work for Islam to make living on this earth meaningful and purposeful? Rest assured, this is the way to peace. *'Alī* the first Muslim boy, accepted this peace — Islam.

Early Muslims

You should know some of the names of great people who accepted Islam and later became the great personalities in the history of Islam.

Early Muslims included : *'Alī bin Abū Ṭālib, Zaid bin Ḥārithah, Abū Bakr bin Abū Quhāfah, 'Uthmān bin 'Affān, Sa' d bin Abī Waqqās, 'Abdur Raḥmān bin 'Auf, Ṭalḥah bin 'Ubaidullāh, Abū Dharr, Zubair bin 'Awwām, Abū 'Ubaidah bin Jarrāh, Arqam bin Abī Arqam, Ṣuhaib Al-rūmī, 'Abdullāh bin Mas'ūd, Khabbāb bin al-'Arat, 'Uthmān bin Maẓ'ūn, Ja'far bin Abū Ṭālib and Nu'aim bin 'Abdullāh.*

Women also were not left behind. Among the great women to be Muslims were : *Khadījah Bint Khuwailid, Fāṭimah Bint Al-Khaṭṭāb, Āsmā' Bint Abū Bakr, Fāṭimah bint Al-Mujallil, Fukaiha bint Yasār, Asmā' Bint 'Umais, Asmā' bint Salamah, Ramlah bint Abū 'Auf, Umaina bint Khalaf.*

End of the first phase

During the first phase of the Islamic Movement, Muḥammad *(pbuh)* preached the message of Allah discreetly and it was spreading gradually among all age-groups especially the youth in Makkah. People of Makkah began to talk about Muḥammad *(pbuh)* and his message. They did not take it seriously in the beginning. They thought the Muslims had a fantasy that would soon die away and the worship of idols would eventually triumph.

Three years passed and the message of Allah continued to spread far and wide in the valley of Makkah.

You will see in the following pages how Truth became victorious and falsehood vanished. Islam is the Truth; worship of idols is falsehood.

Islamic Movement becomes public

Three years after the first revelation, Allah commanded the prophet, *"Proclaim what you have been ordered and turn away from the polytheists."* (15:94). This was the command to make the call to Allah open and public and was the beginning of the second phase of the Islamic movement.

'Alī and the dinner

The Prophet prepared himself to meet the new situation with strong determination and faith. He invited his kinsmen to a dinner and after the dinner addressed them saying :

"O sons of 'Abdul Muṭṭalib, I know of no Arab who has come to his people with a nobler message than mine. I have brought you the best of this world and the next. Allah has ordered me to call you to Him. So, who of you will stand by me in this matter?"

The elders in the dinner were not responsive. They were about to leave when the young boy *'Alī* stood up and said, *"I am the youngest of you; I may be a boy, my feet may not be strong enough, but O Muḥammad (pbuh), I shall be your helper. Whoever opposes you, I shall fight him as a mortal enemy."* The elders laughed loudly and dispersed.

Consider the courage of the boy *'Alī*! How strongly and firmly he spoke about his faith! Should you not as youngsters follow the example of *'Alī*? To uphold the Truth and work for it is the best of everything in this world.

The Prophet on Mount Ṣafā

Muḥammad *(pbuh)* now prepared to call the Makkans to the message of Allah. He climbed on the top of *Aṣ-Ṣafā* and shouted to the people who, seeing him standing there, gathered below. Muḥammad *(pbuh)* told them, *"O men of Quraish, if I were to tell you that I see an army ready to attack on the other side of the mountain, would you believe me?"*

They answered, *"Yes, why not?* We trust you and never found you telling a lie."

Muḥammad *(pbuh)* said, "Know then, that I am a warner and that I warn you of severe punishment. *O Banū 'Abdul Muṭṭalib! Banū 'Abd Manāf! O Banū Zuhrah! O Banū Taim! O Banū Makhzūm! O Banū Asad!* Allah has commanded me to warn you, my nearest kinsmen, that I can assure you of good on this earth and in heaven if you declare that there is no god but Allah". *Abū Lahab*, his uncle, became red with anger and spoke bad of his nephew. He said, *"Damn you! Did you assemble us for this?"*

Muḥammad *(pbuh)* was severely shocked and looked towards his uncle for a moment. Allah comforted His messenger and informed him of the fearful punishment awaiting *Abū Lahab*. Allah revealed. *"May the hands of Abū Lahab perish; doomed he is. His wealth and his properties shall not save him. He shall be thrown into a flaming fire of hell."* (111:1-3).

The open invitation to Allah's message brought hostility and opposition to the Prophet and his followers. A new stage of the Islamic movement began. We will see how the followers of Islam overcame this opposition with valour, vigour and steadfastness. Indeed, it is rare that we find such proof of sacrifices for the noble cause of Allah.

Hostility begins

The *Makkans* who for a long time took no serious notice of the movement became very hostile to the open call of Muḥammad *(pbuh)*. They now realised a threat to their idolatry and began to harass the followers of Islam in order to stop its increasing popularity. Hardly a day passed without some new followers joining the faith. This trend further increased the fury of the idolaters.

The *Quraish* first tried to settle the matter through *Abū Ṭālib* and asked him to withdraw his support from Muḥammad *(pbuh)*. Delegations of the influential people went to meet *Abū Ṭālib* twice for this purpose. He listened to them calmly and sent them back with conciliatory words. *Abū Ṭālib* asked Muḥammad *(pbuh)* not to put him under so much strain, for he was the leader of the *Quraish*. The Prophet faced a dilemma but remained firm and said to his uncle, *"O my uncle, by Allah if they put the sun in my right hand and the moon in my left, and ask me to give up my mission, I shall not do it until Allah has made it victorious or I perish therein!"*

Abū Ṭālib was moved by the firmness of his nephew and said, *"Go and say what you please, for by Allah, I shall never withdraw my support from you."*

The first Muslim to suffer at the hands of the unbelievers of *Makkah* was *Sa' d Bin Abī Waqqās*. He was struck with a sword in a fight with the enemies as they attacked the Prophet and his followers at prayer in a mountain pass. The Prophet was once preaching in the area of the *Ka'bah* and he was attacked. During the encounter *Ḥārith Bīn Abī Hālah* tried to pacify the mob but was attacked and killed. He was the first Muslim to give his life for Islam.

Bilāl bin Rabāḥ, an Abyssinian slave was tortured by his master for accepting Islam. He was thrown onto the sand under the burning sun with a heavy stone laid on his chest for no other reason than his acceptance of Islam. *Bilāl* gallantly faced his torture and used to proclaim, *"Allah, the One; Allah, the One"*, *Abū Bakr* freed him from his infidel master.

Others who suffered terribly in the hands of unbelievers were : *'Ammār, Abū Fukaiha, Ṣuhaib Rūmi* and *Khabbāb*. The infidels even did not spare women Muslims. Among the women tortured were : *Sumaiyyah, Lubainah, Nahdiyyah* and *Umm 'Ubais*.

The Prophet himself was ridiculed, insulted and accused of being a sorcerer, and of being possessed. Once he was almost strangled by an unbeliever while praying. Suddenly *Abū Bakr* arrived to rescue him. *Abū Lahab's* wife, *Umm Jamīl* used to throw rubbish and thorny bushes from her house at Muḥammad's *(pbuh)* door and way, and all that Muḥammad *(pbuh)* was able to do was to remove them.

Muḥammad *(pbuh)* continued his preaching with even more enthusiasm and firmness, and the hostility of the unbelievers also intensified. The Makkans did all they could to stop him and his followers. But nothing worked. The Islamic movement continued to flourish among the Makkans despite the false propaganda, persecution and harassment from the idolaters.

During this period, *Ḥamzah*, the young uncle of the Prophet joined the Islamic movement. His acceptance of the faith added strength to Islam, for *Ḥamzah* was a brave man. His acceptance of Islam compelled the *Quraish* to abandon some of their harassment.

The offer of 'Utbah Bin Rabī'ah

'Utbah bin Rabi'ah a leader of the *Quraish*, put some proposals to the Prophet. He suggested, *"If what you want is money, we will gather for you our property, so that you may be the richest of us; if you want honour, we will make you our chief, so that no-one can decide anything apart from you; if you want sovereignty, we will make you king."*

The Prophet declined these suggestions and recited verses from *Sūrah 41 (Hāmīm As-Sajdah)* of the *Qur'ān*. *'Utbah* returned to his companions with a changed face and reported to them that he heard from Muḥammad *(pbuh)* what he had never heard before. No worldly temptation could keep the Prophet away from the Truth.

Another cunning proposal

The *Quraish* failed in all their attempts to discourage Muḥammad *(pbuh)* and the Muslims from their faith. Harassment, ridicule, torture and false propaganda proved futile, and the Muslims simply became more determined. The leaders of the *Quraish* now hatched a shrewd plot. They proposed to the Prophet that he should adore their gods and they in return would adore his God; in this way there would come about a compromise and hostility would cease.

Allah commanded the Prophet to tell the unbelievers in clear terms that there could be no such compromise on matters of basic principles. Muḥammad *(pbuh)* was asked to declare them, *"You have your religion, and I have mine."* (109:6). The plan of mixing the truth with untruth was defeated.

Emigration (Hijrah) to Abyssinia (Ethiopia)

The infidels, frustrated in their attempts to make a compromise with the Prophet, increased the intensity of their persecutions. The threat to life and property intensified. The poor Muslims were particularly insecure and vulnerable. Muḥammad *(pbuh)* advised those Muslims who felt insecure to emigrate to Abyssinia where *Najjāshī* (Negus), a noble king, ruled. Eighty three Muslims, not counting children, emigrated to Abyssinia in groups. The first group was of ten people. This is the first emigration *(Hijrah)* of the Muslims who had to leave their country for the sake of Allah.

Efforts to get the emigrants back

A delegation of the *Quraish* consisting of *'Amr Ibnul 'Āṣ* and

'Abdullāh Ibn Abū Rabī'ah, went to the Negus and tried to get the emigrant Muslims back.

They bribed the courtiers of the *Negus* and made accusations against the Muslims to succeed in their mission. They alleged that the emigrants were apostates and followers of a new religion which no-one had heard of before. The *Negus* wanted to know the whole matter and called for the Muslims. He asked, "What is the new religion you follow which caused you to leave your country?"

Ja'far bin Abū Ṭālib, answered on behalf of the Muslims, *"O King, we were in a state of ignorance and immorality, worshipping stones and idols, eating dead animals, committing all sorts of injustice, breaking natural ties, treating guests badly, and the strong among us exploited the weak.*

"Then Allah sent us a prophet, one of our own people, whose lineage, truthfulness, trustworthiness and honesty were well known to us. He called us to worship Allah alone and to renounce the stones, the idols, which we and our ancestors used to worship. He commanded us to speak the truth, to honour our promises, to be helpful to our relations, to be good to our neighbours, to abstain from bloodshed, to avoid fornication. He commanded us not to give false witness, not to appropriate an orphan's property or falsely accuse a married woman. He ordered us not to associate anyone with Allah.

"He commanded us to hold prayers, to fast, to pay Zakāh. We believed in him and what he brought to us from Allah, and we follow him in what he asked us to do and forbade us not to do.

"Thereupon, our people attacked us, treated us harshly and tried to take us back to the old immorality and worship of idols. They made life intolerable for us in Makkah, and we came to your country to seek protection to live in justice and peace."

Hearing this, the *Negus* wanted to listen to part of the *Qur'ān* which came down from Allah to the Prophet.

Ja'far recited to him *Sūrah Maryam* (Mary), the 19th *Sūrah* of the *Qur'ān*. The Negus wept until his beard was wet, listening to the *Qur'ān*. Then he said, *"What you have just recited and that which was revealed to Moses must have both issued from the same source. Go forth into my kingdom; I shall not deport you at all."*

Thus the spiteful efforts of the pagans against the Muslims were doomed to failure once again.

'Umar accepts Islam

'Umar bin Al-Khaṭṭāb, a strong and tough person in his late twenties, became a Muslim in the sixth year of the prophethood of Muḥammad *(pbuh)*. His acceptance of Islam is remarkable in the sense that he went out with a vow to kill the Prophet. On his way to kill Muḥammad *(pbuh), Na'īm* told *'Umar* that he should rather take care of *Fāṭimah* and *Sa'īd* who had become Muslims. *Fāṭimah* and *Sa'īd* were 'Umar's sister and brother-in-law. *'Umar* became enraged with anger when he heard this and changed his course to arrive at his sister's house.

As he approached the house, he heard the recitation of the *Qur'ān. Khabbāb bin al-'Arat* was reading *Sūrah Ṭā Hā* (the 20th chapter) to them. 'Umar entered the house without knocking and angrily cried out, *"What is this balderdash (nonsense) I heard?"*

Faṭimah and *Sa'īd* refused to say. They had hiden *Khabbāb* before *'Umar* came in. *'Umar* was furious and began to hit his brother-in-law, and injured *Fāṭimah* when she tried to protect her husband.

Seeing his sister blood-stained, *'Umar* paused for a while and wanted to see the sheet of the *Qur'ān* from which they were reciting. *Fāṭimah* asked him to cleanse himself. *'Umar* washed himself before he was given the sheet.

While reading he was deeply moved at the rhyme and rhythm and the content. He decided to accept Islam and said, *"Lead me to Muḥammad (pbuh), so that I may accept Islam." Khabbāb* came out from hiding and led him to *Arqam's* house where the Prophet was staying at that time. *Arqam's* house was the centre of Islam at the time. The Prophet welcomed *'Umar* at the gate and asked him his intention. *'Umar* expressed his wish to be a Muslim and the Prophet was very pleased.

'Umar was a very powerful man. His entry into Islam gave a strong impetus to the Muslims. Before him, *Ḥamzah*, the prophet's uncle, became a Muslim. He was also a powerful man. The entry into Islam of these two great and brave men was a turning point in the history of the early Islamic movement.

Boycott and confinement

The *Quraish* were seething at the gradual increase in the strength of the Muslims. They plotted another assault and decided on a total boycott of the family of *Hāshim* and *Muṭṭalib*. They were confined in a pass named *Shi'bi Abī Ṭālib*. The boycott continued for three years and the clans of *Hāshim* and *Muṭṭalib* suffered badly during that time. Eventually the boycott had to be withdrawn because of differences among the *Quraish* themselves. The clans of *Hāshim* and *Muṭṭalib* demonstrated great firmness during the boycott.

The document of boycott which was kept in the *Ka'bah* was eaten up by white ants, all except the name of Allah.

The Prophet continued his work amid intimidation and persecution. Truth must prevail over falsehood. The call to Allah must subdue paganism. The popularity and strength of Islam were on the increase.

Year of sorrow

Time passed and Muḥammad *(pbuh)* at the age of fifty, in the tenth year of his prophethood, had to face more sorrow and grief.

His uncle *Abū Ṭālib* died. It was *Abū Ṭālib* who always gave protection to his nephew. Muḥammad *(pbuh)* was heartbroken. Still more sadness was in store. The Prophet lost his most loving and caring wife, *Khadījah*, who had stood by him like a solid rock, to comfort, support and encourage him at times when no-one else did so. And she was the first to accept him as the messenger of Allah.

It was a terrible blow to Muḥammad *(pbuh)*. But the Prophet had to endure. Death is an undeniable fact of life. All men and women die and so must we, one day.

The Prophet had become used to shocks and grief, ever since his childhood. Providence tested him all through his life. The responsibility of prophethood needed unmatched endurance and patience. The Prophet passed all the most difficult tests of life, including persecution, torture and death blows.

Ṭā'if — the most difficult day

The stone-heartedness of the people of *Makkah* saddened the Prophet. He now decided to try the people of *Ṭā'if*, a city sixty miles to the west of *Makkah*, to see if they would support him.

On arriving in *Ṭā'if*, accompanied by *Zaid bin Ḥārithah*, he went to three important people of the city and invited them to Islam. All three refused and insulted him. They even incited street urchins to drive him out of the city.

The urchins pelted stones at the Prophet's legs and feet. They hooted at him and drove him out. He was weary, sad and very unhappy and took shelter in a garden where he prayed.

The owners of the garden witnessed the whole episode and felt sorry for him in his tired and bruised condition. They offered him hospitality and sent grapes for him through their servant, *'Addās*.

The Prophet used to say that the day in *Ṭā'if* was the most difficult day of his life. But look at his greatness; he was bruised, hurt, blood-stained, yet never pronounced one word of curse for the people who had abused him.

Al-Mi'rāj (The Ascent)

After the severe shocks of the death of *Abū Ṭālib* and *Khadījah*, and the cruel treatment received at *Ṭā'if*, Muḥammad *(pbuh)* longed for some comfort. It was not long before he got it. It happened in the form of a remarkable and eventful night journey to *Jerusalem* called *Al-Isrā'*, and the ascent to heaven in the same night called *Al-Mi'rāj*.

Mi'rāj was a memorable event for the Prophet. Allah honoured him by this unique and extra-ordinary journey. During the journey Muḥammad *(pbuh)* saw with his own eyes the glory of Allah and the working of the universe. It was a great moral boost which he needed most. It further strengthened his faith that Allah was always with him. No amount of shock could prevent him from his task of calling people to Allah.

The Prophet himself gave vivid details about the journey and the ascent. He said that one night the angel *Jibrā'īl* awoke him from sleep and took him to *Jerusalem* riding an animal which looked like a horse with large wings. The name of the animal was *Buraq*.

At Jerusalem, he met all the prophets including *Ādam, Ibrāhīm, Mūsā, 'Isā* and *Hārūn*.. He led them in prayer. He was then taken to different heavens and he saw the *Paradise* and the *Hell*. The most important of all was his experience of the Glory and the Majesty of Allah. He had many more experiences. It is beyond the grasp of ordinary people like us to understand every aspect of the journey. But it was not impossible for the last messenger of Allah to grasp the significance of these things. He had to have such experiences to act as Allah's messenger.

Five times daily prayers were laid down for Muslims at the time of *Mi'rāj*. The whole miraculous journey lasted for a short time of the night.

Next morning, when Muḥammad *(pbuh)* related his experience, the *Makkans* laughed at him and started saying that Muḥammad *(pbuh)* must have gone crazy. The Muslims believed him, however. But some of the new entrants to the faith became a bit doubtful and the unbelievers, as usual, refused to accept the truth. Muḥammad *(pbuh)* gave graphic details of the journey and a caravan which he had met on his way to *Jerusalem* confirmed the details he gave.

Remember here that Muḥammad *(pbuh)* was nicknamed by his own people as *Al-Āmīn* (the Truthful) and *Aṣ-Ṣādiq* (the Trustworthy). Later, these same people behaved quite strangely. Muḥammad *(pbuh)* after receiving his prophethood had done everything according to Allah's wish.

First covenant of Al-'Aqabah

During his open, public preaching, Muḥammad *(pbuh)* met a group of people from *Madīnah* (then called *Yathrib*) at the time of *Ḥajj*, and he invited them to accept Islam. They responded to his call and became Muslims. There were six of them. They returned to *Madīnah* as believers and invited others of their tribes to join the new faith.

Next year twelve people from *Madīnah* came during *Ḥajj* and the Prophet entered into an agreement with them at a place called *Al-'Aqabah* in 621 CE. This agreement is known as *'the Covenant of Al-'Aqabah'*. In this pledge, they agreed to obey none but Allah, neither to steal nor commit adultery, neither to kill their children nor commit any evil, and not to disobey Allah. They were told by Muḥammad *(pbuh)* that if they lived under this covenant, Allah would be pleased with them and reward them with *Paradise.*

Second covenant of Al-'Aqabah

A second covenant with the Muslims of *Madīnah* was concluded in *622 CE* in the same place, *Al-'Aqabah*. In all, seventy three people including two women took part in this pledge. This covenant was an extension of the first. It was agreed that the Muslims of *Madīnah* would protect and help the Prophet against all odds, as they would protect their own women and children. All dangers which would arise out of this covenant were explained by *Al-'Abbās*, prophet's uncle, to the Madinite Muslims in clear terms. But still the Madinite Muslims said, *"We take him (the Prophet) despite all threats to property, wealth and life. Tell us O Prophet of Allah! what will be our reward if we remain true to this oath?"*

The Prophet answered, *"Paradise"*.

They stretched out their hands to him and he to them, and in this way the covenant was concluded.

The second covenant included clauses about war situations which made it a duty of the Madinite Muslims to defend the Prophet in the event of external attack from *Makkah*.

Emigration to Madīnah

The conclusion of the second covenant of *Al-'Aqabah* was another turning-point in the history of the Islamic movement. The Muslims now had a place in which to take shelter, an ally in time of war and danger.

The unbelievers eventually came to know about the covenant after it had been concluded. It was done in secrecy so that the infidels could not have an opportunity to foil it. When they found out, they reacted in anger and resorted to torturing some of the people from *Madīnah*.

The prophet now changed the strategy of his work. For thirteen years, he had tried his best to preach the message of Allah to the people of *Makkah*. But the Makkan soil was not fertile for this. *Madīnah* provided him with fresh, receptive ground in which to sow the seed of Islam, and he planned to use this opportunity.

He commanded the Muslims of *Makkah* to start emigrating to *Madīnah* and strengthen the bond with the Muslims there. The Muslims of *Madīnah* are known as *Anṣār* (helpers) and those of Makkah as *Muhājirūn* (emigrants) in Islamic history. Following the command of the prophet, the Makkan Muslims started moving to *Madīnah* individually and in small groups. The unbelievers tried ferociously to stop this and became even more malicious.

Think of the emigration! Muslims left their homes for the sake of Allah and His pleasure! At the moment of need, this was what was required of them. As Muslims, we also must be ready to do the same for the sake of our faith. Life on this earth will have meaning and purpose only when we can attain this attitude.

The Hijrah of the Prophet

After most of his companions had left for *Madīnah* Muḥammad *(pbuh)* was waiting for permission from Allah to emigrate himself. *Abū*

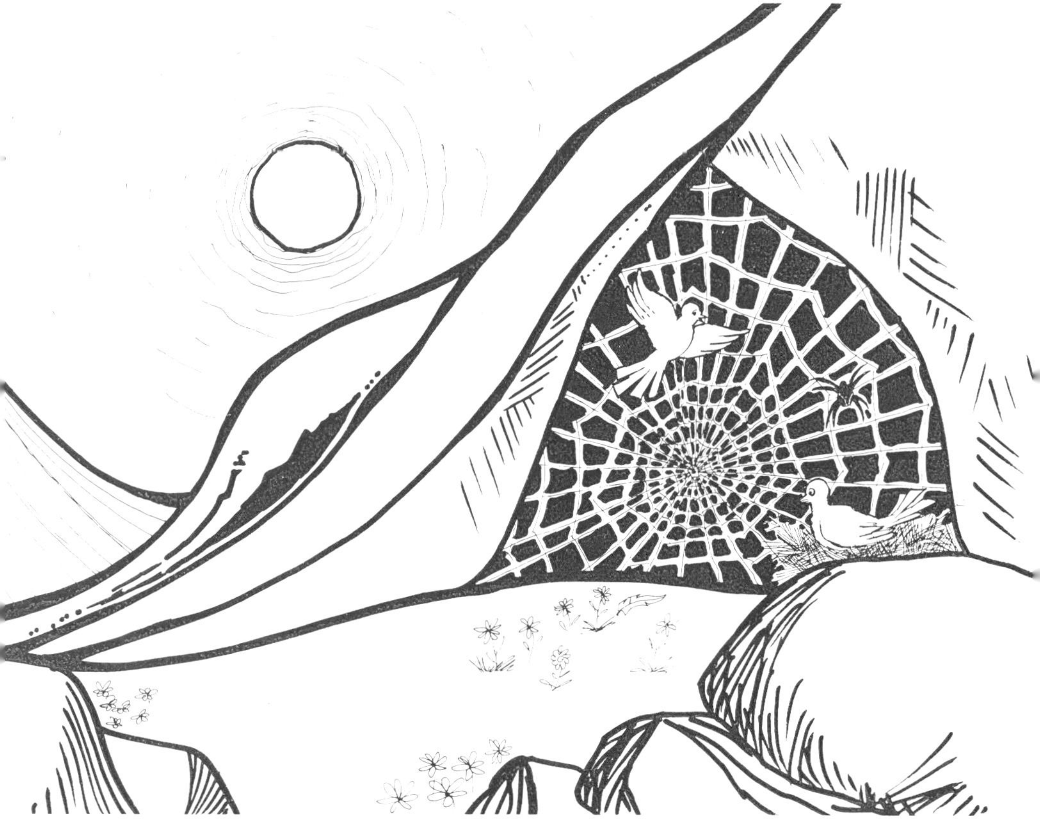

Cave Thawr

Bakr, his closest friend sought permission to leave for *Madīnah* but stayed behind on the Prophet's advice. *'Alī*, the cousin of the Prophet also stayed behind. Abū Bakr was to accompany the Prophet later on. He was very lucky.

The unbelievers now plotted to kill Muḥammad *(pbuh)*. The permission to migrate to *Madīnah* also had come. Muḥammad *(pbuh)* secretly left Makkah at night in *622 CE* with *Abū Bakr*. A specially-formed group of unbelievers laid in wait at night around the Prophet's house to kill him as he came out. *'Alī* was left behind to sleep in the Prophet's bed and the Prophet quietly left, making the unbelievers look very foolish. In the morning, they found *'Alī* in the Prophet's bed and were dumb-founded.

The Prophet and his companion *Abū Bakr* had left just before dawn and proceeded to the cave *Thawr*, to the south of *Makkah*. They stayed in the cave for three days where *Abū Bakr's* servant brought them food in the evening. They left the cave *Thawr* on the third day and started for *Madīnah*.

The unbelievers, fooled by the wit of the Prophet, now organized a thorough search on the road to *Madīnah* and offered a prize of 100 camels for the capture of Muḥammad *(pbuh)*. One *Surāqah* was almost successful, but failed in the end. His horse fell down three times in his pursuit to kill Muḥammad *(pbuh)* and in the end he gave up his sinister aim, taking the falls as bad omens.

After a tiresome, exhausting and very difficult journey, the Prophet accompanied by *Abū Bakr* reached *Qubā'*, a place near *Madīnah*. They stayed there for two weeks and the Prophet founded a mosque in *Qubā'* where *'Alī* had joined them.

The prophet entered *Madīnah* and allowed his camel to kneel where it liked. It knelt first in a place which was owned by two orphans, and got up to kneel finally in front of the house of *Abū Ayyūb Anṣārī* which became the first residence of the Prophet in *Madīnah*.

The people of *Madīnah* who had anxiously awaited the arrival of Muḥammad *(pbuh)*, became very happy and excited when they found him among them. They gave him a hero's welcome.

The *Hijrah* of the Prophet started a new chapter in the history of the Islamic movement. It has two sides : the sad and heart-breaking scene of leaving the beloved birth place on one side, and a feeling of security and hope for the work of Islam more freely than before, on the other.

The *Islamic calendar* starts from the day of the Hijrah of the Prophet Muḥammad *(pbuh)* from *Makkah* to *Madīnah*.

Hijrah was the beginning of the new role for the Prophet as a statesman and a ruler. With this ended his fifty three years of life in *Makkah*, of which he spent thirteen eventful years as the Prophet of Allah.

The Prophet of Madīnah

Muḥammad's *(pbuh)* arrival in *Madīnah* was a memorable event for the people of the city. They felt elated and were jubilant because they had Allah's messenger among them.

Madīnah was known at that time as *Yathrib*. It came to be known as *Madīnatun Nabī* — the Prophet's city — after Muḥammad's *(pbuh)* arrival. Later it became known simply as *Madīnah* — The City.

The Makkan migrants added a new dimension to the life of *Madīnah*. The city now had three communities : the *Anṣār* (the Helpers) of the tribes of *'Aws* and *Khazrāj*, the Jews from the tribes of *Qainuqā', Naḍīr* and *Quraiẓah*, and the migrants from *Makkah*. The migrants *(Muhājirūn)* had to be absorbed by the local community of the *Anṣār*.

The companion of the Prophet had reached *Madīnah* before Muḥammad *(pbuh)* himself, and were living with the *Ansār* as guests. With the arrival of the Prophet, this situation changed to a more stable one. The migrants *(Muhājirūn)* had brought almost nothing with them.

The Prophet's first task was to form a solid bond of faith and brotherhood between the *Anṣār* and the *Muhājirūn*.

He called a meeting of both communities and asked the *Anṣārs* to become brothers of the *Muhājirūn*. He also suggested that they should share their property and other belongings with their migrant brothers. The *Anṣār* did as they were asked by the Prophet. This was a rare event unmatched in human history; such was the powerful influence of Islam.

The *Anṣār* practically shared their property with the *Muhājirūn* equally, on the basis of a shared faith.

Muḥammad *(pbuh)* became the leader of the city. With the cementing of the bond of brotherhood, he had virtually inaugurated the Islamic Society. *Madīnah* now was the capital of the Islamic community, the first Islamic state.

The Islamic State of *Madīnah* knew no distinction between the ruler and his subjects. Every citizen belonged to Allah and enjoyed equal rights. Islam does not recognise any preference of one over another except on the basis of piety *(Taqwā)*. *"The noblest among you to Allah is the one who is the most virtuous,"* says the *Qur'ān*. In the Islamic state of *Madīnah*, there was no discrimination on the basis of colour, class or descent.

After laying the foundations of the Islamic state, Allah's messenger took steps to secure the internal peace of the new state. A treaty with the Jews was signed, but the Jews, did not live up to their pledge and later betrayed it.

Masjīdun Nabī in Madīnah

The Prophet now decided to construct a mosque in *Madīnah*. Soon, work began at a place which was purchased from its orphan owners. This was the place where the prophet's camel had first knelt before it finally knelt in front of the house of *Abū Ayyūb Anṣārī*. The Prophet's residence was built next to the mosque.

Muḥammad *(pbuh)* himself took part in the construction as an ordinary labourer. In fact it was difficult to identify him from other workers on the site. Muḥammad *(pbuh)* never hesitated to do any ordinary work. He used to mend his own clothes, repair his own shoes, do the shopping and milk the goats. In this respect he left for us a shining example.

Adhān (call to prayer)

You may recollect that prayer of five times a day was laid down for Muslims at the time of the *Mi'rāj* (the Ascent). In *Madīnah*, Muslims were now a cohesive and united community and the Prophet felt it necessary to call the believers to pray in congregation. Muslims would collect themselves together for prayer when the time came. Many suggestions were put forward, and the Prophet finally asked *Bilāl*, the Abyssinian Muslim who had a melodious voice, to shout aloud the following words :

Allah is the Greatest! (4 times)
I bear witness that there is no god but Allah! (twice)
I bear witness that Muḥammad is the messenger of Allah! (twice)
Rush to Prayer! (twice)
Rush to success! (twice)
Allah is the Greatest! (twice)
There is no god but Allah.

This is the **Adhān** *(the call to prayer).* The introduction of *Adhān* with its beautiful and magnetic appeal, made possible the pronouncement of the Greatness of Allah five times a day in *Madīnah*. This system of Adhān is still in use in all the Muslim countries. The rhyme and rhythm of the words chanted are really marvellous.

More Islamic duties laid down

Madīnah, the first Islamic state, began to thrive under the dynamic leadership of Muḥammad *(pbuh).* The Islamic society of *Madīnah* needed more guidance and training for its development, welfare and prosperity.

This society which was passing through its infant stage at this time, later went on to make a tremendous impact on the history of mankind.

The programme of training introduced during the second and third years of *Hijrah* included *Ṣawm* (fasting in the month of *Ramaḍān*), *Zakāh* (welfare contribution), prohibition of wine drinking and transaction involving interest *(Ribā).* Also during this period, laws regarding orphans, inheritance, marriage and the rights of married women were revealed.

In the second year of Hijrah (the month of Sha'bān) the direction of prayer (Qiblah) was changed by revelation from Bait ul-Maqdis in Jerusalem to Al-Ka'bah in Makkah.

Hard task

The society was growing and the task of making it strong, solid and dynamic also continued. Muḥammad *(pbuh)* during this time was virtually fighting on four fronts :

i To maintain cohesion and discipline among the rank and file of the Islamic society;

ii To guard against the intrigues and conspiracies of the Hyprocrites (Munāfiqūn);

iii To remain alert to the dangers from the Quraish of Makkah, and

iv To remain vigilant about the sinister motives of the Jews in Madīnah.

History shows how wonderfully Allah's messenger faced all these dangers and led the Islamic state towards more and more success and victory.

The Battle of Badr

Muḥammad *(pbuh)* was a wise and practical man. He took steps to counter the dangers from both inside and outside the city of *Madīnah*. He left no stone unturned to make the small community of Muslims a solidly united force, to combat any threat to its existence.

He did not have many resources. The economy of *Madīnah* was under strain from absorbing the migrants from *Makkah*, but the messenger of Allah was full of hope and confidence. He knew Allah's help would be coming at the right moment. What counted was the strength of faith and not the material resources.

The unbelievers of *Makkah* were raging in anger at the comparative safety to the Muslims in *Madīnah*. All their previous attempts to finish off Muḥammad *(pbuh)* had failed. Their trade route to Syria was now within easy reach of the Muslims. They became restless and were burning within themselves, unable to find a way to tackle Muḥammad *(pbuh)*. They were looking for some excuse to attack the new Islamic society and get rid of it once and for all.

Such was the situation when news came of an unusual caravan with about a thousand camels laden with goods and arms, travelling to *Makkah* from Syria. The leader of the caravan was Abū Sufiān — a chief of the *Quraish* of *Makkah. Abū Sufiān* feared there might be an attack from the Muslims and lost no time in sending for just such a message and soon an army of a thousand was ready to march to *Madīnah* to attack the Muslims on any excuse.

News of the Makkan army reached the Prophet and he had decided to face them outside *Madīnah* with the help of Allah. The aggression of the unbelievers must not go unchallenged. A small army of three hundred and thirteen people, including young boys, ill-equipped with arms and ammunition, started from *Madīnah* under the Prophet's command and camped at a place called *Al-Badr*, eighty miles from *Madīnah*. The Muslim army had only a few horses and a small quantity of armour, but they were full of faith, courage, valour and determination. They knew they were on the right side.

Meanwhile, *Abū Sufiān's* caravan changed its route and was out of any danger. But the Makkan army would not leave until they had finished off the Muslims. An encounter between the two armies took place on the *17th of Ramaḍān* of the second *Hijrah*.

The Muslims responded to the Makkan attack with unmatched bravery and determination. They repelled the Makkan army and the unbelievers were decisively defeated. They left seventy dead and a further seventy were taken prisoner by the Muslims.

The Battle of Badr proved beyond doubt that real strength lies in faith in Allah and not in arms and ammunition. The battle decided the course of future history of the Muslims.

On that day, in spite of their meagre resources, the soldiers of the truth turned out triumphant and the military might of falsehood was humiliated, defeated and tarnished. *"Truth prevails, faleshood vanishes"*, (17:81) declares the *Qur'ān*.

In the battle of *Badr*, each Muslim soldier had to face three infidels, because the size of the Makkan army was three times that of the Muslim army. Still the Muslims won.

The defeat of the Muslims in this battle would have been fatal.

But the Makkans in this battle left with a grudge of defeat and humiliation. Another encounter was not far off.

The Battle of Uḥud

The Makkans could not forget the shattering blow inflicted on them by the Muslims at *Badr*. They were planning for revenge. The year that followed was their year of preparation.

The Muslims were consolidating the gains they had made at *Badr* and strengthened their community ties. The Prophet sent messengers and delegations to various parts of Arabia during this time.

Al-'Abbās, one of the uncles of the Prophet, still lived in Makkah though he accepted Islam. His feelings for his nephew and the Muslims were very strong. He was watching all the preparations the unbelievers were making and sent an envoy to Muḥammad *(pbuh)* in Madīnah with the details of the moves by the Makkans.

The Prophet received news that an army three thousand strong, including two hundred horsemen, was marching towards *Madīnah*. Muḥammad *(pbuh)* called for the elders and consulted them on the matter. The elders of Madīnah, among them *Anṣār* and *Muhājirūn*, favoured defence from inside *Madīnah*. But the younger men, alive with faith and vigour, wanted a manly combat outside *Madīnah*. They saw it as an opportunity to be *Shahīd* (martyrs).

After *Jumu'ah* prayer on a Friday, the Prophet started out for *Mount Uḥud* with an army of seven hundred Muslims. The *Quraish* of *Makkah* had already camped there. The Prophet reached *Uḥud* and after dawn prayer put the Muslim army into position. He took particular care to place fifty archers under the command of *'Abdullāh Bin Jubair*, to protect a strategic mountain pass, and ordered them not to leave their position under any circumstances.

The two armies faced each other in the morning. Fierce fighting broke out and soon the Muslim army got the upper hand and the Makkan army was forced to retreat. The Muslims captured the supplies and baggage of the Makkans.

Before the battle was really over, most of the archers stationed in the mountain pass joined in the collection of booty, despite the repeated pleas of *'Abdullāh Bin Jubair*. This indiscipline provided *Khālid Bin Walīd*, one of the Makkan commanders, with a rare opportunity to make a counter attack from the rear. *'Abdullāh Bin Jubair* and six other archers who had not left their position, put up a desperate fight, until finally all of them were martyred.

Khālid's men took the Muslim army by surprise and soon the Muslim's celebration ended in grief. They found themselves surrounded and in the fighting that followed, *Ḥamzah*, the Prophet's uncle and a great warriar was martyred by *Waḥshī*. Many other Muslims became Shahīd and the Prophet himself suffered injury.

A rumour that Muḥammad *(pbuh)* was dead caused the Muslims to flee, and drained them of morale. The Prophet was taken by some of his followers to a position on the hill, and he called to the Muslims at the top of his voice. He ordered them to reunite and before long the scattered and battered Muslims again regrouped, once they saw the Prophet was alive.

In the battle, the enemy violated all norms of civilised behaviour. They mutilated the dead bodies of Muslims and *Hind*, the wife of *Abū Sufiān*, was so terrible that she took out the liver of *Ḥamzah* and chewed it raw.

By the end of the day the regrouped Muslim army was ready for a counter attack, but the Makkan army had already left, satisfied that they had taken revenge for *Badr*. The Muslim army pursued them.

On his return to *Madīnah*, the Prophet sent out a contingent of Muslims to pursue the Makkans, to ensure that they did not come back. When *Abū Sufiān* heard of it, he quickened his pace to Makkah.

The overall result was almost a draw — neither side could claim victory. But the battle had some very costly lessons for the Muslims. The disobedience and indiscipline of the archers at the mountain pass caused the Muslims to suffer badly in a battle which they almost had won.

Discipline and obedience to the commander are very important in a battlefield.

The Battle of Aḥzāb

Muḥammad *(pbuh)* had a very busy life. Hardly a day passed without some incident taking place somewhere in the new state. Skirmishes, plots, conspiracies and violation of treaties were rife. So was molesting and mockery of the Muslims and the Prophet. All this happened by the collusion of the Jews and Makkan infidels. They joined together against Muslims.

The Jewish tribe of *Banū Naḍīr* violated treaty conditions and plotted to kill the Prophet. So action had to be taken against them. They were given options either to fight or be deported. At first they refused to leave *Madīnah* but later they were expelled for their treachery. They moved to *Khaibar* and turned the place into an enemy den against the Muslims. They incited the Makkans to make a new offensive against the Muslims and try decisively to finish them.

Badr had been a fatal blow to the dreams of the Makkans; at *Uḥud*, their mission remained unfulfilled. But it gave them new impetus to launch another attack, because their impression of the invincibility of the Muslims had been shaken. The incitement by *Banū Naḍīr* added fuel to their evil objectives.

Emissaries were sent on secret trips between the Makkans and the Nadirites. Finally agreement was reached about the new assault on *Madīnah*. Forces were gathered to make the assault, drawing on people from *Makkah, Ghaṭafān, Ṭā'if, Fazara* and other towns.

News of these sinister moves reached the Prophet, and he consulted his companions about preparations to counter the latest enemy offensive. The decision was made to face the enemy from within the city and *Salmān al-Fārsī*, a Persian Muslim, advised digging trenches round the city to hold the enemy hordes outside. This novel idea was put into effect.

Deep, wide trenches were dug round the whole of *Madīnah* and it took twenty days to complete the digging. Muḥammad *(pbuh)* himself took part in the digging. After the trenches had been completed, the Prophet placed the Muslims in position to defend the city from inside.

An allied force ten thousand strong marched against *Madīnah* in the fifth year of the *Hijrah*. The number was so large, it appeared as if the enemy forces were advancing from all directions — the north, the south, above and below. They alighted on the outskirts of the city beating drums and chanting their war songs. But they found themselves separated from the Muslims by the very deep and wide trench, and this took them by surprise.

The enemy could not understand this new war technique. They were greatly astounded. They had no other alternative but to wait and see. But for how long?

A long and boring wait for about four weeks made them very weary, tired and restless. Nothing happened during this long siege except a few exchanges of arrows. Some desperate efforts to cross the trench were made, but the vigilant Muslims silenced these attempts for ever.

The stocks of food and other supplies of the enemy were dwindling and they felt worried and anxious.

A treacherous plot was now hatched by the enemy to instigate a surprise attack on the Muslims at night, by the Jews of the *Banū Quraiẓah* who were still in *Madīnah* at the time. The Prophet heard of the plot and took measures to foil it. The Prophet sent a message to the Jews in *Madīnah*, asking them to think over the consequences of their treachery should the allied enemy forces be defeated! After the battle of *Aḥzāb*, the Jews of *Banū Quraiẓah* were besieged for about two to three weeks and later on, all adults were killed on a judgment by *Sa'd* chief of the *'Aws* tribe — an ally of the *Quraiẓah*.

Allah, the Almighty, is always with the lovers of Truth. His help is crucial for the success. It was time the Muslims, besieged in *Madīnah*, badly needed such help. Indeed, they did get that help.

The weather changed suddenly. Strong winds, thunder and heavy rain storms made the enemy flee in disarray. Soldiers were trampled under foot by horses and camels in the rush. The hordes eventually fled in a wild frenzy. What a scene it must have been! And what a timely intervention by Allah!

The enemies were greatly dispirited, while the Muslims were equally relieved and elated. The Muslims expressed their gratitude to Allah, the Merciful for His timely help.

Ḥudaibiyah agreement

In the sixth year of the *Hijrah*, the Prophet announced his intention to pay a visit to *Al-Ka'bah* in *Makkah for short pilgrimage ('Umrah)*. He set out with 1400 of his followers who were under strict orders not to carry any weapons, except their traveller's sword.

The *Quraish* of Makkah knew fully well that the only purpose of the Prophet's visit was pilgrimage, but how could they let the Muslims enter Makkah when they had not been able to enter Madīnah? The Muslims, they decided, must be stopped.

Plans were put in hand. The top generals — Khālid and *'Ikrimah* — were alerted to be ready with their armies to stop the Prophet and his followers from entering *Makkah*.

The Muslims continued their journey to *Makkah* until they had reached a place called *Ḥudaibiyah*. Steps were taken to find out what sort of mood the Quraish were in, and it was clear they were in the mood for battle.

The *Quraish* on their part gathered information about the strength and armoury of the Muslims, and realised they had come for no other purpose than the pilgrimage to *Al-Ka'bah*. Envoys were sent from each side. The Prophet made his intentions crystal clear to the *Quraish* through his envoy. But the *Quraish* maltreated the Muslim envoy and threatened the Muslims. The patience of the Muslims was put to severe test. They could teach the *Quraish* a good lesson even with their traveller's sword, but Allah's Prophet ordered them to show extreme restraint.

The *Quraish* were in no mood to allow the Muslims in for the pilgrimage that year. They made it an issue of prestige and pride. It was humiliating for the Muslims, but what could they do? Allah's messenger was their leader and all his steps were guided by Allah, so they had to be followed.

Eventually, after intense negotiations, an agreement between the *Quraish* and the Prophet was signed. This agreement is the *Ḥudaibiyah agreement.*

The conditions were :

A *The Muslims would not visit Makkah that year, but would come a year later and remain there for three days only.*

B *There would be one-sided extradition — the Makkans taking refuge with the Prophet would be handed over on demand to the Quraish, but Muslims taking refuge in Makkah would not be handed over to the Prophet.*

C *There would be peace for ten years and during this period, Muslims could go to Makkah and Ṭā'if and the Quraish could go to Syria through the Muslim areas.*

D *Each party would remain neutral in the event of a war between the other and a third party.*

E *Any tribe wishing to sign an agreement with either the Muslims or the Quraish would be able to do so.*

The terms of the agreement were apparently very unfavourable for the Muslims, but it turned out to be a favourable one for them in the end.

The Muslims were disheartened but they were soon given the news of victory by Allah. It was revealed : *"Surely we have granted you a clear victory."* (48:1).

In what way was this one-sided treaty a victory? The treaty eased the years long tension and made possible the intermingling of the two parties. The Makkans could now come to Madīnah, stay with the Muslims and this provided an opportunity for the Muslims to influence the stone-heartedness of the Makkans. In fact, during the years that followed the *Ḥudaibiyah* treaty, the number of new Muslims increased dramatically. *Khālid Bin Walīd*, who later became the most famous general in Islamic victory, and *'Amr Ibnul 'Āṣ*, the conqueror of Egypt, became Muslims during this time.

The treaty proved beyond doubt that the Prophet and the Muslims stood for peace. It also later paved the way for the escape of the detained Muslims in *Makkah*, as the extradition clause was later dropped on the initiative of the Makkans.

The *Ḥudaibiyah* agreement also opened the way to the conquest of *Makkah* in *630 CE* — the eighth year of *Hijrah*.

The Conquest of Makkah

During the years that followed the *Ḥudaibiyah* treaty, the Prophet sent emissaries to the *Roman Emperor*, the *Persian Emperor*, the *ruler of Egypt*, the *King of Abyssinia,* the *chiefs of Syria* and other leaders, inviting them to accept Islam.

In the seventh year of *Hijrah*, an expedition was made against the Jews of *Banū Naḍīr* who were expelled to *Khaibar. Khaibar* became the centre of anti-Islamic activities and the Prophet decided to take action against trouble-makers there. After a long siege and protracted battles in a number of different places, the fortress of the Jews was conquered and a centre of anti-Islamic activities destroyed.

The strength of the Muslims was on the increase, and new followers were joining.

The *Ḥudaibiyah* treaty gave freedom to the tribes to make agreements with either the *Quraish* or the Muslims. The tribe of *Banū Khuzā'ah* sided with the Muslims, while *Banū Bakr* went on the side of the *Quraish*.

Two years after the agreement, *Banū Bakr* attacked *Banū Khuzā'ah* while they were asleep. *Banū Khuzā'ah* took refuge in *Al-Ka'bah*, but were butchered in the sacred precincts. The news of this violation of the treaty reached the Prophet, and he sent an ultimatum to the *Quraish* asking them to accept any of the following options :

1 *To pay compensation for the victims of the Banū Khuzā'ah;*
2 *To withdraw their support for Banū Bakr;*
3 *To declare that the Ḥudaibiyah agreement no longer holds valid.*

The *Quraish* did not agree to the first two options, and declared the

Ḥudaibiyah treaty to be null and void.

The Prophet then had no alternative but to take action against the *Quraish*. He set forth for *Makkah* with an army of ten thousand and took care to see that the news of his advance remained a secret. It was the tenth of the month of Ramaḍān, in the eighth year of *Hijrah*.

The *Quraish* had no power to resist the mighty Muslim advance. All the famous warriors were now on the Muslim side. How could the *Quraish* fight? They were totally demoralised by the might of the Muslim army.

Abū Sufiān, the arch-enemy of the Prophet saw that there was no route to escape. He asked *Al-'Abbās*, the prophet's uncle, to take him to the Prophet. Muḥammad *(pbuh)* granted an unconditional pardon to *Abū Sufiān*.

The Muslim army entered *Makkah* without incident. Inside, Makkans locked themselves within their homes and only a few who were unable to accept the new situation put up vain resistance.

The Prophet declared a *general amnesty* for the entire community of *Makkah*. He forgave them for their past crimes. It was a unique scene! The *Quraish* could not believe it! But even if they were unable to understand, it was the beauty and splendour of Islam which Muḥammad *(pbuh)*, Allah's messenger, was trying to make them comprehend. Now they saw it with their own eyes. It was Muḥammad *(pbuh)* whom they compelled to migrate, called a sorceror, crazy and an apostate. Now, it was the same Muḥammad *(pbuh)* who granted pardon to them.

Now *Makkah* was safe, peaceful and free of vengeance and enmity. Everyone enjoyed peace.

The conquest of *Makkah* without any bloodshed is a memorable event in Islamic history. The amnesty granted by the Prophet was unique and unmatched. The greatness of Islam and its Prophet is proved splendidly in the conquest of *Makkah*. Where can you find an example of such forgiveness and mercy? It is only in Islam which is the only way to real peace and happiness.

The Prophet stayed at *Makkah* until the *9th Shawwāl* of eighth *Hijrah*.

The farewell address

The Prophet completed his mission. He sustained every sort of trial and tribulation for the sake of his Lord and Creator. For twenty long years he worked hard to make the rule of Allah supreme on earth. He carried out this onerous duty on the soil of Arabia, a country which was most reluctant to accept the rule of the One Allah.

The system to guide mankind for all eternity was now completed. The Prophet could feel that his days were coming to an end.

After the performance of the last Ḥajj, he delivered his farewell speech at *'Arafah* before about *120,000* of his followers. This speech was one of the most memorable in the whole history of Islam.

The Prophet delivered his speech sitting on his camel and devoted followers listened intently to every word of it.

Praising and thanking Allah, the Prophet said : "*O people, listen to my words carefully, for I know not whether I would meet you again on such an occasion.*

"O people, just as you regard this month, this day, this city as sacred, so regard the life and property of every Muslim as a sacred trust. Remember that you will indeed appear before Allah and answer for your actions.

"Return the things kept with you as a trust (Amānah) to their rightful owners. All dues of interest shall stand cancelled and you will have only your capital back; Allah has forbidden interest, and I cancel the dues of interest payable to my uncle 'Abbās bin 'Abdul Muṭṭalib.

"O people, your wives have a certain right over you and you have certain rights over them. Treat them well and be kind to them, for they are your partners and committed helpers.

"Beware of Satan, he is desperate to divert you from the worship of Allah, so beware of him in matters of your religion.

"O people, listen carefully! All the believers are brothers. You are not allowed to take the things belonging to another Muslim unless he gives it to you willingly.

"O people, none is higher than the other unless he is higher in obedience to Allah. No Arab is any superior to a non-Arab except in piety.

"O people, reflect on my words. I leave behind me two things, the Qur'ān and my example, and if you follow these, you will not fail.

"Listen to me carefully! Worship Allah and offer Ṣalāh, observe Ṣawm in the month of Ramaḍān and pay Zakāh.

"O people, be mindful of those who work under you. Feed and clothe them as you feed and clothe yourselves.

O people, no prophet or messenger will come after me and no new faith will emerge.

"All those who listen to me shall pass on my words to others, and those to others again.

"Have I conveyed the message of Allah to you, o people?" asked the Prophet facing towards the heavens. The audience answered in one voice, *"Yes, you have; Allah is the witness."*

As the Prophet finished the following revelation came to him :

"Today I have perfected your religion for you, completed my favour upon you and have chosen for you Islam as the way of your life." (5:3).

The sad news

Back in *Madīnah*, the Prophet was taken ill. His health deteriorated and the illness became serious. He was unable to lead *Ṣalāh*. So, he asked *Abū Bakr*, his closest friend, to lead *Ṣalāh* for him.

During the last days of illness, he had terrible headaches and a very bad fever. The disease eventually took the life of the Prophet, the most illustrious personality in the history of mankind.

It was heart-breaking news for the Muslims. At first, they could not believe it; *'Umar*, one of the well-known companions of the Prophet became so furious about the news that he threatened to kill anyone who said Muḥammad *(pbuh)* was dead. It was the depth of his love and attachment to the Prophet that made him behave this way.

The Prophet was a man. He was mortal. He died. However painful and upsetting the news was for the Muslims, they had to believe it. *Abū Bakr*, pale and saddened with grief, went in and kissed the Prophet's forehead. He came out weeping to the waiting crowd outside the mosque. He heard what *'Umar* had said. He addressed the crowd with tears in his eyes but with a firm voice :

"Surely he who worshipped Muḥammad (pbuh) should know that Muḥammad (pbuh) is dead, but he who worshipped Allah should know that Allah is alive and never dies."

He then recited the verse of the *Qur'ān*, *"Muḥammad is but a messenger and messengers have passed away before him. Will it be that when he dies or is slain you will turn back on your heels? He who turns back does no harm to Allah and Allah will reward the thankful."* (3:144).

These words of *Abū Bakr* brought the Muslims back to face hard reality, and instilled in them confidence and hope, for Allah was there to help them and the *Qur'ān* and the *Sunnah* of the Prophet were there to guide them.

Muḥammad *(pbuh)*, Allah's last messenger on earth and supreme example for mankind, breathed his last on *12 Rabī'ul-Awwāl*, 11 AH *(8th June, 632 CE)*, at the age of *sixty three.*

Mission accomplished

The victory at *Makkah* was followed by an expedition of *Khālid* to demolish the Temple of *Al-'Uzzā*, the battle of *Ḥunain*, the siege of *Ṭā'if* and the battle of *Tabūk*. During the last two years of the Prophet's life, laws regarding *Zakāh, Jiziah* (non-Muslim tax), *Ḥajj* and interest dealings were revealed.

Muḥammad *(pbuh)* had a mission, a goal to achieve. It was to make the Law of Allah hold supreme in all human affairs. His duty was to call people to worship Allah alone, and none other. His task was to form a society based on the worship and obedience of *Tawḥīd*, belief in the *Risālah* and a firm conviction in *Ākhirah*.

Muḥammad *(pbuh)*, the Prophet of Allah, accomplished his assigned mission very successfully. He started preaching in the centre of idolatry, suffered torture, faced strong opposition, tolerated harassment and finally had to leave his own home and birth place for the sake of the Truth and the pleasure of Allah, the Creator.

He fought evil and untruth and never compromised on matters of basic principles. He was offered all kinds of worldly allurements and temptations, but he was not drawn into such traps.

He practised meticulously what he preached. His character and demeanour had a magnetic quality about them. His conduct and behaviour impressed even his bitterest enemy. He had a superb personality. His life was the perfect example of the total obedience to Allah's commands.

He was loved by his companions more than anybody else. His was the life of an unrivalled leader, teacher, general, statesman, husband, friend and brother and above all a true, real servant of Allah.

When he had to fight, he fought for the Truth, and never violated the principles of war. He showed the highest degree of patience in the face of strongest provocation and incitement. He loved his companions so deeply that they did not hesitate to give their lives at his call.

Muḥammad's *(pbuh)* life is the shining example for us to follow. He left for us teachings for all areas and affairs of our life. His life is the complete embodiment of Islam, based on the Qur'ān, the complete book of guidance from Allah.

Muḥammad *(pbuh)* was raised for mankind, to show them the best way to worship Allah and during his twenty-three years as Allah's messenger, he demonstrated infallibly this assigned task.

PROPHET MUḤAMMAD'S (pbuh) LIFE AT A GLANCE

Life at MAKKAH

Birth	Monday, 22nd April, 571 CE*
	12 Rabī'ul Awwāl
	Father *'Abdullāh* died before the Prophet's birth
At Six years of age	Death of mother *Āminah*
Eight	Grandfather *'Abdul Muṭṭalib* died
Twelve	First business trip to Syria
Fifteen	Battle of *Al-Fujjār*
Sixteen	Member of *Ḥilf-ul-Fuḍūl*
Twenty four	Second business trip to Syria
25	**Marriage with Khadījah**
35	Settlement of *Al-Ḥajr ul-Aswad* dispute
40	**Prophethood in** *610 CE*
1st Year of Prophethood	*Fajr* and *'Aṣr* prayers 2 Raka'h each
1st-3rd year	Secret preaching of Islam
	Centre : *Arqam Makhzūmi's* house
At the end of 3rd year	Open Call to Islam from Mount *Ṣafā*

*The Prophet's biographers differ about the exact year of his birth. Some have taken it to be 570 CE while others 569 CE. I have preferred 'Allāma Shiblī Nu'mānī's view from his famous 'Sīratun Nabī : 571 CE.

3rd-5th year	Hostility of Makkan infidels
5th year	Migration of Muslims to Abyssinia (Ethiopia)
6th year	*Ḥamzah* and *'Umar* accept Islam
7th-9th year	Boycott and Confinement by Makkan Infidels at *Shi'bi Abī Ṭālib*
10th year	**Year of Sorrow** — *Uncle Abū Ṭālib and wife Khadījah died*
10th year	Visit to *Ṭā'if*
10th year	**Mi'rāj, 27 Rajab**
10th year	Five times daily prayers made obligatory during *Mi'rāj*
11th year	First Covenent of *Al-'Aqabah,* 621 CE
12th year	Second Covenent of *Al-'Aqabah,* 622 CE
13th year	**Hijrah to Madīnah** *27 Ṣafar (622 CE)*

End of life in Makkah

Life at MADĪNAH

1st Year of Hijrah	Arrival at *Qubā', 8 Rabī'ul-'Awwāl* Arrival at *Madīnah, Friday, 622 CE* Construction of *Masjīdun Nabī* **Establishment of First Islamic State** Treaty with the Jews
2nd Hijrah	**Jihād ordained, 12 Ṣafar** *Adhān* and *Zakāh* introduced Revelation about the change of *Qiblah*, Monday, *15th Sha'bān* *Ramaḍān* prescribed *'Īdul Fiṭr, 1st Shawwāl* **Battle of Badr,** *17 Ramaḍān* Marriage of *'Alī* and *Fāṭimah*, after Badr Siege of *Banū Qainuqā'*
3rd Hijrah	1st restriction on drinking wine revealed **Battle of Uḥud,** *5 Shawwāl* First order about *Ribā* (Interest) revealed

	Revelation of Laws about orphans, after *Uḥud*
	Laws of Inheritance revealed
	Revelation of the Laws about marriage and the rights of wives
4th Hijrah	Order of *Ḥijāb* (Veil) for women revealed
	Revelation about the Prohibition of drinking wine
5th Hijrah	Battle of *Dumatul Jandal* and Battle of *Banū Al-Muṣṭalīq*
	Laws about Adultery and Slander revealed
	Battle of Aḥzāb
	Punishment of *Banū Quraiẓah*
6th Hijrah	**Ḥudaibiyah agreement**
	Khālid and *'Amr Ibnul 'Āṣ* accept Islam
7th Hijrah	*Letters to rulers of different countries including Iranian and Roman emperors*
	Battle of Khaibar
	Performance of postponed *'Umrah*
	Laws about Marriage and Divorce revealed
8th Hijrah	Battle of *Mu'tah*
	Conquest of Makkah, *20 Ramaḍān*
	Battle of *Ḥunain*, month of *Shawwāl*
	Siege of *Ṭā'if*
	Final order prohibiting *Ribā* (Interest) revealed
9th Hijrah	Battle of *Tabūk*
	Order of *Jiziah* (Protection Tax on minorities) revealed
	Ḥajj prescribed
10th Hijrah	**Farewell Address, 9 Dhū'l-Ḥijjah**
Death	*12 Rabī'ul-Awwāl, 11 Hijrah (632 CE)*

Note : The Prophet Muḥammad (pbuh) is the last and the final prophet of Allah. There will be no prophet after him. Those who do not believe Muḥammad (pbuh) as the last and the final prophet are not Muslims. For example, Qadiyanis or Aḥmadis who do not believe in the finality of the Prophet Muḥammad (pbuh) have been officially declared as non-Muslims in Pakistan.

Exercise : 7

1st Form

1. Answer the questions :
   a. Who was *Muḥammad* (pbuh)?
   b. Where was he born?
   c. When was he born?
   d. Who were his father and mother?
   e. When and to whom was he married?
   f. When did he become *Prophet of Allah?*
   g. What was his message?
   h. When did he leave *Makkah?*
   i. When did he die?
   j. What did he leave behind for us?
2. Write in your own words the story of *'Alī and the Dinner.*
3. Write in your own words the story about *'Umar's* acceptance of Islam.

2nd and 3rd Forms

1. Describe in your own words how ten year old *'Alī* accepted *Islam.*
2. Answer the questions :
   a. What was the duty of Prophet *Muḥammad* (pbuh)?
   b. When and where was he born?
   c. Who was *Baḥīrā?*
   d. Who was *Khadījah?*
   e. When and where *Muḥammad* (pbuh) received the revelation from *Allah?*
   f. What were the titles given to *Muḥammad* (pbuh) by the *Makkans?*
   g. Why did the Prophet leave *Makkah?*
   h. Where is *Masjīdun Nabī?*
   i. When was the battle of *Badr* fought?
   j. What did *Muḥammad* (pbuh) leave behind for our guidance?
3. Write in your own words the story of *The Prophet on Mount Ṣafā.*

4th, 5th and 6th Forms

1. Describe the incidents relating to the *Search for the Truth* and *Receiving the Truth* by the Prophet *Muḥammad* (pbuh).
2. Describe the circumstances which led to the *Hijrah* of the Prophet *Muḥammad* (pbuh) from *Makkah* to *Madīnah.*

3. Write down the main points from the farewell address of the Prophet *Muḥammad* (pbuh).
4. What lessons can we learn from the topic *Mission accomplished?*

Exercise : 8

1st Form

1. Fill in the blanks :
   No other ________ in the history of ________ has left so deep an ________ on the life of his ________ as ________ (pbuh), the last ________ of ________ .
   His life is the best ________ for us to ________ . He has ___ us how to ________ *Allah,* the Lord of the universe.
2. Write down the names of five early *male Muslims* and five *female Muslims.*

2nd and 3rd Forms

1. Write in your own words about the following :
   a. The Prophet's business trip to Syria.
   b. Prophet as a shepherd.
   c. Hostility begins.
2. Fill in the blanks :

   The Prophet was a ________. He was ________ . He________.
   However, painful and________the news was for the________,
   they had to________it. *Abū Bakr*, pale and ________
   with grief ________ in and ________the Prophet's forehead.

3. Make a list of the important events of the life of the Prophet *Muḥammad* (pbuh).

4th, 5th and 6th Forms

1. *"Indeed in the Messenger of Allah, you have for you, the best example"* (33:21). Explain in your own words the meaning of this verse of the *Qur'ān.*
2. Find out the reasons which led to the hostility of the *Makkans* to the message of the Prophet *Muḥammad* (pbuh).
3. Write an account of the events of the Prophet's life both at *Makkah* and *Madīnah.*

Exercise : 9

1st Form

1. Answer these questions :
   a. Who was *Maysarah?*
   b. What is the Arabic of the Black Stone?
   c. Who brought the first revelation?
   d. Who was *Warqah bin Nawfal?*
   e. Who was *Zaid Bin Ḥārithah?*
   f. Who was *Khabbāb?*
   g. Which was the most difficult day in the life of the Prophet?
   h. What is *Mi'rāj?*
2. Write in your own words about the Hijrah of the Prophet.

2nd and 3rd Forms

1. Why was *Adhān* introduced? Write the sentences which are said loudly at the time of *Adhān* in English.
2. Fill in the gaps :
   The ________ of *Makkah* were ________ in anger at the ________ safety of the ________ in ________. All their ________ attempts to ________ off ________ *(pbuh)* had ________. Their ________ route to ________ was now ________ easy ________ of the ________. They became ________ and were ________ within themselves, unable to ________ a way to ________ Muḥammad *(pbuh).*

4th, 5th and 6th Forms

1. Write an account of the *Battle of Badr* and comment on the outcome of this battle.
2. What lessons should we learn from the *battle of Uḥud?*
3. Describe the *Conquest of Makkah* and comment on the general *amnesty* declared by the Prophet at the time of this conquest.

Exercise : 10

2nd and 3rd Forms

1. Answer these questions :
   a. What is the meaning of the word *Muḥammad?*
   b. What is *Ḥilful Fuḍūl?*
   c. Who was *Najjāshī?*
   d. Who was the leader of the first emigrants to *Ethiopia?*
   e. Which *Sūrah* was recited by the leader of the emigrants before *Najjāshī?*
   f. What is *Al-Isrā?*
   g. Where is *Mount Thawr?*
   h. What is the English of *Muhājirūn?*
2. Write in your words about the *Ḥudaibiyah* agreement.

4th, 5th and 6th Forms

1. Discuss the role of young Muḥammad *(pbuh)* in social welfare activities. What lessons can you learn out of this?
2. Write an account of *Al-Mi'rāj.*
3. What were the main features of the *Ḥudaibiyah agreement.* In what way was it helpful for the Muslims in the long run?
4. Comment on the teachings of the day of the Prophet at *Ṭā'if.*

4

Khulafā' Ur Rāshidūn

(Rightly guided Caliphs)

Abū Bakr (RA)*

NOW that the prophet is no more, who will lead the Islamic community? That was the question in the minds of all those present at the *Masjīdun Nabī*. It was a crucial matter. A community cannot continue without a leader. Something must be decided before Allah's messenger was finally put to rest in the grave.

It proved the importance of leadership, without which a community becomes disarranged and indisciplined, and then loses its potential and prospects.

There was much discussion on the question of leadership. After discussion and argument, *Abū Bakr* was elected unanimously as the leader of the Muslim community. He was the first to succeed the Prophet, and was the **first Khalīfah** *(Caliph or successor to the Prophet)* of the Muslims. Who else could lead the Muslim community at this crucial moment except *Abū Bakr*? He was the closest friend of the Prophet and he acted as the Prophet's deputy, leading the prayers when the Prophet was ill.

After the election of the *Khalīfah*, the Prophet was buried, on the night of 13 *Rabī' ul-Awwāl* of the *11th Hijrah*.

Abū Bakr's real name was 'Abdullāh, and he was given the title of *Aṣ-Ṣiddīq (testifier to the truth)*. His father, *'Uthmān* was known as *Abū Quḥāfah* and his mother *Salmā*, was known as *Ummul Khair*. He was two and a half years younger than Muḥammad *(pbuh)*.

After his election as the *Khalīfah, Abū Bakr* addressed the Muslims with these words :

"O people, I have been chosen by you as your leader, although I am no better than any one of you. If I do any good, give me your support. If I do any wrong, set me right.

"Listen, truth is honesty and untruth is dishonesty.

"The weak among you are the powerful in my eyes, as long as I do not get them their due. The powerful among you are weak in my eyes, as long as I do not take away from them what is due to others.

---

*RA stands for Raḍiyallāhu 'Anhu (may Allah be pleased with him).

"Listen carefully, if people give up striving for the cause of Allah, He will send down disgrace upon them. If a people become evil-doers, Allah will send down calamities upon them.

"Obey me as long as I obey Allah and His messenger. If I disobey Allah and His messenger, you are free to disobey me."

Abū Bakr was asking people to obey him only if he obeyed Allah and His messenger. Such was the first *Khalīfah* of the Muslims! Indeed, the world would be a better place to live in if we had leaders like *Abū Bakr*.

He was the first among the Prophet's friends to accept Islam, at the beginning. He accompanied the Prophet during the *Hijrah* to *Madīnah*.

Abū Bakr was a merchant. He freed many slaves, including *Bilāl* and *Umayya Bin Qahāf*. He participated in all the battles which the Prophet had to fight against unbelievers.

Abū Bakr loved his faith more than anything else. At *Badr*, his son, *'Abdur Raḥmān* was fighting on the side of the unbelievers. After accepting Islam, *'Abdur Raḥmān* once said to his father, *"O father, at Badr, you were twice under my sword, but my love for you held my hand back."* To this, *Abū Bakr* replied *"Son, if I had you only once under my sword, you would have been no more."* He was so uncompromising in his faith.

At the time of the battle of *Tabūk*, he donated all his belongings to the War Fund, and when the Prophet asked, *"What have you left for your family?"*, he replied, *"Allah and His messenger."*

Before his death, the Prophet nominated *Usāmah Bin Zaid* to lead an expedition to Syria against the Roman *(then called Byzantine)* army on the northern border of Arabia. The Romans killed the envoy of the Prophet and refused to accept any negotiated settlement. *Usāmah* could not go on because of the death of the Prophet. *Abū Bakr* sent *Usāmah* on the expedition even though he had to attend to all the internal problems of the Islamic state.

The news of the Prophet's death made some new Muslims think that the Islamic state would crumble and they refused to pay the *Zakāh*. These new Muslims could not get used to their new faith and its requirements until then. *Abū Bakr* declared, *"By Allah! Even if a single kid is due from a man, he must give it. If he refuses I will declare war against him."*

Some others became renegades and imposters. *Ṭolaiḥah, Musailimah, Mālik Bin Nuwairah, 'Aswad 'Ansī* and a woman named *Sajāh* claimed they were prophets and created a great deal of confusion. *Abū Bakr* was quick to take strong action against these imposters. *Khālid Bin Wālīd* was sent to deal with *Ṭolaiḥah* who fled to Syria and later became a Muslim. *Mālik Bin Nuwairah* was killed.

'Irkimah and *Shurahbil* were sent to take action against *Musailimah*, but they were defeated and *Abū Bakr* dispatched *Khālid* to tackle the notorious *Musailimah* who married *Sajāh*. In the fight that followed, *Waḥshī*, the killer of *Ḥamzah* at *Uḥud*, killed *Musailimah*. *Waḥshī*, who became a Muslim after the conquest of Makkah had regretted killing the Prophet's uncle *Ḥamzah* at *Uḥud*, and killing *Musailimah*, he felt, compensated for his earlier mistake.

Musailimah and *'Aswad* claimed to be prophets while Muḥammad (pbuh) was alive. *'Aswad* was taken care of by the Muslims of *Yemen* during the Prophet's life.

Abū Bakr's swift and bold steps saved the Islamic state from serious danger of chaos and confusion. He could now attend to other urgent problems.

During his Khilāfah *(Caliphate)*, *Abū Bakr* had to take action against the Iranian empire. The emperor of Iran, Khusru Parvez, *(Chosroe)* tore up the letter the Prophet sent to him through *'Abdullāh bin Ḥudhāfah* and demanded that the Prophet be arrested. In the mean time, *Khusru* was murdered by his son and the whole empire fell into chaos and disorder. *Hurmuz*, the Persian governor in *'Irāq* was very hostile to Arabs and he was cruel to the Muslims living in his area.

Abū Bakr sent *Muthannā* to take action against the Iranians in *'Irāq*. His forces were insufficient and *Khālid* was then sent with reinforcements. The Muslim army captured vast areas of the Iranian empire in several battles.

Khalīfah Abū Bakr then turned his attention to the Romans who were causing trouble on the North-West frontier. The prophet himself led an expedition against the Romans and this is known as *Battle Mu'tah*.

Abū Bakr dispatched four separate armies under *Abū 'Ubaidah bin Jarrāḥ, 'Amr Ibnul 'Āṣ, Yazīd bin Abū Sufiān* and *Shuraḥbil bin Ḥasnah* to deal with Roman power.

The four generals merged themselves into a unit to face the Romans most effectively. The Romans had amassed *150,000* soldiers but the total Muslim army was only *24,000*. Reinforcements were requested and *Abū Bakr* asked *Khālid* to handover the charge of Iraqi front to *Muthannā* and rush to the Syrian front to help fight the colossal Roman army. The armies met in *Yarmūk* after *Abū Bakr's* death during the *Khilāfah* of *'Umar* and *the Romans* were defeated.

Abū Bakr fell ill during this time and he died on *21 Jumadiul-Ākhir 13 AH* (22 August 634 CE). His rule lasted two years and three months.

One of the many contributions of *Abū Bakr* was the collection and compilation of *Al-Qur'ān*.

Abū Bakr lived a simple, pious and upright life. He was a true servant of Allah and a meticulous follower of the Prophet.

Abū Bakr's advice to the Muslim Army

1. *Always fear Allah; He knows what is in men's hearts.*
2. *Be kind to those who are under you and treat them well.*
3. *Give brief directions; directions that are too long are likely to be forgotten.*
4. *Improve your own conduct before asking others to improve theirs.*
5. *Honour the enemy's envoy.*
6. *Maintain the secrecy of your plans.*
7. *Always speak the truth, so that you get the right advice.*
8. *Consult your men when you are free to do so; this will develop participation.*
9. *Take suitable measures to keep a watch on the army.*
10. *Be sincere to all with whom you deal.*
11. *Give up cowardice and dishonesty.*
12. *Give up bad company.*

'Umar *(RA)*

Before his death, *Abū Bakr* consulted the senior companions of the Prophet and selected *'Umar* as the second *Khalīfah* of the Muslims.

'Umar was the son of *Khaṭṭāb* and he is famous in Islamic history as *Al-Fārūq* (one who distinguishes between right and wrong). His acceptance of Islam is notable and we mentioned it earlier in the Prophet's biography.

'Umar was a very brave and straight-forward person. He was tough in his attitude and uncompromising in basic principles. He was a great and talented ruler. During his Caliphate, the frontiers of the Islamic state expanded enormously.

'Umar was a strong disciplinarian. He noticed the tremendous popularity of *Khālid*, the commander-in-chief of the Muslim forces, and feared the people might think too highly of him. So he removed *Khālid* and appointed *Abū 'Ubaidah* as the Commander-in-Chief. The other reason for this bold decision was to make it clear that no-one was indispensable and victory in war was actually due to Allah's help. According to *Allāma Shiblī Nu'mānī* the deposition of *Khālid* took place in 17 AH after the conquest of Syria. Some historians, however, maintain that this was the first mandate of *Khalīfah 'Umar*.

Khālid, who had been given the title of the *'Sword of Allah'* (Ṣaifullāh) by the prophet, gracefully accepted Khalīfah's order and worked as an ordinary soldier under *Abū 'Ubaidah*. This is an example of the Islamic teaching of obedience to leadership.

Khālid had left *Muthannā* in command of the Muslim forces on the Iraqi front when he rushed to *Yarmūk*. *Muthannā* was finding it difficult to counter the enemy and went personally to *Madīnah* to ask *Abū Bakr* for reinforcements. *Abū Bakr* was by then on his death-bed.

Muthannā's absence from 'Irāq made things worse. The Iranians regrouped and under the command of *Rustam*, recaptured the Muslim-occupied areas. *Rustam* sent two columns of his army, one to *Ḥirah* and the other to *Kaskar*.

'Umar sent *Abū 'Ubaidah*, the Commander, to deal with the situation and he defeated both the Persian columns. *Rustam* despatched a still larger force, including elephants, under the command of *General Bahman*. The two armies fought and the Muslims were defeated.

Khalīfah 'Umar raised another large army and *Muthannā* regrouped the defeated troops. They put up a valiant fight and the Persians were defeated this time.

But the Persian court raised a larger army still, and forced *Muthannā* to withdraw. The report of the new situation was sent to *'Umar* and reinforcements were sent under *Sa'd Bin Abī Waqqās*.

The Persian army and the Muslim army met at *Qādisiyah*. After a prolonged battle on several fronts, the outnumbered Muslim army defeated *120,000* Persian troops and recaptured the Ḥirah and other areas in 14 AH (636 CE).

Muslims laid siege to *Damascus* during *Khalīfah Abū Bakr's* term of office. It continued, after *Abū Bakr's* death and lasted 70 days during the rule of *'Umar*. After the long siege, *Khālid* took the Romans by surprise and entered the city. The Governor surrendered and a peace treaty was signed.

Meanwhile, *'Amr Ibnul 'Āṣ* was laying siege to *Jerusalem*. Later, *Khālid, Abū 'Ubaidah* and others joined him there. The Christians had little hope, and decided to give in. They put forward a proposal to the Muslims that they would hand over the city if *Khalīfah 'Umar* himself came to *Jerusalem*.

The proposal was relayed to *Madīnah* and the *Khalīfah* agreed to go to *Jerusalem*. He started out for the city with one attendant, riding a camel. They would ride the camel in turn. Sometimes the *Khalīfah* would walk and the attendant would ride and another time the *Khalīfah* would ride and the attendant would walk by the camel. This is Islamic Justice. The ruler and the ruled have equal rights. The rulers of the Islamic state must acknowledge the rights of the citizens over their own rights.

The *Khalīfah* of the Muslims entered *Jerusalem* dressed in ordinary clothes and flanked by the Muslims generals. *The Christians* could hardly believe the Muslim rider had arrived; such was the simplicity of *'Umar*. He used to live like a very humble ordinary man. But he was tough, and the most able ruler of his time. He had no pride, no pomp and no grandeur. This is the teaching of Islam. This is what present day Muslim rulers have forgotten, and is what we must restore and get back.

An agreement was signed that guaranteed the safety and security of the *Christians* in *Jerusalem*.

During the *Khilāfah* of *'Umar*, vast areas of the *Roman*, and *Persian* empires and the whole of *Egypt* were brought under Islamic rule. *'Umar* was a gifted orator. He was very concerned for the welfare of the citizens under his rule. He left a memorable legacy for Muslims after him.

The second *Khalīfah 'Umar* died after being stabbed by a Persian non-Muslim *Fīroz* nick-named *Abū Lu'lu'*. *Fīroz* complained to *'Umar* about his master *Mughīrah bin Shu'bah* who imposed a tax on him. *'Umar* heard the details of the complaint and told *Fīroz* that the tax was reasonable. This made *Fīroz* angry and the next day during dawn prayer he struck the *Khalīfah* with a dagger six times wounding him fatally. *'Umar Al-Fārūq* died three days later in 23 AH *(644 CE)*.

Before his death, *'Umar* had appointed a six-man Committee to elect his successor from among themselves. The six members of the Committee were : *'Uthmān bin 'Affān, 'Abdur Raḥmān bin 'Auf, 'Alī bin Abū Ṭālib, Zubair bin 'Awwām, Sa'd bin Abī Waqqās*, and *Ṭalḥah bin 'Ubaidullāh*.

'Umar Al-Fārūq ruled the Islamic state for *ten years six months and four days*.

'Umar's advice

1. *Do not be misled by someone's reputation.*
2. *Do not judge a person only by his performance of Ṣalāh and Ṣawm; rather look into his truthfulness and wisdom.*
3. *One who keeps his secrets controls his affairs.*
4. *Fear the person whom you hate.*
5. *Prudent is he who can assess his actions.*
6. *Do not defer your work for tomorrow.*
7. *He who has no idea of evil can easily fall into its trap.*
8. *Judge a man's intelligence by the questions he asks.*
9. *Less concern for material well-being enables one to lead a free life.*
10. *It is easier not to indulge in sins than to repent.*
11. *Contentment and gratitude are two great virtues; you should not care which one you are gaining.*
12. *Be grateful to him who points out your defects.*

'Uthmān *(RA)*

The six member committee appointed by *'Umar Al-Fārūq*, after long deliberations and consultation, elected *'Uthmān the son of 'Affān* as the third *Khalīfah* of Islam.

'Uthmān was born six years after the Prophet and he belonged to the Umayyah tribe of the *Quraish*. He was a cloth merchant and was very rich. He was known as *Al-Ghanī* (the rich).

He had accepted Islam on Abū Bakr's invitation and migrated to Abyssinia with his wife *Ruqaiyyah* (Prophet's daughter). He acted as the Prophet's envoy during Ḥudaibiyah agreement.

His state policy can be understood from his letter to the officers of the Islamic army. He wrote :

"You are the protectors of Islam from the onslaughts of the enemies. 'Umar had issued some regulations which are known to me. In fact, they were drafted in consultation with me.

"Beware! I do not want to have reports from anyone of any transgression by you. If you do so, you will be replaced by someone better. You should always be mindful of your conduct. I will watch over whatever Allah has entrusted to my care."

He once spoke to the Tax Collectors with these words :

"Allah has created everything with fairness and justice. He accepts only what is right and just. Give what is right and take what is right. Trust produces trust. Follow it strictly and do not be of those who fail to discharge it. Faithfulness begets faithfulness. Do not oppress the orphans and those with whom you have covenanted. Allah will punish those who will do so."

Sa'd bin Abī Waqqās was the Governor of *Kufā* in 'Irāq. *'Uthmān* dismissed him for non-payment of a state loan. He was succeeded by *Mughīrah*.

During the Caliphate of *'Uthmān*, the rebellion in *Ādharbaijān* and *Ārmenia* was quelled. *Mu'āwiyah*, Governor of Syria, with the help of *Abī Saraḥ*, the Governor of *Egypt*, made a naval attack on *Cyprus* and brought it under Islamic rule. Vast areas of North Africa including *Tripoli, Tunisia* and *Morocco* were brought under Islamic rule during the *Khilāfah of 'Uthmān.*

The Romans, although defeated several times by the Muslim army in the past, made another attempt during the *Khilāfah of 'Uthmān* to recapture the territories they had lost.

Constantine, then *Emperor of Rome* made great preparations and attacked *Alexandria* with a naval fleet five to six thousand strong. But, the *Romans* were decisively defeated by the new Muslim naval force under the commands of *Abī Saraḥ* and *Mu'āwiyah*.

During the last six years of his Khilāfah, *'Uthmān* faced internal dissension and trouble. This trouble took the shape of civil war which eventually led to the killing of the third *Khalīfah 'Uthmān* by an unruly and angry mob.

'Uthmān's Khilāfah lasted *twelve years*. He was murdered by rioters

on *Friday, 17 Dhū'l Ḥijjah in 35 AH* (656 CE).

'Uthmān was a simple and a very kind-hearted man. His simplicity and kindness did not allow him to take strong action against the trouble-makers and rioters. Above all, because of his simple mindedness, his administration was not as disciplined as it had been during *'Umar*.

'Uthmān was a generous man. He used to spend a lot of money for Islam and to free the slaves. He was a great pious man who feared and loved Allah above everything else.

'Alī (RA)

"I am the youngest of you. I may be a boy, my feet may not be strong enough, but O messenger of Allah, I shall be your helper. Whoever opposes you, I shall fight him as a mortal enemy."

These were the words of *'Alī*, the cousin of the Prophet and then a boy of only ten. He spoke these words before the elders of *Quraish* during the dinner hosted by the Prophet to invite them to Islam.

'Alī was the person who risked his life for the Prophet and slept in the Prophet's bed when the unbelievers laid a siege around the Prophet's house to kill him on the night of the Prophet's migration.

The same *'Alī* was elected the fourth Khalīfah of Islam after *'Uthmān*. He was the son of *Abū Ṭālib*, the Prophet's uncle.

'Alī was married to the Prophet's daughter *Fāṭimah* and they had two sons, *Ḥasan* and *Ḥusain*, whom the Prophet loved very dearly as his grandsons.

He took part in the battles of *Badr, Aḥzāb* and *Khaibar*. At *Khaibar*, it was *'Alī* who subdued the Jews by his furious assault.

'Alī held many important positions during the life of the Prophet and the three Caliphs *(Khulafā')* before him.

He was elected *Khalīfah* at a very delicate time when the *Muslim Ummah* (community) was torn by internal strife and the sad incident of the murder of *'Uthmān*, the third *Khalīfah* had taken place.

'Alī first concentrated on consolidating his administration and pledged then to take action against *'Uthmān's* murderers. But the supporters of *'Uthmān* would not listen to the *Khalīfah*, until he took action against *'Uthmān's* murderers.

The murder of *'Uthmān* by a group of riotous Muslims had a

tremendous effect on the later history of the Muslims. It divided the once cohesive, united and determined *Muslim Ummah* (Community), and factions fought bloody battles among themselves.

The once powerful Islamic army which fought the wrong-doers and rescued those suffering from the exploitation and tyranny of the mighty *Persian* and *Roman* empires had now become seriously involved in internal clashes.

The talented and able ruler, *'Alī*, had to spend much of his time pacifying the warring factions of the Muslims. He tried his best to reconcile the opposing groups and restore peace, without much success. The *Ummah* was dangerously divided and catastrophic consequences followed. Groupings developed and mutual trust and confidence were undermined.

During this turmoil, *'Alī*, the fourth Khalīfah of Islam was fatally wounded during *Ṣalātul-Fajr* by one *Ibn Muljim. 'Alī* died on *Friday, 20 Ramaḍān AH 40* (659 CE).

'Alī's rule lasted for four years nine months and the whole of that time was a period of unrest.

'Alī lived a very simple and austere life. He was a very generous and courageous person and had a sharp sense of justice.

He had a love of learning and he was a great and learned person himself. He had been given the title of *"Gate of learning"* by the Prophet. He was also called *Asadullāh* (Lion of Allah).

Some important sayings of 'Alī

1 *One who knows himself, knows his creator.*
2 *If you love Allah, tear out your heart's love of the world.*
3 *The fear of Allah makes one secure.*
4 *How can you rejoice about life that grows shorter each hour?*
5 *World-wide reputation can be undone by an hour's degradation.*
6 *Three defects make life miserable :*
1 Vindictiveness 2 Jealousy 3 A bad character.
7 *One who is proud of worldly possessions of this fleeting existence, is ignorant.*
8 *Joy is followed by tears.*
9 *Each breath of a man is a step nearer to death.*
10 *The best man is he who is most helpful to his fellow-men.*
11 *One who thinks himself the best is the worst.*

12 *The hated person is one who returns evil for good.*
13 *Virtue is the key to success.*
14 *Learned men live even after death, ignorant men are dead although alive.*
15 *There is no treasure like knowledge.*
16 *Knowledge is wisdom and the educated man is the wise man.*
17 *Experience is knowledge gained.*
18 *Who never corrects himself will never correct another.*
19 *Listen, and you will teach yourself : remain silent, and you risk nothing.*
20 *One who reflects on Allah's gifts, succeeds.*
21 *Ignorance harms a man more than a cancer in the body.*
22 *One of the signs of a stupid man is the frequent change of opinion.*
23 *Never speak when it is not the time for speech.*
24 *Beware of back-biting : it sows the seeds of bitterness, and separates you from Allah and man.*
25 *The best truth is the keeping of promises.*
26 *Better be dumb than lie.*
27 *Do not flatter, it is no sign of faith.*
28 *A hypocrite's tongue is clean, but there is sickness in his heart.*
29 *Better to be alone than with bad company.*
30 *Whoever sows good reaps his reward.*

Conclusion

Abū Bakr Aṣ-Ṣiddīq, 'Umar Al-Fārūq, 'Uthmān Al-Ghanī, 'Alī Al-Murtaḍā were the consecutive successors of the Prophet. These four *Khulafā'* are called *Khulafā'-ur-Rāshidūn* or the rightly guided *Khulafā'*.

Together, these four *Khulafā'* ruled the Islamic State for about *thirty years*. They are called, *'rightly guided'* because they ruled the people of their time exactly in accordance with the teachings of the *Qur'ān* and the *Sunnah* of the Prophet.

Despite the unpleasant happenings, this period of Islamic rule is the golden period of justice unrivalled in human history. Islamic principles were put into practice in full during this time.

A detailed and serious study of the lives of the Khulafā'-ur-Rāshidūn would open before us a treasure of knowledge and experience about the Islamic system of life which is the only solution to the present and future problems of mankind. We need to follow the Islamic teachings most faithfully in order to get the promised good out of it. Mere lip service to the greatness and beauty of

Islam would deliver nothing. It is the practice of the system which counts.

Let us resolve to understand, practise and preach Islam. Only then shall we ourselves find peace and happiness and the whole of humanity also will be freed from unhappiness and oppression.

Exercise : 11

1st Form

1. Answer these questions :
   a. What are the meanings of *Khalīfah* and *Khilāfah?*
   b. What is the title of *Abū Bakr?*
   c. What should you say after the name of a male companion of the Prophet?
   d. What is the name of *Abū Bakr's* son who fought on the side of unbelievers at the time of *Badr?*
   e. When did *Abū Bakr* die?
   f. What is the title of *Khalīfah 'Umar?*
   g. Who was the commander of Muslim army at the time of *'Umar?*
   h. Who killed *Khalīfah 'Umar?*
   i. How long did *Khalīfah 'Umar* rule the Muslims?
   j. When did *Khalīfah 'Umar* die?
2. Write down *Khalīfah Abū Bakr's* twelve points of advice.

2nd and 3rd Forms

1. Answer these questions :
   a. What is the meaning of *Khulafā'ur Rāshidūn?*
   b. Who was the father of *Khalīfah Abū Bakr?*
   c. Who were the false prophets against whom *Khalīfah Abū Bakr* fought?
   d. What did *Khalīfah Abū Bakr* say to his son at the time of the battle of Badr?
   e. Who was *Khalīfah 'Umar's* father?
   f. How did *Khalīfah 'Umar* go to Jerusalem?
2. Write down *Khalīfah 'Umar's* twelve points of advice.

4th, 5th and 6th Forms

1. Discuss the importance of *leadership* in Islamic community.
2. Write down the speech of *Khalīfah Abū Bakr* which he delivered after his election as *Khalīfah.*

3. Why was *Khālid Bin Walīd* replaced as *Commander-in-Chief* of the Muslim army?
4. Who were the members of the committee formed by *Khalīfah 'Umar* to elect his successor?

Exercise : 12

1st Form :

1. Fill in the blanks :

   "Allah has ________ everything with ________ and justice. He ________ only what is ________ and ________. Give what is ________ and take what is ________. Trust produces ________. Follow it ________ and do not be of ________ who fail to ________ it."
2. Write down ten points from *Khalīfah 'Alī's* 30 points of advice.
3. Who were the *Khulafā'ur Rāshidūn?*

2nd and 3rd Forms

1. What did *Khalīfah 'Uthmān* write to the officers of the Islamic Army?
2. Answer these questions :
   a. What is the title of *Khalīfah 'Uthmān?*
   b. Who was *Khalīfah 'Uthmān's* wife?
   c. What was Mu'awiyah's post during the *Khilāfah of 'Uthmān?*
   d. Which countries came under muslim rule during the *Khilāfah of 'Uthmān?*
   e. Who was the father of *Khalīfah 'Alī?*
   f. Who was *Khalīfah Alī's* wife?
   g. Who were the sons of *Khalīfah 'Alī?*
   h. Who killed *Khalīfah 'Alī?*

4th, 5th and 6th Forms

1. Describe in your own words the *Khilāfah* of *'Uthmān.*
2. What observations could you make about the *Khilāfah* of *Khalīfah 'Alī?*
3. Why are the four caliphs of Islam called *Khulafā'ur Rāshidūn?*

5

Three Great Muslim Women

*Khadījah (RA)**

"When none believed me, Khadījah did. She made me a partner in her wealth."

THOSE are the words of the Prophet Muḥammad *(pbuh)* about his first wife — the great Muslim lady, *Khadījat ul-Kubrā'*.

Khadījah, the daughter of *Khuwailid*, was born 15 years before the year of the elephant in 555 CE. Her mother was *Fāṭimah bint Zaidah*.

She was a noble, fine-natured wealthy lady of *Makkah*. She married the Prophet when she was *40* and he was *25*. They had six children : two boys, *Qāsim* and *'Abdullāh* (also known as *Ṭāhir* and *Ṭayyib*), and four girls, *Zainab, Ruqaiyyah, Umm Kulthūm* and *Fāṭimah*.

Khadījah lived with the Prophet for 25 years and was the Prophet's only wife during that time.

When the revelation came from Allah and Muḥammad *(pbuh)* was made Prophet, it was *Khadījah* who accepted the faith and became the first Muslim. She was 55 years old at that time. Her acceptance of Islam greatly helped its spread among the Makkans. She stood by the Prophet all the time. In moments of trial and difficulty the Prophet used to come to her and she consoled and comforted her husband and encouraged him.

Khadījah's wealth was used for the cause of Islam. The Prophet remained busy in preaching Islam and his devoted and loving wife looked after the children and family affairs.

The Prophet and *Khadījah* had many sorrows. They had to bear the death of their sons *Qāsim* and *'Abdullāh* in their infancy, and in the fifth year of the prophethood, their daughter *Ruqaiyyah* left them and migrated to Abyssinia with her husband, *'Uthmān bin 'Affān*.

Ruqaiyyah left her parents at the age of 12 and returned after four years, and that time was a long and painful separation for her mother, *Khadījah*.

During the prophethood, the *Quraish* did all they could to stop the

*RA here stands for Raḍiyallāhu 'Anhā (may Allah be pleased with her).

Prophet preaching Islam. Nothing worked. The Prophet continued his mission, relying on Allah. *Khadījah* was his source of encouragement and comfort. She also had to bear enormous strain and suffering during the boycott at *Shi'bi Abī Ṭālib* for three years.

The great Muslim lady *Khadījah*, the first Muslim, died on *10 Ramāḍan* in the tenth year of the prophethood, in *620 CE*, at the age of 65. Her death was a great loss to Muḥammad *(pbuh)*. He said, *"I cannot bear the scene. I believe that Allah has kept much good in it"*. He loved *Khadījah* so dearly that after her death he used to remember her very often.

The angel, *Jibrā'īl*, used to bring salām for her from Allah.

Fāṭimatuz Zahrā' became so sad at her mother's death that she stuck to her father and continued crying, *"Where is my mummy? Where is my mummy?"*. The Prophet consoled her and told her of the good news of *Khadījah's* acceptance by Allah in Paradise.

Young Muslim girls should know how devoted *Khadījah* was to her husband, and how much she did for him for the cause of Allah. The Muslims of the present day would feel proud to have such a wife. The world could be changed by great Muslim ladies like *Khadījah*.

Fāṭimah (RA)

Fāṭimah, the youngest of the four daughters of the Prophet, is known as *Sayyidatun Nisā'* (Leader of the women). She was born five years before the prophethood of Muḥammad *(pbuh)*, and migrated to *Madīnah* after the Prophet, with her sisters and step mother *Sawdah*.

After the death of her mother *Khadījah*, she served her father with total devotion and love. The Prophet loved her very much and kept her with him in deep affection. She was loved by all the wives of the Prophet. She looked like her mother *Khadījah* and this reminded people of her great mother.

Fāṭimah was married to *'Alī* after the battle of *Badr*, in a simple marriage ceremony. The guests were served dates and drinks made from honey. She was about *18* years old, though some say she was only 15 at the time.

Her married life was happy and peaceful. *'Alī*, her husband, respected her, and the Prophet always used to advise *Fāṭimah* to obey and serve her husband in every respect. She kept her house neat, clean and tidy and gave it a simple, pure and peaceful look where happiness and good fortune prevailed.

Fāṭimah and her husband had five children : three sons, *Ḥasan, Ḥusain* and *Muḥassin*, and two daughters, *Zainab* and *Umm Kulthūm*. *Muḥassin* died while still a baby.

According to *Aḥādīth* (plural of Ḥadīth), *Fāṭimah* was regarded as a great and respected lady by the women of her day, because of her personality, kindness, politeness and dignity.

The Prophet said, "Among the women of the whole world, four are great : *Khadījah, Fāṭimah, Maryam* (Mary) and *Āsiyah* (wife of *Fir'awn* (Pharaoh))."

Fāṭimah resembled her father very closely in habits, traits and in conversation. When she came to any meetings of the Prophet, he used to get up for her and make room for her to sit by his side.

Fāṭimah took part in the battle of *Uḥud* and nursed the wounded Muslim soldiers. She bandaged the wound sustained by the Prophet during the battle. She also took part in the battle of the conquest of *Makkah*.

The Prophet was always seen off by *Fāṭimah* when he was going out from *Madīnah* and was met by her when he returned home.

Fāṭimah died after a few months of the death of the Prophet, on *3 Ramaḍān* in 11 AH at the age of 30. Before her death she willed that her body be carried for burial prayers in such a way that no-one could recognise whether it was the body of a male or female.

Since she died so soon after the death of the Prophet, she could narrate no more than eighteen or nineteen *Aḥadīth*.

Fāṭimah was an ideal Muslim daughter, wife and mother. Her life should be an example for Muslim girls of all ages.

'Ā'ishah (RA)

This great Muslim lady was married to the Prophet after the death of his first wife, *Khadījah*. She was born in 613 or 614 CE, the fourth year of the Prophet's mission, and was married to the Prophet when she was nine, but only went to live with him when she was 12 (some say at 15).

Her father was *Abū Bakr*, the closest friend of the Prophet and the first Khalīfah of Islam. Her mother was *Umm Rūmān*.

'Ā'ishah was a great Muslim lady. She was very talented and had a wonderful memory. She had a great love of learning and became noted for her intelligence, learning and sharp sense of judgment.

She grew up in an Islamic environment. Her father was a great Muslim and the Prophet himself was a frequent visitor to their house. She became a Muslim as soon as she reached an age of reason and understanding.

During her childhood, *'Ā'ishah* memorised quite a number of *sūrahs* of the Qur'ān. Her father was a man of learning and she inherited his love of knowledge.

'Ā'ishah and her elder sister, *Asmā'*, helped in packing for the famous *Hijrah* of the Prophet.

'Ā'ishah had the good fortune to be trained under the care of the greatest teacher of mankind, the Prophet Muḥammad *(pbuh)*. This training made her one of the most notable Muslim ladies in Islamic history. She was totally devoted to the Prophet, her husband, and he loved her very dearly.

She loved and enjoyed serving her husband. She used to do the household work, including grinding flour and baking bread. She would make the beds and do the family's washing. She always kept water ready for the Prophet's ablutions, before prayer.

The Prophet did not love her only for her physical beauty but for her intelligence, sound judgment and personality. She liked what the Prophet liked and disliked what he disliked.

If *'Ā'ishah* loved anyone more than her husband Muḥammad *(pbuh)*, it was Almighty Allah. This was the teaching of the Prophet.

The Prophet used to live a very simple life. There were occasions when the family had nothing to eat, and times when guests were served with whatever they had while they went hungry themselves. They believed the comfort of the life after death was more important to them than the comforts of this world. This also is the teaching of Islam.

'Ā'ishah used to accompany the Prophet in prayers. They used to remain standing for long periods in prayer, weeping and asking Allah's forgiveness.

The Prophet fell ill in 11 AH and *'Ā'ishah* nursed him with all the love and care of a devoted wife. He died in her lap.

'Ā'ishah was present also at her father's death bed. *Abū Bakr* asked her how many pieces of cloth were used to bury the Prophet and she told him three. He asked his daughter to wrap him also in three sheets for burial.

'Ā'ishah saved the place beside the father's grave for her own burial, but after a fatal injury, *'Umar* the second Khalīfah of Islam, sent his son *'Abdullāh* to *'Ā'ishah* to ask her permission for him to be buried beside *Abū Bakr*. She agreed to *'Umar's* wish and commented "I prefer 'Umar to myself", which shows how great she was.

'Ā'ishah always stood for the truth. She taught Islam to many people. She was an authority on many matters of Islamic Law, especially those concerning women. She narrated *2,210 Aḥādīth* (plural of *Ḥadīth*). She died at the age of *67 on 17 Ramaḍān, 58 AH.*

Her life shows to what high status a Muslim woman can rise. Before Islam, women had no status in society; Islam gave them a very important position.

Islam wants to see a woman develop her talents and contribute to society as a mother or a wife and to remain obedient and chaste. Muslim women can rise to prominence within Islam. Allah the Creator has fixed their rights and duties according to their nature and biological make-up.

'Ā'ishah's life is an example for young Muslim girls, who should try to follow her devotion and love for her husband, and her special liking for knowledge and learning.

Exercise : 13

2nd and 3rd Forms

1. Answer these questions :
   a. Who was *Khadījah?*
   b. Who was her father?
   c. How long did she live with the Prophet?
   d. When did she die?
   e. Who is called *Sayyidatun Nisā'?*
   f. Who were the four great women of the world according to the Prophet?
   g. In which battle did *Fāṭimah* take part?
   h. Who was *'Ā'ishah's* father?
   i. How many Ahādīth did *'Ā'ishah* narrate?
   j. When did *'Ā'ishah* die?
2. Fill in the blanks :
   Young ________ girls should ________ how devoted ________ was to her ____________ , and how much ____________ did for him for the ____________ of ____________ . The ____________ of the ________ day would ________ proud to have such a ________ . The world could be ________ by ________ Muslim ________ like ________ .

4th, 5th and 6th Forms

1. Discuss the contribution of the great Muslim *Lady Khadījah* towards the cause of Islam.
2. Describe the special qualities of *Fāṭimah*, the youngest daughter of the Prophet.
3. Write down a short narrative on the life of *'Ā'ishah.*

6

Stories of Prophets

"There is a lesson for the men of understanding in their stories" (12:111).

Ādam and Ḥawwā' (Eve) (pbut)*

LONG long ago, none lived on the earth. Allah then decided to create man to worship Him and live on the earth. Of course, *Angels* and *Jinn* were created before *Ādam*.

Allah said to the angels : *"I am going to send my Khalīfah (deputy or agent) to earth."* (2:30).

The angels said, *"Will you send there some-one who will make mischief and shed blood, while we praise you and glorify you." (2:30).* Allah said, *"Surely I know what you do not know." (2:30).* The angels were silent.

Allah also said to the angels, *"I am going to create a mortal (Bashar) from clay. When I have fashioned him and given him life, you must prostrate before him" (38:71-72).*

Allah created *Ādam* from clay and gave him the nicest shape. He then commanded the angels and the Jinn to prostrate before *Ādam*.

The angels obeyed the command. *'Iblīs* refused to prostrate and disobeyed Allah. *'Iblīs* was from among the *Jinn*. Allah asked, *"What prevented you from prostrating before that which I have created?" 'Iblīs* replied, *"I am better than him. You have created me from fire but him you created from clay." (7:12, 15:32-33).*

Allah then said, *"Get out of here. You are cast out. My curse is on you till the Day of Judgment." (15:34-35).*

'Iblīs vowed to misguide *Ādam* and his children. *(7:14-18).* But, as you know, Allah has given man knowledge and guidance to distinguish between *right* and *wrong* to avoid being misguided.

Allah then taught *Ādam* some names and asked the angels to say those names. (2:31). The angels said, *"Glory to you, we do not know more than you have taught us. Surely you are All-knowing and the Most Wise". (2:31).* Allah then asked *Ādam* to say those names, and he did so. (2:33).

Turning to the angels Allah said, *"Did I not tell you that I know every-*

---

* Pbut means peace be on them.

thing that is in the earth and the heavens and I also know whatever you disclose and whatever you hide." (2:33).

Allah then asked *Ādam* to live in *Al-Jannah* (the Paradise). He had everything to enjoy. But he was alone. So Allah created *Ḥawwā'* (Eve) as his wife. Now, *Ādam* was happy and living in *Al-Jannah*.

Allah said to *Ādam, "Live with your wife in Al-Jannah. Eat freely whatever you like in here. But do not go near that tree." (2:35).* This was intended to test them and teach them self-control. Also Allah wanted to see whether they used the knowledge given to them to save themselves from the evil tricks of *'Iblīs*.

'Iblīs was trying hard to misguide Ādam and *Ḥawwā'*. At last, he succeeded and tempted *Ādam* and Eve to go to that tree. As soon as they approached the forbidden tree, *Ādam* and *Eve* became naked. Until then, they did not know what nakedness was. They had no cause to be ashamed of it. But now they felt ashamed. They tried to cover themselves with leaves and tried to hide. But there was nowhere they could hide from Allah, the All-knowing.

Ādam and *Ḥawwā'* asked Allah's forgiveness and it was granted. They prayed :

"Our Lord, we have wronged ourselves; and if you forgive us not and have not mercy on us, surely we are of the lost." (7:23).

He then commanded *Ādam* and *Ḥawwā'* to go down to earth and live there. But He was very kind and taught them the way to seek forgiveness. *(2:38-39).*

He also told them that he would send guidance for them, so that they would not deviate from the *Right Path*.

Allah revealed guidance to *Ādam* and he was made the *first prophet on earth.*

Prophet Nūḥ (Noah) (pbuh)

Many hundreds of years passed after *Ādam*, and the earth was filled with his children. As time passed, the children of *Ādam*, forgot Allah and started to worship statues made of stones. They became bad and would lie, steal and some became mean and greedy.

Allah, the most Merciful, sent *Nūḥ* to these people to bring them back to His worship. *Nūḥ* invited the people to come back to *Tawḥīd*. He asked them to give up idol worship and all other vices which they had developed. He warned them about the Day of Judgment. *(7:59-64).*

Nūḥ tried his best for many years to make people come back to the worship of Allah. But the people would not listen. They laughed at him, mocked him, despised him and called him crazy and a liar. *(26:105-118, 54:9).*

Nūḥ lived *950* years *(29:14)* and within this long period, only a few people responded to his call. Even his sons and wife did not believe in him.

Nūḥ was tired and shocked to see the stone heartedness of his people. He became so fed up with the stubborness of their opposition to the truth that he ultimately prayed to Allah, *"Leave not upon the land any one from the unbelievers." (71:26)*. So, he cried unto his Lord saying : *"I am vanquished, so give help." (54:10).* He also prayed to Allah to save him and his followers *(26:118).*

Almighty Allah accepted *Nūḥ's* prayers and asked him to build an *ark*. *Nūḥ* started to construct the *ark*. It was not an easy task. But Prophet *Nūḥ* persevered. *(11:37)*.

When the people saw *Nūḥ* building the ark, they laughed at him and thought that *Nūḥ* must have gone mad. They could not see the reason for building so huge an *ark*, hundreds of miles away from the sea. *(11:38)*.

What was the *ark* for? they exclaimed! Soon they were to realise. It was Allah's plan to destroy the whole land of unbelievers except the ones who believed and helped *Nūḥ*.

Nūḥ told the mockers that a flood would soon overcome them and they would have no place to take shelter. The people laughed even more. But Allah's plans soon materialised and the disbelievers saw it happen before their own eyes.

After many days of hard work, the *ark* was complete and Allah asked *Nūḥ* to take *a pair* (one male one female) of all the animals, into the *ark*. He and his followers boarded afterwards. *(11:40-41)*.

Suddenly the skies became dark and thunder and rain followed. It rained and rained and the whole land became flooded. There was water everywhere. Every living thing drowned except those that were in the *ark* which was floating on top of the water. *(54:11-15)*.

The flood water lasted five months and it destroyed all the disbelievers. Even *Nūḥ's* own son — an unbeliever was not saved. *Nūḥ* had asked permission of Allah to take his son in the ark but was refused. He was told an unbelieving son was no part of his family. *Nūḥ* felt sorry and Allah forgave him. *Nūḥ* and his followers were safe in the *ark*. *(11:45-47)*.

At last, the skies began to clear and the *ark* halted at *Mount Judi* (in Turkey). *Nūḥ* and his followers disembarked. *(11:44)*. Thus Allah saved *Nūḥ* and his followers. *(29:15)*.

Allah bestowed prosperity and abundance on *Nūḥ's* children. They spread over the earth and filled it. *(11:48)*.

Such is the dreadful punishment meted out to the disbelievers. Allah says in the *Qur'ān*, *"We drowned who denied our signs. Lo! they were blind folk." (7:64)*.

Prophet Ibrāhīm (Abraham) (pbuh)

Ibrāhīm known as the *Khalīlullāh* (friend of Allah) (4:125) lived in the country south of present day 'Irāq. His father *Āzar* used to make idols and sell them.

The people of the area used to worship these idols made by themselves. They had a temple for these idols which they worshipped.

Ibrāhīm was an intelligent boy. It was strange for him to see people bowing down before the stone-made idols which could neither move nor talk. They could not even drive away the flies which sat on their eyes and nose. *Ibrāhīm* wondered why people worshipped such powerless statues.

He once asked his father, *"O my father, why do you worship idols which can neither speak or hear?"*. *Āzar* became angry and warned *Ibrāhīm* not to ask such questions.

Ibrāhīm had an idea. He thought he would give the people a practical lesson. Once when people were busy celebrating a festival, *Ibrāhīm* went to the temple where the idols were kept.

He asked the idols, *"How do you do? Here is the food and drink. Why don't you help yourselves?"* The stone idols were silent, of course.

Ibrāhīm now took an axe and began to break all the idols except the biggest which he spared with a purpose. When he had finished, he left the axe hanging round the neck of the biggest idol. (21:58).

On their return from the festival, people came to the temple to worship the idols but were astonished to see the pitful condition of their gods. They were shocked, grieved and furious. *"Who has done this mischief?"* they asked themselves.

They thought of *Ibrāhīm* — the only one who talked disrespectfully about the idols.

Soon *Ibrāhīm* was found out. They asked him, *"Who broke the idols?"* *Ibrāhīm* calmly replied, *"Ask the biggest idol."* The people knew that the idols could not talk. They said, *"O Ibrāhīm, don't you know that the idols can't talk?" Ibrāhīm* retorted, *"Why do you worship them, then? They can't talk, move or understand anything. Why do you ask them for favour?"* The people had no answer. They were sure that it was *Ibrāhīm* who broke the idols. They could not let the matter go easily. They called a meeting and decided to burn *Ibrāhīm* alive. They had to defend their gods. (21:59-68).

But Allah was in his favour, and nothing could harm *Ibrāhīm* as he did the right thing.

A big fire was set up and *Ibrāhīm* was thrown into it. But a miracle happened! The fire did no harm to him. Allah protected him. People were amazed to see it and they could not believe their eyes. But it was so. *Ibrāhīm* was happy and his persecutors felt sad and helpless. (21:69-70).

Ibrāhīm's enquiring mind was in search of Allah. He thought and thought. It occurred to him that the shining Moon might be his Lord. But when the moon vanished he said to himself, "No, a vanishing thing cannot be my Lord." He looked at the sun and said, "It is the biggest and it is my Lord." But when the sun also went down, *Ibrāhīm* said to himself, "No, this cannot be my Lord." He came to the conclusion that only the ever-lasting, ever-present and All-knowing, Almighty can be his Lord. The stars, the moon, the sun cannot be the Lord. (6:76-79).

In this way, *Ibrāhīm* was given the light of truth by Allah. *Ibrāhīm* was a messenger and servant of Allah. (16:120-122, 19:41). He loved Allah more than anything else. He was ready to sacrifice his son Ismā'īl on Allah's command. Allah accepted *Ibrāhīm's* readiness and sent a lamb to be sacrificed instead. (37:101-107).

We observe the festival of *'Īdul Aḍḥā* to commemorate this.

It was prophet *Ibrāhīm* who rebuilt the *Ka'bah* in *Makkah* with his son *Ismā'īl*. (22:26-27, 2:125-129, 14:35-37).

Prophet Mūsā (Moses) (pbuh)

Mūsā, the son of *'Imrān* was born in Egypt 450 years after *Yūsuf* (Joseph). In Egypt, at that time the kings were known as *Fir'awn* (Pharaoh).

The followers of the prophet *Ya'qūb* (Jacob), father of prophet *Yūsuf* are called *Banī Isrā'īl* (Israelites). *Banī Isrā'īl* had lived in Egypt since the days of the prophet *Yūsuf*. Prophet *Ya'qūb* was known as *Isrā'īl*.

Fir'awn or the ruler of Egypt looked upon the *Banī Isrā'īl* as 'foreigners' and treated them harshly. The rulers feared that one day the *Banī Isrā'īl* would grow in number and be powerful. So, *Fir'awn* issued orders to kill every male child born in the family of *Isrā'īl*. (28:4-6).

Mūsā was born during this critical time. His mother managed to conceal him for three months and when she could not manage any more, she was inspired by Allah to put *Mūsā* into a specially made box and threw it into the river (20:38-39). *Maryam, Mūsā's sister* was asked to watch the floating box from a distance to avoid suspicion (28:11).

The box reached the other shore and one of the members of *Fir'awn's* family picked it up and got excited to find a lovely baby boy inside. *Mūsā* was then taken to *Fir'awn's* wife and she was very glad to have the baby and adopted him (28:8-9). *Mūsā's* sister went to *Fir'awn's* palace and suggested a nanny look after the baby, a woman who would be suitable to suckle him. This woman was none other than *Mūsā's* mother (28:12).

So *Mūsā* came back to his mother's lap. In this way, it has been proved that none could destroy a person whom Allah would protect.

Mūsā was growing up in *Fir'awn's* house and during this time he came across an Egyptian who was beating an Israelite. *Mūsā* gave the Egyptian a blow and killed him accidentally. (28:15).

He left *Fir'awn's* house and went to Midian (28:22-28). He stayed there for ten years before moving on to Ṭuwā, a valley at the foot of the mountain *Aṭ-Ṭūr* in Sinai. Here, *Mūsā* was given the divine guidance by Allah, and was selected as a messenger of Allah. (28:30).

Allah bestowed on *Mūsā* two signs : a *'stick'* which when thrown down would turn into a living serpent and the ability to make his hand shine, after it was drawn out from under his arm. (20:17-22).

Allah commanded *Mūsā* to go to *Fir'awn* and invite him to *Tawḥīd* (20:42-44). He begged Allah to make his brother *Hārūn* his helper and Allah granted his prayer. (20:24-36).

Mūsā and *Hārūn* went to *Fir'awn* and they argued with him, telling him that Almighty Allah had chosen *Mūsā* to save the Israelites from the oppression of the Egyptians. *Fir'awn* refused to let the Israelites go. (20:47-54, 26:16-17).

Fir'awn made fun of *Mūsā*. *Mūsā* showed his signs to impress upon

Fir'awn that his message was true. He threw his stick on the ground and it changed into a serpent. *Mūsā* picked it up and it turned again into a stick. *Fir'awn* and his followers were amazed to see this. But he thought that *Mūsā* was a magician and challenged him to face his own magicians who could show even more stunning magic. (26:23-37).

But on the appointed day, the magicians of *Fir'awn* were badly defeated. The false snakes they produced by their sticks were all swallowed up by the serpent of *Mūsā's* stick. *Fir'awn* and his magicians could hardly believe their eyes. His magicians bowed to the truth and professed their faith in Allah. (26:38-47).

Fir'awn became angry and began to torture the *Banī Isrā'īl* even more.

It was during this time that Allah commanded *Mūsā* to leave Egypt with his followers (20:77). *Mūsā* asked his followers to get ready and they set out at night to avoid *Fir'awn's* notice and reached the shore of the Nile. They were chased by *Fir'awn* and his soldiers. They almost reached the Israelites. In front of them was the mighty Nile and behind were *Fir'awn's* soldiers. At this moment, Allah ordered *Mūsā* to throw his stick in the water and as he did so, the Nile was divided into two and a road was ready in the middle, allowing the Israelites to cross it. (26:52-65).

Fir'awn was following, but when the Israelites reached the other shore and *Fir'awn* was in the middle of the *Nile*, water from both sides suddenly poured in and the road was no more.

Fir'awn and his soldiers were drowned there (26:66). This is how Allah punishes transgressors and helps his servants.

Prophet 'Īsā (Jesus) (pbuh)

The *Banī Isrā'īl* were given many favours by Almighty Allah. But they were very ungrateful. They violated Allah's orders, ridiculed the prophets and killed some of them. They started to worship idols and made Allah's message a mockery.

Allah, the Merciful again sent a prophet to bring them to the right path. This prophet was *'Īsā* son of *Maryam* (Mary), (2:87). Allah bestowed on him *Injīl* (Gospel) and *'Īsā* confirmed what was in *Tawrāt* (Torah), (5:46, 61:6).

The birth of *'Īsā* was a miracle. He was born of the virgin *Maryam* without a father, by Allah's command (19:17-21). Allah can do anything he likes. Everything is possible for Him. When He wants to get something done, He only says, *'Be'* and there it is (2:117).

We know that *Ādam* was created by Allah without a father and a mother. So, it was easy for Him to create *'Īsā* without a father.

Baby *'Īsā* born of virgin *Maryam* could talk even as a baby. He was commissioned as a prophet when he was 30, and he acted as a prophet for three years (19:29-34).

Allah endowed him with some miraculous powers. He could make birds out of clay, heal leprosy within minutes, restore the eyes of the blind, and he could also make the dead come alive. All these miracles were given to him by Allah. The Qur'ān mentions the miraculous powers and the birth of *'Īsā* in *Sūrah Āle 'Imrān : "(And remember) when the angels said : O, Mary! Allah gives you the glad tidings of a word from Him, whose name is the Messiah, Jesus, Son of Mary, illustrious in the World and the Hereafter and one of those brought near (unto Allah)."*

"He will speak to mankind in his cradle and in his manhood, and he is of the righteous." (3:46).

"She (Mary) said : My Lord! How can I have a child when no mortal has touched me? He said, So (it will be). Allah creates what He wishes. If He decrees a thing, He says to it only : Be, and it is. (3:47).

"And He will teach him the Scripture and wisdom, and the Torah and the Gospel (3:48).

"And will make him a messenger to the Children of Isrā'īl, (saying) : I come to you with a sign from my Lord. See! I fashion for you out of clay the likeness of a bird, by Allah's leave. I heal him who was born blind and the leper, and I raise the dead, by Allah's leave. And I announce to you what you eat and what you store up in your houses. Here truly is a portent for you, if you are to be believers (3:49).

"And I come to you confirming what was before me of the Torah, and to make lawful some of what was forbidden to you. I come to you as a sign from your Lord, so keep your duty to Allah and obey me (3.50).

"Allah is my Lord and your Lord, so worship Him. That is a straight path." (3:51).

He asked people to obey Allah alone. But his followers made fantasies about him and they considered him a part of Allah, even a son of Allah (5:116-117).

We believe in *'Īsā* as a prophet and a servant of Allah (43:59). We don't believe in him as son of Allah. Allah can have no son or daughter. He is above any such notion. Allah is One and Indivisible. There is no idea of unity in *Trinity* in Islam (4:171). *Trinity* is clear partnership *(Shirk)*. It is a big sin to say anyone is the son of Allah (5:17, 19:35).

According to the *Qur'ān*, Prophet *'Īsā* was not crucified to death rather he was taken up by Allah, the Almighty and the Most Wise (4:157-158). Everything is possible for Allah. It was He who saved *Ibrāhīm* from fire and *Mūsā* from *Fir'awn.*

Exercise : 14

1st Form

1. Answer these questions :
   a. Who lived on earth before human beings?
   b. Who was *Ādam?*
   c. Who was *Ḥawwā'?*
   d. Where did *Ādam* and *Ḥawwā'* live in the beginning?
   e. Who refused to prostrate before *Ādam?*
   f. What mistakes did *Ādam* and *Ḥawwā'* make when they were in *Heaven?*
2. What was the prayer of *Ādam* and *Ḥawwā'* to Allah after they were trapped by devil?
3. Write in your own words about Prophet *Nūḥ's* ark.

2nd and 3rd Forms

1. What is the Quranic verse about the creation of *Ādam?*
2. What did *'Iblīs* say when commanded by Allah to prostrate before *Ādam?*
3. What was the fault of *Ādam* and *Ḥawwā'* in *Al-Jannah?*
4. Draw a picture of *Nūḥ's* ark.
5. Why was the Prophet *Nūḥ* commanded to built an ark by Allah?

4th, 5th and 6th Forms

1. Narrate the story of *Ādam* and *Ḥawwā'* in your own words and write some notes about the theory of creation.
2. *"The story of the Prophet Nūḥ is the story of a disobedient people and their punishment by Allah."* — Explain.

Exercise : 15

1st Form

1. Answer these questions :
   a. Who was *Khalīlullāh?*
   b. Who was Prophet *Ibrāhīm's* father?
   c. What did the Prophet *Ibrāhīm* say to his father about the worship of idols?
   d. What did the Prophet *Ibrāhīm* do on the day of festival?
   e. Did the fire burn Prophet *Ibrāhīm?*
   f. Who saved the Prophet *Ibrāhīm* from fire?
2. Fill in the blanks :
   Fir'awn or the ________ of ________ looked upon the________ as ________ and treated them ________. The rulers ________ that one day Banī ________ would ________ in number and be ________.
3. Draw a picture of the baby Mūsā in a box in the river Nile.

2nd and 3rd Forms

1. Write the story of Prophet *Ibrāhīm* in your own words.
2. Fill in the gaps :
   a.________ was the ruler of Egypt.
   b.________ was the father of the Prophet *Ibrāhīm.*
   c. Prophet ________ was the ________ of *'Imrān.*
   d.________ was the sister of the Prophet *Mūsā.*
   e. ________ was the brother of the Prophet *Mūsā.*
   f. Allah bestowed *Mūsā* ____ ____: a stick which when thrown ________ would________ into a living________ .

4th, 5th and 6th Forms

1. Why is idol worship foolish and unreasonable?
2. What was the significance of the incident of the Prophet *Ibrāhīm's* not being burnt by the fire of the idol worshippers?
3. What lessons can we learn from the story of the Prophet *Mūsā?*

Exercise : 16

1st Form

1. Answer the following :
   a. Who was *'Īsā?*
   b. Who was Prophet *'Īsā's* mother?
   c. What book was revealed to Prophet *'Īsā* by Allah?
   d. Was Prophet *'Īsā* crucified to death?
   e. What is *Trinity?*
2. What were the especial things about Prophet *'Īsā?*

2nd and 3rd Forms

1. Fill in the blanks :
   ________ endowed him with ______ ______powers. He could make________out ________, heal ________within ________, restore the________of the blind, and he________ also ________ the________come ________.
2. What was the teaching of Prophet *'Īsā?* Did he ask his followers to worship him?

4th, 5th and 6th Forms

1. Compare the birth of Prophet *Ādam* with the birth of Prophet *'Īsā.*
2. Explain the doctrine of *Tawḥīd* and the doctrine of Trinity. Can you reconcile the two? Give your reasons.
3. *"Risālah was the channel of communication between man and Allah."* — Discuss.
4. *"There is a lesson for the men of understanding in their stories. (12:111)".* Discuss this verse of the Qur'ān.

7

Sharī'ah (ISLAMIC LAW)

SHARĪ'AH is the code of law for the Islamic way of life which Allah has revealed for mankind and commanded us to follow. The word *Sharī'ah* means a clear straight path or example.

Sharī'ah or Islamic law consists of the code of conduct for Muslims and is based on two main sources : The *Qur'ān* and the *Sunnah* of the Prophet. It aims towards the success and welfare of mankind both in this life and life after death.

Sharī'ah prescribes a complete set of laws for the guidance of mankind so that Good *(Ma'rūf)* may triumph and Evil *(Munkar)* disappear from society. It provides a clear and a straight path which leads to progress and fulfilment in life and the attainment of Allah's pleasure.

The *Qur'ān* is the main basis of the *Sharī'ah*. It states the principles, while the sunnah of the Prophet provides the details of their application. For example, the *Qur'ān* says : establish *ṣalāh*, observe *ṣawm*, pay *zakāh*, take decisions by consultation, do not earn or spend in wrong ways — but it does not describe how to do these things. It is the sunnah of the Prophet which gives us the details.

The *Qur'ān* is the main book of guidance and the Prophet taught how to follow it. The Prophet not only told us how to follow the guidance, he also practised it himself.

The *Sharī'ah* has rules for every aspect of life. It is complete and perfect, and guarantees us success, welfare and peace in this life on earth and life after death.

Man-made laws differ from *Sharī'ah* in a number of significant ways.

	Man-made Law	**Sharī'ah or Allah's Law**
1	Men make laws when they feel the need; these laws start from a few and then grow in number over the years.	Islamic Law is complete, perfect and includes all aspects of human life.

2	Man-made laws are not permanent; they can be changed according to the time and circumstances. For example, in a particular country at a particular time, drinking alcohol may be banned; but this can change when public pressure grows. The American Government once banned alcoholic drink but removed the ban after a time because it could not be applied.	*Sharī'ah* is permanent for all people all the time. It does not change with time and conditions. For example, drinking wine and gambling are not allowed under Islamic law. And no-one can change this; it is a law that is valid for all time and for all places.
3	Man does not have knowledge of the future. Hence, man-made laws cannot stand the test of time.	Allah is All-knowing and All-powerful; He is the most Wise and His laws are the best and are complete.
4	Man is a created being. His laws are the creation of the created.	Allah is the Creator and his laws are for Man, His creation.
5	Man-made laws may be suitable for a particular nation or country. They cannot be universal.	Allah's laws are for all nations, all countries and for all time. They are universal.
6	Men make laws to suit their own needs. Suppose, members of parliament want to decrease the rate of tax on the rich, they would do so, even if the majority of the people suffered and there was high unemployment in the country.	Allah is above all needs. He is not dependent on anything, so His laws are for the good of all people and not for a few, selfish people.

The *Sharī'ah* has two other sources : The *Ijmā'* (consensus) and The *Qiyās* (analogy or reasoning on the basis of similar circumstances). These sources must still be based on the *Qur'ān* and the *sunnah*.

Ijmā' or consensus applies to a situation where no clear conclusion can be made from the *Qur'ān* and the *sunnah*. In this situation the representatives of the people who are well-versed in the *Qur'ān* and the *sunnah* will sit together and work out an agreed formula to solve the particular problem. *Ijmā'* developed during the period of the *Khulafā'ur Rāshidūn*.

Qiyās means reference or analogy or a comparison of one thing with a similar one. It is applied in circumstances where guidance from the *Qur'ān*, the *sunnah* is not directly available. A solution to a problem is reached by a process of deduction from a comparison with similar situations.

Sunnah

The word *sunnah* means a system or a path or example. In Islam it refers to the practice of the Prophet, his life example. It is embodied in the *Aḥādīth* (plural of *Ḥadīth*) which are the Prophet's sayings, actions and the actions done with his approval. *Aḥādīth* have been very carefully collected and compiled since the death of the Prophet. *Six* collections of *Ḥadīth* are regarded as the most authentic. They are :

1 *Saḥīḥ Al-Bukhārī*	(Collected and compiled by *Muḥammad bin Ismā'īl*, known as *Imām Bukhārī*, born 194 AH, died 256 AH).
2 *Saḥīḥ Muslim*	(*Muslim bin al-Ḥajjāj*, known as *Imām Muslim*, born 202 AH, died 261 AH).
3 *Sunan Abu Dāwūd*	(*Sulaimān bin Ash'ath*, known as *Abū Dāwūd*, born 202 AH, died 275 AH).
4 *Sunan Ibn Mājah*	(*Muḥammad bin Yazīd*, born 209 AH, died 273 AH).
5 *Jami' At-Tirmidhī*	(*Muḥammad bin 'Īsā*, born (not known) died 279 AH).
6 *Sunan An-Nasā'ī*	(*Aḥmad bin Shu'aib*, born 215 AH, died 303 AH).

In addition to this, *Muwaṭṭa'* of *Imām Mālik* (born 93 AH, died 179 AH) *Mishkāt Al-Maṣabīḥ* of *Abū Muḥammad al-Ḥusain bin Mas'ud* (died 516 AH), and *Musnad* of *Aḥmad bin Ḥanbal* (born 164 AH, died 241 AH), are also well known.

Fiqh

Fiqh is the science of Islamic law or jurisprudence. It refers to the collection and compilation of Islamic laws based on the *Qur'ān* and the *Sunnah* of the Prophet. The word *Fiqh* means knowledge and understanding.

Some great Muslims devoted themselves to the task of developing the science of understanding Islamic law and its practice. The four best-known compilers of Islamic law or *Sharī'ah* are :

1 *Abū Ḥanīfah Nu'mān bin Thābit*, known as *Imām Abū Ḥanīfah* (born 80 AH, died 150 AH).
2 *Mālik bin Ānas*, known as *Imām Mālik* (93-179 AH).
3 *Muḥammad bin Idrīs Al-Shafi'ī*, known as *Imām Shafi'ī* (150-240 AH).
4 *Aḥmad bin Ḥanbal*, known as *Imām Ḥanbal* (164-241 AH).

Islamic law divides human activities into : (1) *Farḍ* or *Wājib* (duty or obligatory) — performance of these actions are rewarded and their omission is punished. (2) *Mandūb* (recommended) — actions the performance of which is rewarded but omission of which is not punished. (3) *Mubāḥ* (silent) — actions permitted by silence. (4) *Makrūh* (disliked) — actions disapproved but not punished. (5) *Ḥarām* (forbidden) — actions punishable by law.

The scholars and experts on Islamic Law have made the *Sharī'ah* easier to understand and practise, by the science of Fiqh. Fiqh is the explanation of the Islamic laws, based on the *Qur'ān* and the *Sunnah*.

Islamic Law or the *Sharī'ah* embodies the Islamic ideal life. Islam is the complete way of life and *Sharī'ah* is the means to arrive at the ideal life recommended by Islam. *Sharī'ah* enables us to bring our life in line with the will of Allah. It is the process of achieving our goal of life.

Exercise : 17

4th, 5th and 6th Forms

1. Answer these questions :
   a. What is *Sharī'ah?*
   b. What are the sources of *Sharī'ah?*
   c. What is *Sunnah?*
   d. What are the six authentic books of *Sunnah?*
   e. What is *Fiqh?*
   f. What are the names of the four most famous compilers of *Islamic Law?*
2. Compare *Sharī'ah* with man-made laws.
3. Divide human activities into five groups according to *Islamic Law.*
4. List the names of the compilers of *Ḥadīth* with the years of their birth and death.

8

Social Life in Islam

Family Life in Islam

FAMILY life is the basis of the Islamic society. Its origin goes back to the beginning of the creation of man and woman — *Ādam* and *Eve*. So, it is an institution founded by Allah's will. Allah says in the *Qur'ān :*

"O mankind, be mindful of your duty to your Lord who created you from a single soul and from it created its mate and from the two created many men and women." (4:1).

Marriage is the basis of the Islamic family. A good and sound society can only grow if a man and a woman are bound in a solid relationship through the sacred contract of marriage.

Marriage develops love and care and co-operation between the husband and wife. It gives peace of mind and provides a secure atmosphere for the growth and progress of the whole human race. Without marriage, the human race would come to a standstill. Marriage was the practice of most of the prophets including Muḥammad *(pbuh)*.

MARRIAGE

Marriage is a sacred social contract between a bride-groom and a bride. A great deal of thought is necessary therefore before the couple decides to marry.

Piety should come before all other considerations. Allah's prophet said, "Do not marry only for the sake of beauty, may be the beauty becomes the cause of moral decline. Do not marry even for the sake of wealth; may be the wealth becomes the reason of disobedience; marry rather on the ground of religious devotion."

A Muslim is expected to marry a Muslim although in some cases Jewish and Christian chaste women can be married. But a Muslim woman is not allowed to marry a non-Muslim man. In Islam, marriage is a religious and social institution and not simply a sexual relationship.

Muslim marriages are traditionally arranged by parents but the final say lies with the boy and the girl.

Islam does not allow free mixing of grown-up boys and girls, nor does it allow sex outside marriage. The Islamic way of life does not approve of the boy-friend/girl-friend system, or mixed parties of the grown-ups and the like.

Islamic society is based on submission and obedience to the will of Allah. Husband and wife, bound by marriage are Allah's servants and representatives *(Khalīfah)*. Marriage must not conflict with the purpose of life (seeking Allah's pleasure), but rather should lead towards its achievement.

Divorce is allowed but is regarded as the least desirable of all lawful acts. Islam encourages adjustment and happiness. But when living together is impossible, the Islamic law does not stand in the way of divorce.

STATUS OF WOMEN IN ISLAM

Women have a very important place in Islamic society. Unlike a number of other religions, Islam holds a woman in high esteem. Her importance as a mother and a wife has been clearly stated by the Prophet Muḥammad *(pbuh)*.

The Prophet said, *"Paradise lies at the feet of your mothers."* Once a person asked the Prophet, *"Who deserves the best care from me?"* the Prophet replied, *"Your mother (he repeated this three times), then your father and then your nearest relatives."*

In his farewell speech at 'Arafah in the tenth year of Hijrah, the Prophet said, *"O people, your wives have certain rights over you and you have certain rights over them. Treat them well and be kind to them, for they are your partners and committed helpers."*

The Prophet also said, *"The best among you is the one who is the best towards his wife."*

These sayings clearly prove the important position given to women in Islam. But there are still people, especially in the West, who have misgivings about the status of women in Islam. To these people, the Muslim woman is seen almost as a *'prisoner in the four walls of the house'*, a *'non-person'*, and *as someone who has no rights and is living always under the domination of a man*. These notions are totally wrong, and are based on ignorance rather than knowledge of Islam.

One of the rites of *Ḥajj* is a fast walk between *Aṣ-Ṣafā* and *Al-*

Marwah, which is observed to remember the event of *Hājirah* (Hagar), mother of Prophet *Ismā'īl*, who ran between these two hills to find water. This is another proof of the importance given to women by Islam.

In order to judge these false ideas held by western people, it would be useful to survey the attitudes to women in different societies in the past.

During *the Roman* civilization, for example, a woman was regarded as a slave. *The Greeks* considered her a commodity to be bought and sold. Early *Christianity* regarded *women as temptresses, responsible for the fall of Adam*[1].

In India, *the Hindus* until recently considered their women worse than death, pests, serpents or even hell. A wife's life ended with the death of her husband. In the past, the widow had to jump into the flames of her husband's funeral pyre[2].

In the pre-Islamic state of *Arabia*, a woman was regarded as a cause for grief and unhappiness, and baby girls were sometimes buried alive after birth.

In *France* in *587 CE*, a meeting was held to study the status of women and to determine whether a woman could truly be considered a human being or not! *Henry VIII* in England forbade the reading of the Bible by women, and throughout the middle ages, the *Catholic Church* treated women as second class citizens. In the Universities of *Cambridge* and *Oxford*, male and female students were not given the same rights until *1964*. Before *1850*, women were not counted as citizens in *England*, and English women had no personal rights until *1882*[3].

If we keep this picture in mind and look into the position of the women in Islam, we must conclude that Islam liberated women from the dark age of obscurity, fourteen hundred years ago!

Islam is a religion of common sense and is in line with human nature. It recognises the realities of life. This does not mean it has recognised equality of man and woman in every respect. Rather, it has defined their duties in keeping with their different biological make-up *(2:228)*. Allah has not made man and woman identical, so it would be

---

1. Encyclopaedia Britannica Vol. 19 (Page 909), 1977 Edition.
2. Islam : belief, legislation and morals — Dr Aḥmad Shalaby (Page 308), 1970 (Cairo).
3. Ibid — Page 312, 314.

against nature to try to have total equality between a man and a woman.

It would destroy the social balance. Society would not prosper, but would instead have insoluble problems such as broken marriages, illegitimate children and the break-up of family life. These problems are already rife in the western society. Schoolgirl pregnancies, an increase in abortions, divorce and many other problems have cropped up because of a permissive outlook and so-called freedom of women.

Rights of Women in Islam

Allah has created every living being in pairs — male and female *(51:49)*, including mankind. Allah has honoured the children of Adam — both male and female *(17:70)*. Men and women who believe are protectors of one another *(9:71)*. Allah will reward both men and women in the life after death *(3:195)*.

In Islam, woman has a distinct and separate identity. Islam has given women a right to own property. She is the owner of her earnings. No-one (father, husband or brother) has a right over them. She can dispose of her earnings and property as she wishes, within the bounds of *Ḥalāl* (lawful) and *Ḥarām* (unlawful).

Islam has given women a right to inheritance. She has a part in the property of her dead father, husband or childless brother *(4:7, 32, 176)*.

She has a right to choose her husband. No-one can impose a decision on her against her will. She has a right to seek separation (Khulā') from her husband if their marriage becomes impossible to sustain.

If any man falsely questions a woman's chastity, that man is declared unfit for giving evidence *(24:4)*. This shows how a woman's honour is safeguarded from false accusations.

The *Qur'ān* asks the Muslims to treat women kindly *(4:19)*. It makes Muslim husbands responsible for their wife's maintenance. The women, in return, are expected to remain obedient and chaste *(4:34)*.

A woman has a right to develop her talents and to work within the limits of Islam. Islam allows a non-Muslim married woman to retain her religion and her husband cannot interfere in this freedom. This applies to Christian and Jewish women with Muslim husbands.

Duties of a woman in Islam

Islam is a fair and a balanced system of life. While it specifies the rights of women it also lays down duties. A Muslim woman is expected to observe the following duties :

1 Belief in *Tawḥid* and the practice of Islam come first. A Muslim woman must perform her *Ṣalāh*, observe *Ṣawm*, pay *Zakāh* on her own wealth (if it is applicable), go on *Ḥajj* if she can afford it. She is exempted from *Ṣalāh* and can defer *Ṣawm* during her period, but she must make up the days lost afterwards. Friday prayer *(Jum'ah)* is optional on women.

2 She is required to maintain her chastity all the time. She must not have any extra-marital relationships. The same is the case with men.

3 It is her duty to bring up children according to the needs of Islam. She has to look after the family and has almost absolute control over domestic affairs, although the family is run by mutual consultation and co-operation. She is the queen of the family and in charge of domestic life.

4 She should dress modestly and should put on *Hijāb* (covering cloak) while going out, meeting adult males beyond her close relatives *(33:59, 24:30-31)*. She should not wear men's clothing.

5 She is her husband's help-mate. A faithful wife is like a garment, a source of peace, happiness and contentment for her husband *(30:21, 2:187)*.

6 If she is asked to go against the commands of Allah, she must defy even her husband, father or brother.

7 She is expected to protect her husband's property and belongings in his absence.

Islam views husband and wife as complementary to each other. Neither dominates the other. Each has his or her individual rights and duties — together they form a peaceful and happy family which is the basis for a sound and prosperous society.

Man and woman are not exactly equal in Islam. They have different physical and biological features. Islam recognises the leadership of a man over a woman *(4:34, 2:228)*, but it does not mean domination.

An average man is stronger, heavier, harder in muscles and taller than an average woman. Women can become pregnant and bear children, but men cannot. Women tend to be sensitive, emotional and tender while men are comparatively less emotional and more practical.

Throughout history, men and women have never been treated the same. Islam has given women the right position, and has not attempted to violate divine laws. Other religions and philosophies have been unable to visualise the exact and right role of women until today. In the West, women have been reduced almost to a commodity of enjoyment and fancy. And women have tended to degrade themselves unwittingly in modern times, for in the name of equality, they have become the objects of exploitation by men, and the slogans of liberty and equality have virtually reduced them to playful commodities. They have neither gained liberty nor achieved equality, rather they have lost their natural place in the home.

POLYGAMY AND ISLAM

Islam is a practical religion. It can answer all human problems. Islam allows restricted polygamy — marriage to more than one woman, to the maximum of four. The normal Muslim practice is monogamy — one man married to one wife — polygamy is the exception.

The *Qur'ān* has imposed strict conditions for marrying several wives. *"And if you fear that you will not deal fairly by the orphans, marry of the women who seem good to you, two or three or four; and if you fear that you cannot be fair to so many, then one only or (the captives) that your right hands possess. Thus it is more likely that you will not do injustice."* (4:3). This verse says that to marry more than one woman, a man must be able to be fair and just to each of them. If he is not able to be so, he should marry only one wife.

Another verse of the *Qur'ān* says, *"You will not be able to deal fairly between your wives, however much you wish. Yet do not turn completely aside (from one) so that you leave another in suspense, if you maintain proper conduct and do your duty, Allah is ever Forgiving and Merciful"* (4:129). This further emphasises fair treatment. But, in special circumstances Islam allows polygamy. These situations are :

1 When a wife is barren and cannot bear children, but the husband wants children. It is better to have a second wife than to divorce the barren one. But a barren wife has the option to seek separation from her husband if she wishes, on the grounds of the second marriage of her husband.

2 If the first wife is chronically ill and she is unable to carry out her marital and household duties, the husband may marry another woman and so help restore family peace.

3 Polygamy may be the solution to the problems of a society which

has more women than men. This happens especially after war. The verse in the *Qur'ān* allowing more than one wife was revealed after the battle of Uḥud in which many Muslim men were martyred.

The proportion of women to men increased considerably in the countries taking part in the First and Second World Wars. A solution to such a situation is the marriage of more than one woman by those men who are able to and can be fair to each wife. This is better than leaving a large number of unmarried women.

Islam strictly forbids any sexual relationships outside marriage. There is no such thing as a *mistress* in Islamic society. Islam has given dignity to women by marriage and has protected them from the exploitation of greedy and selfish men. Having more than one wife is better and more dignified than having a number of mistresses. Islam holds you responsible for your actions. You cannot just enjoy and have no responsibilities of fatherhood. This is sheer injustice and inhuman. There can be no one-parent family or illegitimate child in an Islamic society. It is only possible in a cultural climate of irresponsible permissiveness. A woman who is going to be a second wife could refuse to marry the man on the grounds that he already has a wife.

But if a woman happily consents to her husband marrying again and the second wife agrees, why should anyone else object to it?

The overwhelming majority of Muslims are monogamous — they have only one wife. The fact that a few Muslims have more than one wife has become a matter for propaganda against Islam and such propaganda can give a misleading impression of the Islamic way of life. This is especially so when it is non-practising Muslims who are highlighted on the issue of being married to more than one wife.

As opposed to polygamy, the case of polyandry (having more than one husband by a woman) may be raised. The case of polyandry is impractical and it creates problems rather than solves them. How will paternity be decided? Which husband would claim the fatherhood of the child? How would inheritance be decided? Such questions have no answer in polyandry.

Furthermore, it is possible for a man to live with more than one wife and have children from all of them, but for a woman to please more than one husband seems almost impossible. A woman can bear children from only one husband.

Polyandry is forbidden in Islam.

Islam is a practical way of life. It has responded to reality and necessity. It has also put a check on human tendencies and ensured balance. The system is full of wisdom and is perfectly scientific, completely logical.

Allah, the All-knowing, has prescribed what is best for us. We should not be apologetic in our approach. Islam provides the best answer to all problems. We cannot blame Islam if we do not know it or fail to understand it. We need to look at Islam as a whole, not only at a part of it. This is because Islam views life as a whole, as a unit, and does not divide it.

All areas of life are inter-related; the status of women, marriage and family life are only single aspects of the whole Islamic system.

Exercise : 18

4th, 5th and 6th Forms

1. Discuss the role of *marriage* as the basis of Islamic family. Why does Islam not allow extra-marital relationships? Give your reasons.
2. What status is given to women by Islam? Compare this status with that of the past and present non-muslim societies.
3. Write down the rights and duties of *Women in Islam.*
4. Under what circumstances is *polygamy* allowed in Islam? Discuss the *Practicality* and *Responsibility* of this provision in Islam (sixth form only).

9

Economic System of Islam

ISLAM views life as a compact whole and does not divide it into many separate and conflicting parts. The economic aspect is one of the most important parts of our life, while not being the whole of it. The Islamic system is balanced and places everything in its right place. Islam has given detailed regulations for the conduct of our economic life which concerns mainly the earning and use of wealth.

Man needs bread to live but he does not live for bread alone. This means that earning and spending money is essential for our living, but we do not live only for this. We have a greater purpose of life. We are Allah's agents *(Khalīfah)* on earth. We not only have a body but we have a soul and a conscience as well. Without soul and conscience, we would be considered little more than animals.

Everything in Islam is for the benefit and welfare of mankind. The economic principles of Islam aim at establishing a just society wherein every one will behave responsibly and honestly, and not as *'cunning foxes'* fighting for getting as big a share of something without regard to honesty, truth, decency, trust and responsibility.

The Islamic Economic System is based on the following fundamental principles.

1 Earning and expenditure by Ḥalāl means

Islam has prescribed laws to regulate earnings and expenditure. Muslims are not allowed to earn and spend in just any way they like. They must follow the rules of the *Qur'ān* and the *Sunnah*.

a Any earnings from the production, sale and distribution of alcoholic drinks is unlawful, as are earnings from gambling, lotteries and from interest *(Ribā)* transactions. *(5:90-91, 2:275).*

b Earning by falsehood, deceit, fraud, theft, robbery, and burglary are unlawful. Deceitful acquisition of orphan's property has been particularly banned. *(2:188, 4:2, 6:152, 7:85, 83:1-5).*

c Hoarding of food stuff and basic necessities, smuggling and artificial creation of shortages are unlawful. *(3:180, 9:34-35).*

d Earnings from brothels and from such other practices which are harmful to society are also unlawful. *(24:23).*

Islam strikes at the root of evil and wants to establish a just and fair society. A Muslim must earn his living in *Ḥalāl* ways and he should always bear in mind that whatever he does, is known to Allah. He will be accountable for his actions on the day of judgment. He cannot hide anything from Almighty Allah.

Unlawful expenditure is also not allowed in Islam. It does not at all befit a Muslim to spend money irresponsibly. His actions should be responsible and meaningful. Extravagance and waste are strongly discouraged. *(7:31, 17:26, 19:27-31, 25:68).*

2 Right to property and individual liberty

Islam allows a person to own his earnings. The Islamic state does not interfere with the freedom of speech, work and earnings of an individual provided this freedom is not harmful for the greater good of society. Every individual will be answerable to Allah for his or her actions. *(4:7, 36:71, 16:111).*

3 System of Zakāh (welfare contribution)

Compulsory payment of *Zakāh* is one of the main principles of an Islamic economy. Every Muslim who owns wealth more than his needs, must pay the fixed rate of *Zakāh* to the Islamic state. *Zakāh* is a means of narrowing the gap between the rich and the poor. It helps fair distribution of wealth. It is a form of social security. The Islamic state is responsible for providing basic necessities of food, clothing, housing, medicine and education to every citizen. No-one should have any fear of insecurity or poverty. *(9:69, 103, 98:5).*

4 Prohibition of interest (Ribā)

An Islamic economy is free of interest. Islam prohibits all transactions involving interest. It allows Zero rate of interest.

Interest is neither a *trade* nor a *profit*. It is a means of exploitation and concentration of wealth. The *Qur'ān* says :

"They say, trade is like interest and Allah has allowed trade and prohibited interest." (2:275).

"Whatever you pay as interest, so that it may increase in the property of (other) men, it does not increase with Allah". (30:39).

"O you who believe, do not take interest, doubling and quadrupling, and keep your duty to Allah, so that you may prosper." (3:130).

"O you who believe, observe your duty to Allah and give up what remains (due) from interest, if you are believers. But if you do not do it, then be warned

of war from Allah and His messenger; and if you repent, then you shall have your capital. Do not exploit and be not exploited." (2:278-279).

Interest is the basis of modern capitalism. It is completely opposite to Zakāh. Zakāh channels wealth from the rich to the poor while interest takes away wealth from the poor and hands it over to the rich.

Modern economies are so inter-linked with interest that people may think it is impossible to go without it.

The situation is really very complex. But, we must aim at getting rid of interest. An Islamic state must gradually try to change the present system. It needs careful and systematic planning. Allah has not imposed on us, something impossible. An interest-free economy will be a boon for all peoples of the world.

5 Law of Inheritance *(Mīrāth)*

Islamic law of inheritance is a wonderful system of stopping concentration of wealth. It provides very detailed laws regarding the rights of dependents over the property of the deceased person. The *Sūratun Nisā'* of the *Qur'ān* deals with the Law of inheritance in great detail. *(4:7-12, 4:176).*

Conclusion

In addition to the above basic principles Islam has laid down many more rules about economic life. An Islamic state must bring all productive resources into use, including unemployed man-power, unused land, water resources and minerals. An Islamic state must take steps to root out corruption and all harmful pursuits even if they are economically lucrative. Individual freedom may have to be sacrificed for the social good.

Islam encourages simplicity, modesty, charity, mutual help and co-operation. It discourages miserliness, greed, extravagance and unnecessary wastage.

Here, we have discussed the main points of the Islamic economic system and we have no scope to go into the details and specifics. It would be better for you to study some standard books on Islamic Economics to have a good grasp of this important aspect of our life. You will find a list in the bibliography at the end of this book.*

*Exercise No.19 for this chapter is on page 180.

Bank
interest
MANAGER
MONEY FROM POOR TO THE RICH
Halal
Butcher
ISLAMIC WELFARE HOUSE
MONEY FROM RICH TO THE POOR
zakāh

10

Political System of Islam

RELIGION and *politics* are one and the same in Islam. They are intertwined. We already know that Islam is a complete system of life and politics is very much a part of our collective life. Just as Islam teaches us how to say *Ṣalāh*, observe *Ṣawm*, pay *Zakāh* and undertake *Ḥajj*, it also teaches us how to run a state, form a government, elect councillors and members of parliament, make treaties and conduct business and commerce.

A detailed discussion about Islamic political system would have been much desirable, but we have to content ourselves with its basic principles and main features.

The Islamic Political System is based on the following main principles :

1 Sovereignty of Allah

Sovereignty means the source of power. In Islam, Allah is the source of all powers and laws *(3:154, 12:40, 25:2, 67:1)*. It is Allah who knows what is good and what is bad for His servants. His say is final. All human beings unitedly cannot change His Law. The *Qur'ān* says, *"As for the thief —. male and female, chop off their hands. It is the reward of their own actions and exemplary punishment from Allah. Allah is Mighty, Wise." (5:37)*. According to Islam, this order is unchangeable by any parliament or any government which claims itself to be Islamic. *(5:44, 2:229)*. There are many more laws in the *Qur'ān* concerning our life and those laws must be put into practice by an Islamic state for the greater good of human beings.

2 Khilāfah of Mankind *(Vicegerency of man)*

Man is the *vicegerent or the agent* or the representative of Allah on earth. *(2:30, 6:165)*. Allah is the sovereign and man is His representative. Man should do as Allah commands him to do. But he has a choice to either obey or disobey Allah and because of this freedom of choice, he will be tested on the day of judgment. In the political sense, *Khilāfah* means that human beings would implement the will of Allah on earth as His deputy or agent. As Allah's agent, human beings will carry out the will of Allah on His behalf as a trust *(Amānah). Khilāfah* is a trust. An agent is always expected to behave as his master wants him to behave. *(10:14).*

3 Legislation by Shūrā *(Consultation)*

Islam teaches us to run a government, to make legislations and decisions by the process of *Shūrā. Shūrā* means to take decisions by consultation and participation. *(3:159, 42:38).* This is an important part of the Islamic political system. There is no scope for despotism in Islam. The *Qur'ān* and the *Sunnah* will be the basis of legislation in Islam.

4 Accountability of government

The Islamic political system makes the ruler and the government responsible firstly to Allah and then to people. The ruler and the government are elected by the people to exercise powers on their behalf. We must remember here that both the ruler and the ruled are the *Khalīfah* of Allah and the ruler shall have to work for the welfare of the people according to the *Qur'ān* and *Sunnah.* A ruler is a servant of the people of Islam. Both the ruler and the ruled will appear before Allah and account for their actions on the day of judgment. The responsibility of the ruler is heavier than the ruled.

Any ordinary citizen of an Islamic state has the right to ask any question on any matter to the ruler and the government.

5 Independence of judiciary

In the Islamic political system, the Judiciary is independent of the Executive. The head of the state or any government minister could be called to the court if necessary. They would be treated no differently from other citizens. The *Qur'ān* has many injunctions about justice. One of the main functions of the Islamic state is to ensure justice to all citizens *(4:58, 4:135, 5:8).* The ruler and the government has no right to interfere in the system of justice.

6 Equality before law

The Islamic political system ensures equality of all citizens before the law. It does not recognise any discrimination on the basis of language, colour, territory, sex or descent. Islam recognises the preference of one over the other only on the basis of *Taqwā* (piety or fear of God). One who fears Allah most is the noblest in Islam. *(49:13).*

Conclusion

The duty of an Islamic state is to establish *Ṣalāh, Zakāh* and promote the *right* and forbid the *wrong. (22:41)*. The state is responsible for the welfare of all its citizens — Muslims and non-Muslims. It must guarantee the basic necesseties to all citizens. All citizens of the Islamic state shall enjoy freedom of belief, thought, conscience and speech. Every citizen shall be free to develop his potential, improve his capacity, earn and possess. A citizen shall enjoy the right to support or oppose any government policy which he thinks right or wrong.

The Islamic state is duty bound to implement the laws of the *Qur'ān* and the *Sunnah*. The *Qur'ān* strongly denounces those who do not decide their matters by Allah's revelations. *(5:42-50)*.

The Islamic state shall ensure a fair distribution of wealth. Islam does not believe in equal distribution as it is against the law of creation.

There is not a single perfect Islamic state in the world today. There are many Muslim countries. An Islamic state is based on the model of the Prophet Muḥammad's *(pbuh)* state in Madīnah while a Muslim state is the one which has a majority Muslim population and some Islamic features.

However, organised efforts have been going on in many Muslim countries to establish truly Islamic states. The Ikhwānul Muslimūn in the Middle East, the Jamā'at-e-Islāmī in Pakistan, Bangladesh and Kashmir, the Millī Salāmat Party in Turkey and the Masjūmī Party in Indonesia are some of the Islamic movements and parties which have been working for the establishment of Allah's law on Allah's land.

In Iran, an Islamic revolution has come into being and the Iranian Muslims under the leadership of Āyatullāh Khomeinī have been trying to set up an Islamic state. The Islamic revolution of Iran has rekindled a great hope among the Muslims all over the world. They hope and pray that the leaders of the revolution will shape Iran into a truly Islamic state. Islamic laws are also being gradually implemented in Sudan and Pakistan. Let us pray and hope that a perfect Islamic state will emerge to guide the whole of the human race towards justice, fairplay and peace.

Exercise : 19

4th, 5th and 6th Forms

1. *"Man needs bread to live but he does not live for bread alone."* — Discuss.
2. Write down the English meaning of the Quranic verses regarding earning and expenditure by *Ḥalāl* means.
3. Explain the concept of *Zakāh* and contrast it with *Ribā* (interest).
4. What are the main principles of the *Islamic Economic System?*

Exercise : 20

4th, 5th and 6th Forms

1. *"Religion and politics are one and the same in Islam."* — Discuss this statement.
2. Explain the concept of *sovereignty* in Islam. How does it contrast with the concept of *sovereignty* in a *democracy?*
3. Discuss the institution of *Shūrā* in Islam and the principle of *Khilāfah.*
4. What should be done to establish a real Islamic State in the world according to the model set by the Prophet *Muḥammad* (pbuh).

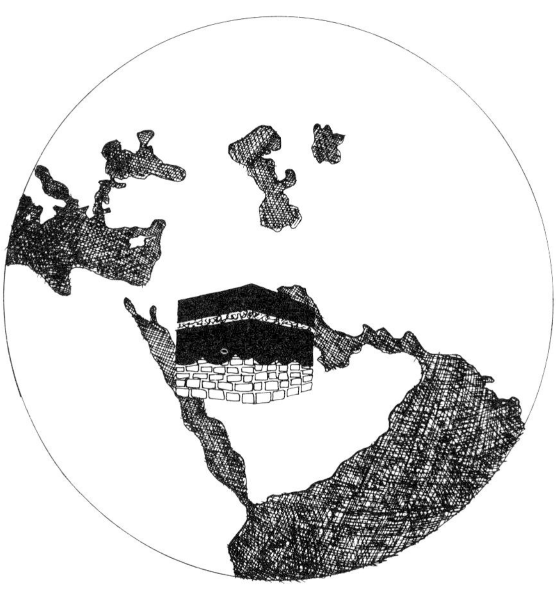

11

Some other aspects of life

Food and Drink

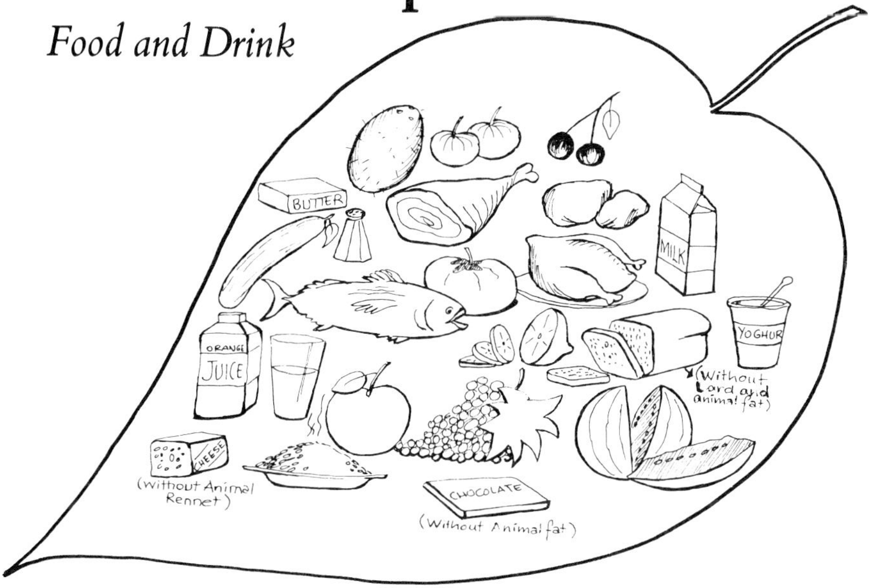

FOOD and drink have direct effects on our health. This is why Islam has given regulations about our food and drink. Islam aims at establishing a healthy society. It lays great emphasis on our physical as well as our moral health. It allows all good and pure things to be taken as food and drink. The *Qur'ān* says :

"O Mankind, eat the lawful and good things from what is in earth and do not follow the foot steps of the devil. Surely, he is your open enemy." (2:168).

Lawful thing are called Ḥalāl and prohibited things are known as Ḥarām in Islamic Law.

Islam forbids eating the meat of the following :

a dead animals and birds

b animals slain without invoking Allah's name

c animals strangled to death

d pigs

e carnivorous animals

f animals devoured by wild beasts

Islam also forbids the eating of :

the blood of an animal

(2:173, 5:3, 6:145, 16:115).

Islamic law requires an animal to be slain by a sharp knife penetrating the inner part of the animal's neck to allow maximum drainage of blood. Allah's name must be invoked at the time of slaying. Meat of the animals not slain in this way is regarded as Ḥarām. Even marrow, rennet and gelatine of these animals are Ḥarām. Effort should be made to obtain Ḥalāl meat from Muslim butchers. But if there is no Muslim butcher nearby, then the 'Kosher' meat of the Jews is regarded as Ḥalāl for Muslims.

Fish and vegetables are, however, quite lawful. All kinds of alcoholic drinks, such as beer, wine and spirits are prohibited. Alcoholic drinks are not at all conducive to a healthy society. The *Qur'ān* says :

"O you who believe, wine and gambling, idols and divining arrows are filthy tricks of satan; avoid them so that you may prosper. Satan wants to incite enmity and hatred among you by means of wine and gambling and prevent you from remembering Allah and from Ṣalāh. So will you not give them up?" (5:90-91).

Alcoholism is a serious social problem. It leads to many vices. Islam aims at rooting out all evils and to ensure that society remains healthy and peaceful.

Muslims begin their meals by saying — *Bismillāhir Raḥmānir Raḥīm* (In the name of Allah, the most Merciful and the most Kind) and should finish by reciting the following Ḥadīth :

اَلْحَمْدُ لِلّٰهِ الَّذِىْ اَطْعَمَنَا وَسَقَانَا وَجَعَلَنَا مِنَ الْمُسْلِمِيْنَ ○

Al ḥamdu lil lāhil ladhī Aṭ'amanā wa saqānā Wa Ja'alanā minal Muslimīn.

(All praise is for Allah who gave us to eat and to drink and made us Muslims).

The Prophet Muḥammad *(pbuh)* asked us to eat with the right hand and to wash our hands before and after meals. It is better not to eat so much as to fill the stomach. The Prophet also asked us not to drink water and other soft drinks at one go, rather we should pause in between and it is better to have three pauses while having any lawful drink.

The Islamic system of life has some fine and very useful regulations for all affairs of life. We should try to follow these rules as best we can for our own benefit.

Dress

Islam enjoins society is one of decency. Allah has created man in the best of forms and He wants His servants to dress nicely and decently. We should bear in mind that we are the best of all creatures and our dress should reflect this. Dress is to cover shame and nakedness and it adds beauty to our personality.

The Qur'ān says : "O children of Ādam, we have revealed to you clothing to conceal your shame and as a thing of beauty but the garment of Taqwā (piety) is the best of all." (7:26).

Islam does not recommend any particular dress for us. But there are guide lines which include :

1 *Men must cover their body from navel to knees.*
2 *Women must cover their whole body except face, hands and feet while inside. But they are also required to cover their whole body including a part of the face while going out or meeting adult males, outside close relatives. Some Islamic jurists allow the face to remain uncovered.*
3 *Women must not wear a dress which reveals the figure and arouses man's base feelings. This includes see-through, skin-tight or revealing dresses.*
4 *Pure silk and clothes decorated with gold are not allowed for men.*
5 *Men are not allowed to wear women's clothing.*
6 *Muslims are not allowed to wear dress which is symbolic of other religions.*

Islam encourages simplicity and modesty. Forms of dress expressing arrogance are disliked. The style of dress depends on local custom and climatic conditions. But the above guidelines apply.

Festivals

Like all other religion, Islam has a number of special occasions of celebration. These occasions are observed with devotion to seek the pleasure of Allah. There is no concept of festival only for pleasure. The festivals are the occasions of thanksgiving, joy and happiness. The two major occasions in Islam in each year are : *'Īdul Fiṭr* and *'Īdul Aḍḥā*.

'Īdul Fiṭr is observed at the end of the month of *Ramaḍān*. On this day, after a month of fasting, Muslims express their joy and happiness by offering a congregational prayer, if possible in an open field, other-

wise in Halls and Mosques. They express their gratitude to Almighty Allah for enabling them to observe fasting which is a very useful rigorous training programme. The day is generally observed as a holiday in Muslim countries. Special dishes are prepared and it is customary to visit friends and relatives and to give presents to children. Muslims generally wear their best clothes on this day.

'Īdul Aḍḥā begins on the 10th of *Dhū'l Ḥijjah* and continues until the *12th day of the month*. It is celebrated to commemorate Prophet *Ibrāhīm's* (Abraham) readiness to sacrifice his son *Ismā'īl* (Ishmael) on the command of Allah. Allah accepted *Ibrāhīm's* devotion and obedience and asked him to sacrifice a lamb instead.

This occasion of great importance comes every year during the days of *Ḥajj* (Pilgrimage to Makkah) and is observed by offering congregational prayer, as in *'Īdul Fiṭr*.

After the prayer, the Muslims, who can afford it, sacrifice animals like goats, sheep, cows or camels to seek Allah's pleasure. The meat of the sacrificed animal is eaten and shared among the relatives, neighbours and the poor. This sacrifice expresses the inner feeling of a

Muslim that, if need be, he will sacrifice his most loved possession for Allah. This is the lesson of the occasion.

We must remember here that what Allah wants is not the animal nor its meat or blood, rather He wants our devotion and submission to His command.

Some other occasions to observe and celebrate include *Lailatul Qadr* (Night of Power), *Lailatul Mi'rāj* (Night of the Ascent), the *beginning of Hijrah*, the *dates for Islamic Battles, the birthday of the Prophet Muḥammad (pbuh)* and *'Ashūrah* (10th of Muḥarram, in memory of the *great martyr Imām Ḥusain).*

The *Jumu'ah Prayer* on each Friday may also be regarded as a weekly festival of Muslims when Muslims gather together for congregational prayer.

Islamic festivals are observed according to the *Islamic calendar* which is based on *Lunar months*. The *Lunar year* is shorter than the *Solar year* by about ten days. Festival dates are determined by the sighting of the moon.

A Muslim's happiest occasion in life is to see the Rule of Allah established on the earth.

Exercise : 21

4th, 5th and 6th Forms

1. What are the dietary rules of Islam? List the things which Muslims are not allowed to eat.
2. Write down the evil effects of *alcoholism.*
3. What are the Islamic regulations for *Dress.* — Discuss the meaning of *modesty* in this context.
4. Write down an essay on the *Festivals* in Islam.

12

Selected verses from the Qur'ān

S*URELY, this Qur'ān guides to that which is the straightest, and gives good news to believers who practise good and they will get a great reward." (17:9).*

"And He (commands you, saying) : This is my straight path, so follow it. Do not follow other paths, which will separate you from His path. Thus He has ordered you so that you may be truly obedient." (6:153).

Tawḥīd

"Allah! There is none worthy of worship except Him, the Living, the Ever Lasting!

Slumber does not overtake Him nor does sleep,
Whatever is in the Heavens and in the Earth belongs to Him.
Who is there to plead to Him except with His permission?
He knows what lies before them and what is behind them, while they grasp nothing of His knowledge except what He may wish.
His Authority extends over Heaven and Earth;
Preserving them both does not overburden Him.
He is the Sublime, the Exalted." (2:255).

Risālah

a *"We have sent a messenger to every nation. Serve Allah (Alone) and turn aside from false gods." (16:36).*

b "Allah has favoured the believers by sending them a messenger from among themselves, to recite His verses to them, to purify them, and teach them the book and wisdom whereas previously they were in clear error." (3:164).

c "He it is who has sent His messenger with the guidance and the religion of truth, that He may make it triumphant over every other religion, how much the idolaters may dislike." (61:9).

Åkhirah

a *"Do you think then that we have created you for nothing and that you would not be returned to us." (23:115).*

b "Those who disbelieve say : when we have become dust like our fathers, shall we truly be raised up again?" (27:67).

c "O mankind! If you are in doubt about the Ressurection then consider that We have created you from dust, then from a drop of seed, then from a clot, then from a lump of flesh shapely and shapeless, so that We may make (our power) clear to you. And We cause what We wish to remain in the wombs for an appointed time, and afterwards We bring you forth as babies, then (give you growth) that you attain your full strength. And among you there is he who dies (young), and among you there is he who brought to the most pitiable time of life (the old age), so that, after knowledge, he knows not (because of infirmity). And you (Muḥammad) see the earth barren, but when We send down rain thereon, it thrills and swell and put forth every lovely kind of growth. This is all because of Allah. He is the Truth. Surely, He makes the dead alive and surely He has the power to do everything; there is no doubt that the Hour will come and truly Allah will raise those who are in graves." (22:5-7).

d "Allah has created the Heavens and Earth with truth and that everyone may be repaid what it has earned. And they will not be wronged." (45:22).

Qualities of Mu'min

a "Successful indeed are the believers,
Who are humble in their prayers (ṣalāh),

Who avoid vain talk,
And who practise the system of Zakāh;
And who guard their modesty except from their wives or the (slaves) that their right hands possess for then they are not blameworthy,
But whoever want beyond that such are the transgressors —
And who faithfully observe their trusts and undertakings,
And who are mindful of their prayers (ṣalāh).
These are the heirs
Who will inherit Paradise wherein
they will live forever." (23:1-11).

b "O believers, Fear Allah as He should be feared and do not die except being one of those who have truly surrendered." (3:102).

Luqmān's advice to his son

(Luqmān was famous for his sound intelligence and wisdom in Arabia. He was most probably an Arab speaking black African).

"O my dear son! Do not make any partner to Allah. Truly, making anyone partner to Allah is a big sin." (31:13).

"O my dear son! Establish ṣalāh and command for the right and forbid the evil and persevere in whatever difficulty you are in. Surely, this is one of those things which have been strongly recommended (31:17).

"Do not turn your face in disgust from people, nor walk arrogantly on the land. Allah does not love the selfish boasters." (31:18).

"Be modest in your behaviour and lower your voice. Truly the harshest of all voice is the voice of the ass. (31:19).

DUTIES AND OBLIGATIONS

Duty towards Parents

1 "Be kind to your parents and the relatives and the orphans, and those in need and speak nicely to people." (2:83).

2 "And we have made it a duty for man to be good to his parents. His mother bears him with one fainting spell after another fainting spell, while his weaning takes two years. Thank Me as well as your parents; towards Me lies the Goal." (31:14).

3 "Your Lord has ordered that you worship none but Him and (show) kindness to your parents, whether either of them or both of them attain old age in your life, never say to them, "Ough" nor be

harsh to them, but speak to them kindly.

"And serve them with tenderness and humility and say : My Lord, have mercy on them, just as they cared for me as a little child." (17:23-24).

4 "We have made it a duty on man to be kind to parents, but if they try to make you associate anything with Me which you have no knowledge of, do not obey them.To me is your return and I shall tell you what you used to do." (29:8).

Relatives, neighbours and the needy

1 "Give your relatives their due and also the needy and the traveller in need and do not squander (your wealth) irresponsibly." (17:26).

2 "Allah commands justice, kindness and giving (their due) to near relatives..." (16:90).

3 "And when near relatives, orphans and the needy are present at the division (of inheritance), provide for them out of it and speak politely to them." (4:8).

4 ...And (show) kindness to (your) parents and to near relatives, orphans, the needy and to the neighbour who is your relative and the neighbour who is not your relative..." (4:36).

5 "Have you seen him who rejects religion? That is the person who pushes the orphan aside and does not encourage feeding the needy." (107:1-3).

Orphan

1 *"The orphan must not be oppressed." (93:9).*

2 "Those who live on orphan's property without having any right to do so only suck up fire into their bellies, and they will (eventually) roast in a blaze." (4:10).

3 "Give orphans their property and do not replace something bad for something good..." (4:2).

4 "Do not approach an orphan's estate before he comes of age except to improve it." (6:152 and 17:34).

SOCIAL MANNERS

Brotherhood

"Believers are but brothers, so set things right between your brothers and observe your duty to Allah so that you may obtain mercy." (49:10).

Greetings

1 "When those who believe in our signs come to you, say : peace be upon you." (6:54).

2 "When you are welcomed with a greeting, then answer back with something finer than it or (at least) return it. Truly Allah takes count of all things." (4:86).

3 "...When you enter houses salute one another with a greeting from Allah, blessed and sweet..." (24:61).

Co-operation

1 "...Co-operate with one another for virtue and piety and do not co-operate with one another for sin and transgression..." (5:2).

2 *"Cling firmly together by Allah's rope (Islam) and do not be divided." (3:103).*

3 "And the believers — men and women are friends of one another, they command for the right and forbid the wrong, establish Ṣalāh and pay Zakāh and obey Allah and His messenger..." (9:71).

Meetings

1 "O you who believe, when you are asked to make room in meetings, then make room. Allah will make room for you (in Ākhirah). And when it is said, "Move up" then move on. Allah will raise in rank those of you who believe as well as those who are given knowledge. Allah knows whatever you do" (58:11).

2 "Truly they are the believers who believe in Allah and His messenger and when they are with him on some common errand, they should not leave until they have asked him for permission to do so. Those who ask for such permission are the ones who believe in Allah and His messenger..." (24:62).

Talking

"Be modest in your behaviour and lower your voice. Truly the harshest of all voices is the voice of the ass." (31:19).

Seek permission before entering someone's house

"O you who believe! Do not enter houses other than your own without first seeking permission and saluting the people inside. That is better for you so that you may be heedful.

And if you find no one therein, still do not enter until permission has been given..." (24:27-28).

Keeping promise

"O you who believe, fulfil your undertakings..." (5:1).

"...Fulfil your promise, every promise will be enquired into." (17:34).

"Of the believers are men who are true that which they covenanted with Allah..." (33:23).

"...And (the pious are those) who fulfil their engagement when they make one..." (2:177).

BASIC VIRTUES

Honesty

"And give full measure when measure out, and weigh with proper scales..." (17:35).

"And measure in fairness and do not weigh unfairly." (55:9).

"Whenever you speak, speak justly even if a near relative is concerned." (6:152).

Truthfulness

"O you who believe! Fear Allah and stand by those who are truthful." (9:119).

"That Allah may reward the truthful for their truth and punish the hypocrites if He will." (33:24).

"Truly Muslim men and Muslim women, believing men and believing women and obedient men and obedient women and the truthful men and the truthful women... Allah has promised them forgiveness and a great reward." (33:35).

"Allah said : This is the day (Day of Judgment) which the truthful will benefit from their truthfulness, for them are the gardens underneath which the rivers flow where they will live forever. Allah is pleased with them and they are pleased with Him. That is the greatest success." (5:119).

Perseverence

"...Seek help from Allah and be patient, the earth belongs to Allah. Anyone He wishes from among His servants shall inherit it..." (7:128).

"...Our Lord, fill us full of patience and make our feet firm. Help us against the disbelievers." (2:250).

"And anyone who acts patiently and forgives, truly he is persevering in affairs." (42:43).

Tolerance

"Tolerate patiently what (unbelievers) say and part from them in polite manner." (73:10).

Firmness against odds and evil

"...and be patient in adversity and troubles and during the time of stress. Such are they who are on the right track and such are the Allah-fearing." (2:177).

"O you who believe! Seek help in firmness and prayer. Surely Allah is with those who are firm." (2:153).

"O you who believe, endure and outdo all others in endurance, be ready, and observe your duty to Allah, so that you may succeed." (3:200).

"Be patient (O Muḥammad) with the finest patience." (70:5).

"Then have patience (O Muḥammad) as the most determined of the messengers (before you) had patience..." (46:35).

Punctuality

"...Surely Ṣalāh at fixed hours has been ordained on to the believers." (4:103).

Courage

"Those to whom people said : Truly the people have gathered against you, so fear them. (The threat of danger) but increased their faith and they cried : Allah is enough for us! Most Excellent is He in whom we trust." (3:173).

"And when the true believers saw the troops they said : That is that which Allah and His messenger promised us. Allah and His messengers told the truth. It strengthened their faith and obedience." (33:22).

Kindness

"It is because of mercy from Allah that you (Muḥammad) have been so kind to them, for if you had been harsh and cruel-hearted they would have dispersed from around you. Pardon them, seek forgiveness for them and consult them on the matter..." (3:159).

"...Be kind as Allah has been kind to you..." (28:77).

Trustworthiness

"Surely, I am a trustworthy messenger to you, so observe your duty to Allah and obey me." (26:107-108).

"Allah orders you to restore things entrusted (to you) to their owners...'' (4:58).

Justice

''We surely sent our messengers with clear proofs and revealed with them books and the standard, so that people may deal with justice...'' (57:25).

Allah commands justice and fairness...'' (16:90).

''...Let not the hatred of others make you to the wrong and depart from justice. Be just, that is next to piety...'' (5:8).

Chastity and cloak for women

''Tell the believing men to lower their gaze and guard their private parts. That is purer for them. Surely Allah knows what you do.'' (24:30).

''And tell the believing women to lower their gaze and guard their private parts and not to display their beauty except which is apparent, to draw cloaks over their bosoms and not to reveal their feminine beauty except to their husbands or fathers or husband's father or their sons or their husband's sons or their brothers or their brothers' sons or sisters' sons or their women or their maids or impotent male attendants or children who do not know of women's nakedness. And let them not walk noisily as to reveal what they preserve of their beauty. And turn to Allah together, O believers! In order that you may prosper.'' (24:31).

''O prophet! Tell your wives and your daughters and the women of the believers to draw their cloaks close round them (when they go out). That will be better, so that they may be recognised and not annoyed. Allah is ever Forgiving and Merciful.'' (33:59).

Hard work

"...Surely Allah does not change the condition of a people if they do not change themselves..." (13:11).

Generosity

''You will not attain piety until you spend what you hold is dear to you...'' (3:92).

''Those who spend their wealth (for the sake of Allah) night and day, both privately and publicly, will get their reward from their Lord, they shall have no cause to fear nor shall they grieve.'' (2:274).

Forgiveness

''Practise forgiveness, command decency and avoid ignorant

people." (7:199).

Reliance on Allah

"If Allah is your helper none can overcome you and if He does not help you, who is there to help you? The reliant rely only on Allah." (3:160).

"...He who relies on Allah, Allah is enough for him..." (65:3).

BAD CONDUCT & PROHIBITIONS

Lying

"...Give up the filth of idols and stop lying." (22:30).

"...Allah's curse will be on him if he is a liar." (24:7).

Back-biting, spying and suspicion

"O you who believe! Shun much suspicion for truly some suspicion is a sin. And spy not, neither back-bite one another. Would one of you love to eat the flesh of his dead brother? You hate that (so hate the other)! And keep your duty to Allah. Surely, Allah is Forgiving and the most Kind." (49:12).

Fraud

"The cheaters will suffer terribly. They insist on full measure when they have people measure something for them; but if they measure or weigh things for them, they give less than their due." (83:1-3).

Extravagance

"...Do not squander (your money) extravagantly. Truly the extravagant are devil's brethren and Satan has always been ungrateful towards his Lord." (17:26-27).

Arrogance

"Do not walk in the earth haughtily. Surely, you can never tear the earth nor can rival the mountains in height." (17:37).

"...Allah does not love prideful boasters." (57:23).

Hoarding

"And let the hoarders do not think that what Allah has bestowed upon them from His bounty is better for them. But it is worse for them. That which they hoard will be a burden for them on the Day of Judgment..." (3:180).

"...Announce a painful punishment to those who hoard gold and silver and do not spend them for Allah's sake..." (9:34).

Mischief and corruption

"...Eat and drink that which Allah has given you and do not act corruptly making mischief in the earth." (2:60).

Mockery and ridicule

"O you who believe! No people should mock or ridicule other people, for the ridiculed ones may be better than those who ridicule them..." (49:11).

Hypocrisy

"And there are people who say : we believe in Allah and the Last Day but actually do not believe." (2:8).

"When the hypocrites come to you (O Muḥammad) they say : We testify that you are indeed Allah's messenger and Allah knows that you are His messenger and Allah declares that the Hypocrites are liars." (63:1).

Abortion and birth control

"Do not kill your children in fear of poverty, we shall provide for them and you. Killing them is a big sin." (17:31).

Usury and interest

"...Allah has permitted trading and forbidden interest and usury..." (2:275).

Wine and gambling

"O you who believe! Liquor and gambling, idols and divining arrows are only a filthy work of satan; give them up so that you may prosper." (5:90).

Adultery

"And keep away from adultery. Surely, it is a hateful filthy work and a very bad thing." (17:32).

"The adulterer and the adulteress, punish each one of them with a hundred lashes..." (24:2).

Theft

"As for the thief, both male and female, chop off their hands. It is the reward of their own deeds and exemplary punishment from Allah. Allah is the Mighty and the Most Wise." (5:38).*

---

*Exercise for this chapter is on page 202.

13

Selections from Ḥadīth

HADĪTH means news or information. It has a special meaning in Islam. It refers to the sayings and doings of the Prophet Muḥammad *(pbuh)* and actions done with his approval.

DUTIES AND OBLIGATIONS

Jihād

"The most excellent man is the one who works hard in the way of Allah with his life and property" (Bukhārī).

"The best Jihād is to speak the truth before a tyrant ruler" (Bukhārī).

Īmān and Islām and Iḥsān

"Faith is that you believe in Allah (Tawḥīd) and His angels and His messengers (Risālah) and in the life after death (Ākhirah).

"Islam is that you worship Allah and not associate anyone with Him, keep up Ṣalāh, pay Zakāh, and observe Ṣawm in Ramaḍān.

"Iḥsān is that you worship Allah as if you see Him and if you do not see Him, surely He sees you" (Bukhārī).

Love of the Prophet (pbuh)

"None of you has faith unless I am dearer to him than his father, and his son and all mankind" (Bukhārī).

Ṣalāh and Ṭahārah

"The key to Paradise is Ṣalāh and the key to Ṣalāh is Ṭahārah (purification)" (Mishkāt).

Parents

A man asked the prophet, "O messenger of Allah! Who deserves the best care from me? The prophet said, "Your mother." The man asked, "Who then?" The prophet said, "Your mother." The man asked once again, "Who then?" The prophet said, "Your mother" (Bukhārī).

"Paradise lies at the feet of your mother" (Nasā'ī).

"A father's pleasure is Allah's pleasure, a father's displeasure is Allah's displeasure" (Tirmidhī).

Wife

"The most perfect of the believers is the best of you in character, and the best of you are those among you who are best to their wives" (Tirmidhī).

Children

"He is not of us who has a compassion for our little ones and does not honour our old ones" (Tirmidhī).

"No father can give his child anything better than good manners" (Tirmidhī).

"Be careful of your duty to Allah and be fair and just to your children" (Bukhārī).

"Whoever properly brings up two daughters until they reach maturity, that man and myself (the prophet) will be so close in paradise as two adjacent fingers" (Muslim).

Guests

"He who believes in Allah and the Last Day should honour his guest" (Bukhārī).

Neighbours

"By Allah, he has no faith (the prophet repeated it three times) whose neighbours are not safe from his wickedness" (Bukhārī).

"He is not a believer who eats his fill while his neighbour remains hungry by his side" (Baihaqī).

"Jibrā'īl has been recommending good treatment towards the neighbours, so much that I thought he would give him the right to inherit" (Bukhārī).

Orphan

"The best house among the Muslims is the house in which an orphan is well treated and the worst house among the Muslims is the house in which an orphan is badly treated" (Ibn Mājah).

The needy

"One who tries to help the widow and the poor is like a warrior in the way of Allah" (Bukhārī).

BASIC QUALITIES

Intention

"Actions shall be judged only by intention, a man shall get what he intends" *(Bukhārī).*

Truthfulness

"Guarantee me six things and I shall assure you of Paradise : When you speak, speak the truth, keep your promise, discharge your trust, guard your chastity and lower your gaze and withhold your hands from highhandedness." (Baihaqī).

"Surely truth leads to virtue, and virtue leads to paradise" *(Bukhārī).*

Keeping promises

"Do not quarrel with your brother Muslim, nor jest with him nor make him a promise which you cannot keep up" *(Tirmidhī).*

Tolerance

"There are two rails in me which Allah likes, toleration and deliberation in undertakings" *(Aḥmad, Tirmidhī).*

Politeness

"Allah is polite and likes politeness" *(condensed from Muslim).*

Modesty

"Modesty is part of faith" *(Bukhārī & Muslim).*

Brotherhood

"Each of you is a mirror of his brother, if you see something wrong in your brother, you must tell him to get rid of it" *(Tirmidhī).*

"Believers are like the parts of a building to one another — each part supporting the others" *(Bukhārī).*

"None of you can be a believer unless he loves for his brother what he loves for himself" *(Bukhārī).*

"A Muslim is he from whose tongue and hands, other Muslims are safe (Bukhārī).

Charity

"Every good action is a charity and it is good action to meet a friend with a smiling face" *(Bukhārī).*

"There is a man who gives charity and he conceals it so much that his left hand does not know what his right hand spends" *(Bukhārī).*

"Removal from a road that which is harmful is charity" *(Bukhārī).*

Contentment

"Wealth does not come from abundance of goods but from a contented heart *(Bukhārī & Muslim).*

Learning

"The best of you is he who has learnt the Qur'ān and then taught it" (Bukhārī).

"The seeking of knowledge is a must for every Muslim man and woman" *(Mishkāt).*

"The learned men are the successors of the prophets. They leave behind knowledge as inheritance. One who inherits it obtains a great fortune" *(Bukhārī).*

Kindness

"Allah is not kind to him who is not kind to people (Bukhārī & Muslim).

"Those who are kind and considerate to Allah's creatures, Allah bestows His kindness and affection on them. Show kindness to the creatures on the earth so that Allah may be kind to you" *(Abū Dāwūd, Tirmidhī).*

Thankfulness

"He who does not thank people does not thank Allah" *(Tirmidhī).*

Steadfastness

"Sufiān bin 'Abdullāh said, 'I asked : O Allah's messenger, tell me something which I should stick to'. He said : 'Say, my Lord is Allah, then remain steadfast'." *(An-Nawawī's forty Ḥadīth).*

Repentance (Tawbah)

"By Allah, I (Muhāmmad) ask Allah's forgiveness and turn to Him in repentance more than seventy times a day." *(Bukhārī).*

Gifts

"Give gifts to one another, for gifts take away malice." *(Mishkāt).*

"The messenger of Allah used to accept gifts and give gifts in return." *(Bukhārī).*

Visiting the sick

"Visit the sick, feed the hungry and free the captives." *(Bukhārī).*

MANNERS

Meeting

"When one of you arrives at a meeting where people are seated, he should say salām to them. And when he wishes to leave, he should say salām to them." *(Abū Dāwūd).*

"Do not sit between two men without permission of both of them." *(Abū Dāwūd).*

"Meetings are like trusts, except three kinds of meeting : for shedding prohibited blood, or for committing adultery or for taking property unlawfully." *(Abū Dāwūd).*

Talking

"He who truly believes in Allah and the last day should speak good or keep silent." *(Bukhārī & Muslim).*

"He who keeps silent, remains safe." *(Tirmidhī).*

Eating and drinking

"The blessing of food is to wash hands at the beginning and washing after taking it." *(Mishkāt).*

"Say Allah's name (Bismillāh) and eat with your right hand and eat from near you." *(Bukhārī).*

"When one drinks, he should not breathe into the vessel (glass)." *(Bukhārī).*

Clothing

"Eat and drink, give ṣadaqah and wear good clothes as long as these do not involve excess or arrogance." *(Nasā'ī, Ibn Mājah).*

"Indeed, he who wears silk in this world (will) have no share in it in the life after death." *(Bukhārī & Muslim).*

"Gold and silk are lawful to the women of my Ummah and forbidden to the men." *(Tirmidhī, Nasā'ī).*

"Allah's messenger cursed the man who puts on women's clothes and the women who put on men's clothes." *(Abū Dāwūd).*

The prophet said to Asmā', the daughter of Abū Bakr, "When a woman reaches puberty, it is not right that any part of her body (should) be seen but this and this and he pointed to his face and two hands." *(Abū Dāwūd).*

Greeting

"When one of you meets his brother, he should say salām to him." *(Abū Dāwūd).*

"The young should say salām to the old, the passer-by to the one sitting, and the small group to the large one." *(Bukhārī).*

"The best (way) of saying salām is shaking hands." *(Tirmidhī).*

Leave that which does not concern you

"An excellent Islamic practice is to give up what is not one's business." *(Mālik, Aḥmad).*

BAD CONDUCT

Lying

"Woe to him who tells lies to make people laugh! Woe to him! Woe to him!" *(Aḥmad, Tirmidhī).*

"It is great treachery that you tell your brother something he accepts as truth from you, but you are lying." *(Abū Dāwūd).*

Back-biting

"If anybody pledges to me that he will keep his tongue under control, guard his chastity, will not speak ill of others not indulge in *slander* or *back-biting* and refrain from adultery and similar sins, I shall assure him of Paradise." *(Bukhārī).*

Suspicion

"Beware of suspicion, for suspicion may be based on false information, do not spy on another, do not disclose others' hidden defects." *(Bukhārī).*

Jealousy

"Keep away from jealousy for as fire burns wood, so jealousy consumes good actions." *(Abū Dāwūd).*

"Nothing is more atrocious than injuring unjustly a Muslim's reputation." *(Tirmidhī).*

Anger

"He is not strong who throws down another, but he is, who controls his anger." *(Bukhārī & Muslim).*

"If anger rouses anyone, he should sit down and if that does not help, he should lie down." *(Tirmidhī).*

Pride

"If anyone has got an atom of pride in his heart, he will not enter Paradise." *(Bukhārī).*

Abuse

"Abusing a Muslim is sinful and killing him is disbelief (kufr)." *(Bukhārī & Muslim).*

Hypocrisy

"The signs of the hypocrite are three : When he speaks, he lies; when he promises, he breaks it; when any trust is kept with him, he misuses it." (Bukhārī).

Taunting

"A believer neither taunts, nor curses nor speaks foul nor chats nor babbles." *(Tirmidhī).*

"Do not rejoice over the distress of a brother Muslim for Allah may relieve his distress and place you in his position." *(Tirmidhī).*

"Beware, in everybody there is a piece of flesh, if it is healthy, the whole body is healthy, and if it is sick, the whole body is sick. Beware, it is the heart." *(Bukhārī & Muslim).*

Exercise : 22

4th, 5th and 6th Forms

1. What does the *Qur'ān* say about *Tawḥīd, Risālah* and *Ākhirah?* Find out as many verses as you can on these three topics from the *Qur'ān.*
2. What were the advice of *Luqmān* to his son as mentioned in the *Qur'ān?*
3. Write down the Quranic commands about the duties towards *parents, relatives, neighbours* and the *needy.*
4. What lessons do you learn from the *Qur'ān* about *social manners?*
5. List ten *basic virtues* which the *Qur'ān* asks us to acquire.

Exercise : 23

4th, 5th and 6th Forms

1. Write down the sayings of the Prophet about duties and obligations.
2. Write down ten *Aḥādīth* which ask us to avoid *bad habits* and conduct.
3. Explain the concept of *brotherhood* in the context of the Prophet's (pbuh) sayings.

14

Muslim Countries of the World

Population and Resources

MUSLIMS wherever they are, form one nation (Millātun Wāḥidah). It is faith which decides nationality in Islam, and not the geographical territory, colour, race or language. Citizenship of an Islamic State may be determined by geographical boundaries.

There are 46 Muslim countries in the world on the basis of majority of population. The total Muslim population in the world is over 1,000 million, which is a formidable human power.

The Muslim countries together produce two-third of the world's oil, about 70 per cent rubber, about 75 per cent jute, 67 per cent spices, two-third of palm-oil, 50 per cent phosphate, 40 per cent tin. They also produce a large quantity of the world's cotton, tea, coffee, wool, uranium, manganese, cobalt and many other commodities and minerals. There is also a huge amount of natural gas in the Muslim countries.

If we look at a world-map, we find the Muslim countries occupying a very strategic position. 60 per cent of the Mediterranean Sea is bounded by Muslim countries. The Red Sea and the Gulf are fully within the Muslim region.

In the course of history, Muslims lost their essential unity, but it should be restored once again for the greater good of all mankind.

Muslims who once contributed tremendously to the science and civilisation of the world could once again do so if they truly get united on the basis of Islam. Real human progress can only be achieved by the faithful observance of the teaching of Islam. We should consciously try to restore the glory of Islam and make the present day problem-torn world a happy and peaceful place to live in. Pride in the past will be meaningful if the present can be shaped in the light of the past with a promise for the future. The *Muslim Millah* has the potential and the need is for faithful practice of the teachings of Islam.

MUSLIM COUNTRIES OF THE WORLD

	Name	*Area (Sq. Km.)*	*Population (million)*	*Percentage of Muslims*
1	**Afghanistan**	**652,015**	**18 m.**	**99%**
2	Albania	28,860	2.3 m.	75%
3	**Algeria**	**1,500,212**	**18 m.**	**98%**
4	Bahrain	1,118	.22 m.	99%
5	**Bangladesh**	**143,328**	**90 m.**	**85%**
6	Cameroon	477,277	6.2 m.	55%
7	Central African Republic	618,420	2 m.	55%
8	Chad	1,289,080	4 m.	85%
9	Dahomey	115,154	3 m.	60%
10	**Egypt**	**1,005,321**	**36 m.**	**93%**
11	**Ethiopia**	**1,221,900**	**27 m.**	**65%**
12	Gambia	10,246	.4 m.	85%
13	Guinea	245,857	4.3 m.	95%
14	Guinea-Bissau	36,125	.81 m.	70%
15	**Indonesia**	**1,491,564**	**140 m.**	**95%**
16	**Iran**	**1,648,000**	**35 m.**	**98%**
17	**Iraq**	**438,446**	**12 m.**	**95%**
18	Ivory Coast	322,500	5 m.	55%
19	Jordan	94,500	2.6 m.	95%
20	Kuwait	17,800	1 m.	98%
21	Lebanon	8,806	3 m.	57%
22	Libya	1,759,500	2.2 m.	100%
23	**Malaysia**	**286,000**	**13 m.**	**52%**
24	Maldive Islands	235	12 m.	100%
25	Mali	1,239,998	6 m.	90%
26	Mauritania	1,030,000	1.3 m.	100%
27	**Morocco**	**446,550**	**18 m.**	**99%**
28	Niger	1,271,896	4.5 m.	91%
29	**Nigeria**	**927,339**	**80 m.**	**75%**
30	Oman	213,000	.75 m.	100%
31	**Pakistan**	**1,041,375**	**80 m.**	**97%**
32	Qatar	10,000	.18 m.	100%

	Name	*Area (Sq. Km.)*	*Population (million)*	*Percentage of Muslims*
33	Saudi Arabia	2,158,000	8 m.	100%
34	Senegal	196,192	4 m.	95%
35	Sierra Leone	72,605	3 m.	65%
36	Somalia	702,000	4 m.	100%
37	South Yemen	291,200	1.5 m.	95%
38	**Sudan**	**2,515,500**	**17 m.**	**85%**
39	Syria	186,808	7 m.	87%
40	**Tanzania**	**943,332**	**15 m.**	**65%**
41	Togo	56,600	2.1 m.	55%
42	Tunisia	165,150	6 m.	95%
43	**Turkey**	**780,580**	**46 m.**	**99%**
44	U.A.E.	85,800	.32 m.	100%
45	Upper Volta	275,259	6 m.	56%
46	North Yemen	195,000	6 m.	99%

Exercise : 24

6th Form

1. Comment on the material and numerical potential of the Muslims all over the world.
2. Study a map giving the location of Muslim countries in the world and present your own observations.
3. Write down an essay on the Muslims in *Britain.*

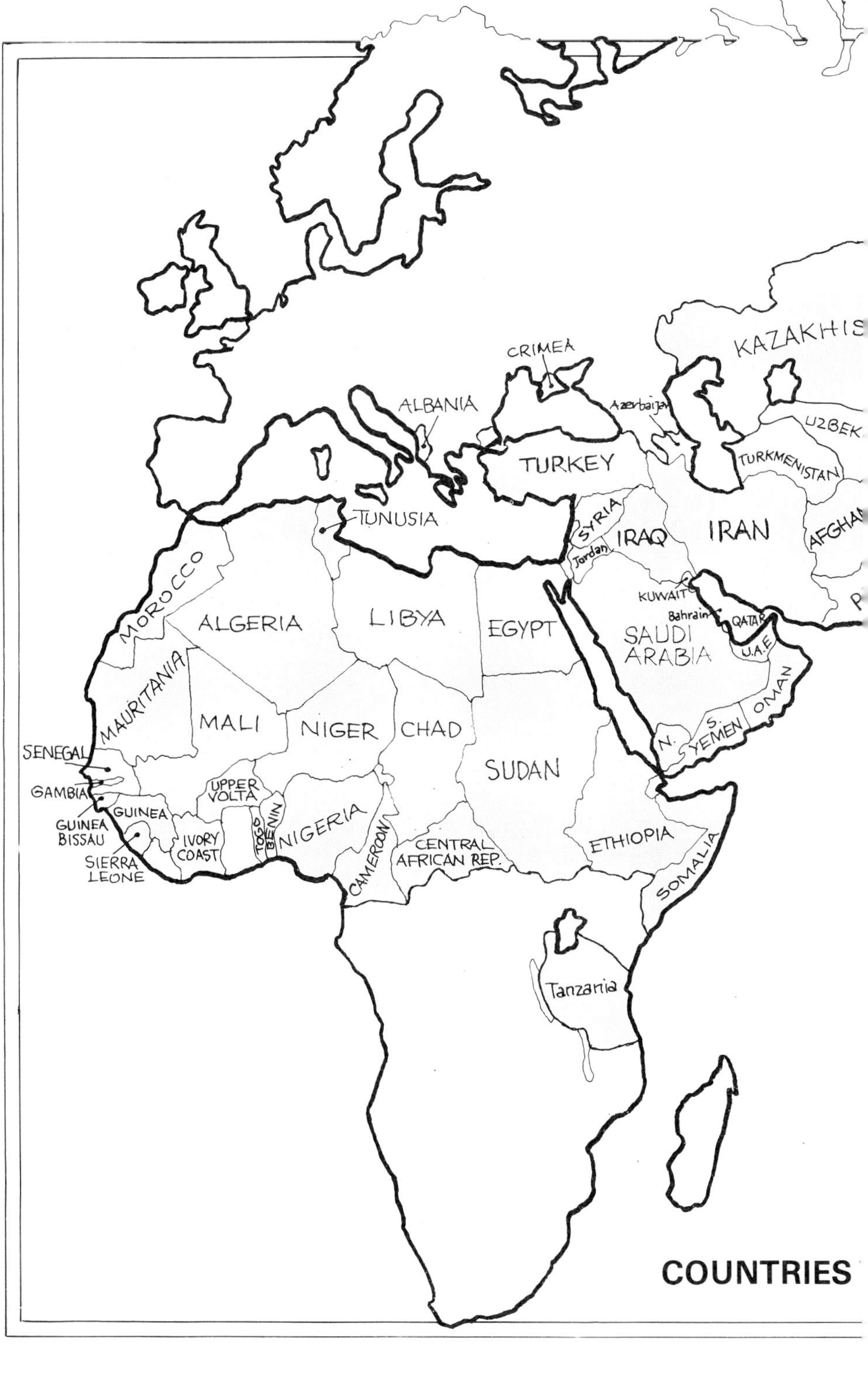
CRIMEA
KAZAKHIS
ALBANIA
Azerbaijan
UZBEK
TURKEY
TURKMENISTAN
TUNUSIA
SYRIA
IRAQ
IRAN
AFGHAN
Jordan
KUWAIT
MOROCCO
ALGERIA
LIBYA
EGYPT
Bahrain
QATAR
SAUDI ARABIA
U.A.E.
MAURITANIA
OMAN
MALI
NIGER
CHAD
N.
S. YEMEN
SENEGAL
SUDAN
GAMBIA
UPPER VOLTA
GUINEA
NIGERIA
GUINEA BISSAU
IVORY COAST
TOGO
BENIN
CAMEROON
CENTRAL AFRICAN REP.
ETHIOPIA
SOMALIA
SIERRA LEONE
Tanzania

COUNTRIES

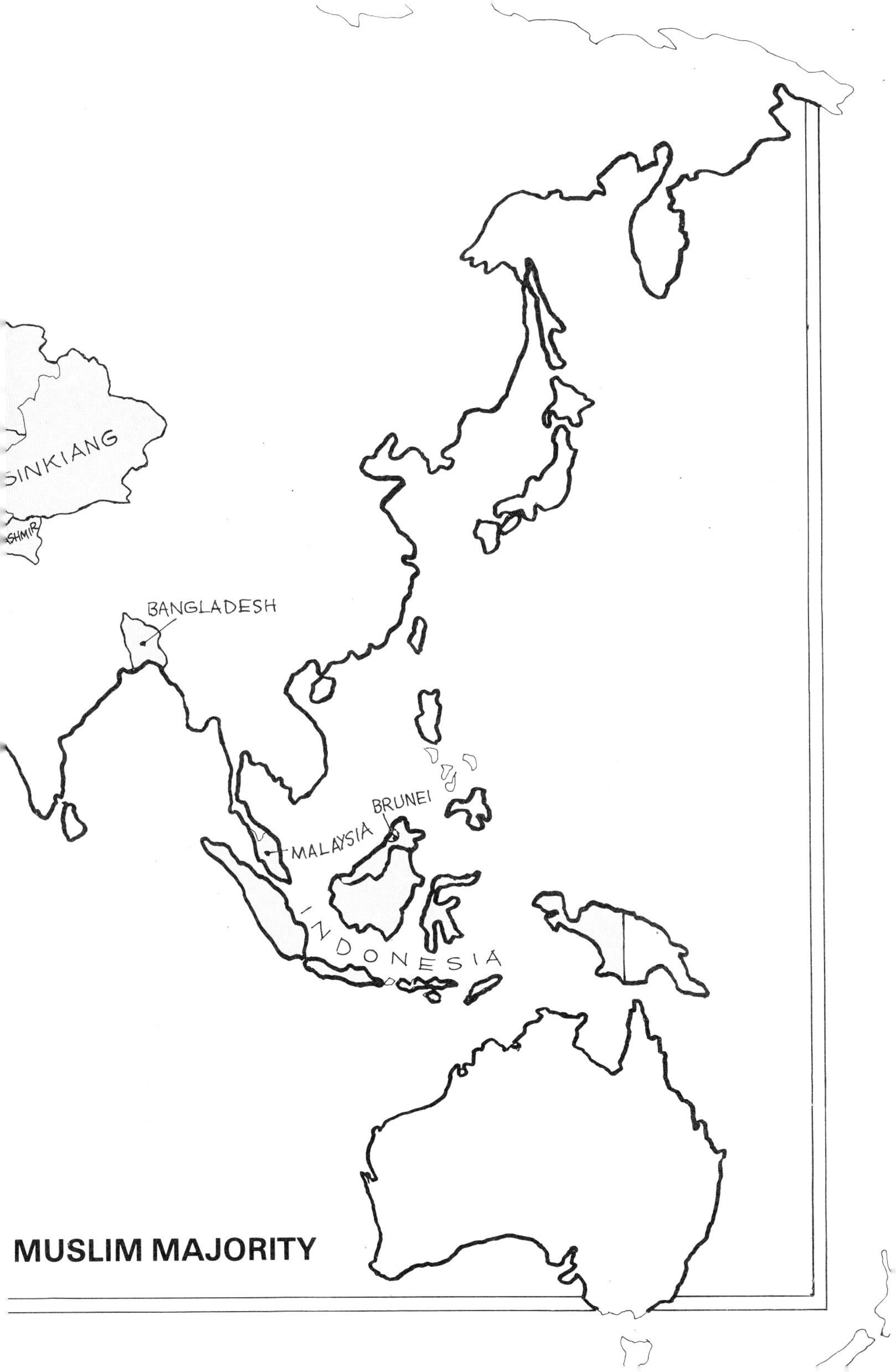

MUSLIM MAJORITY

Muslims are spread in almost all parts of the world. The countries having Muslim minorities are :

Name	*Muslims*	*Percentage of total population*
Angola	**1.5 m.**	**25%**
Argentina	.5 m.	2%
Australia	.13 m.	1%
Bhutan	.05 m.	5%
Botswana	.03 m.	5%
Brazil	.21 m.	0.2%
Bulgaria	**1.3 m.**	**14%**
Burma	3 m.	10%
Burundi	**.7 m.**	**20%**
Cambodia	.07 m.	1%
Canada	.1 m.	0.5%
China	**90 m.**	**11%**
Congo	.15 m.	15%
Cyprus*	**.21 m.**	**33%**
Equatorial Guinea	.07 m.	25%
Fiji	.06 m.	11%
France	**2 m.**	**3.8%**
Germany (West)	**1.5 m.**	**2.4%**
Ghana	**3 m.**	**30%**
Gibraltar	.003 m.	10%
Greece	.27 m.	3%
Hong Kong	.004 m.	1%
Guyana	.01 m.	15%
India	**100 m.**	**12%**
Italy	.55 m.	1%
Japan	.01 m.	1%
Kenya	**4 m.**	**29.5%**
Liberia	**.5 m.**	**30%**
Lesotho	.12 m.	10%
Malagsy Republic	**1.4 m.**	**20%**

* Cyprus is now divided in two separate states : Muslim majority part called Turkish Federated State of Cyprus and the other part Republic of Cyprus.

Malawi	**1.7 m.**	**35%**
Malta	**.045 m.**	**14%**
Mauritius	**.14 m.**	**19.5%**
Mozambique	**2.2 m.**	**29%**
Namibia	.034 m.	5%
Nepal	.5 m.	4%
Netherlands	**.2 m.**	**1.5%**
Panama	.05 m.	3.6%
Phillipines	**5 m.**	**12%**
Portuguese Timor	**.012 m.**	**20%**
Reunion	**.09 m.**	**20%**
Rumania	**.2 m.**	**20%**
Zimbabwe	**1 m.**	**15%**
South Africa	.5 m.	2%
Sri Lanka	**1.2 m.**	**9%**
Surinam	**.1 m.**	**25%**
Swaziland	.046 m.	10%
Thailand	**6 m.**	**14%**
Trinidad & Tobago	.127 m.	12%
Uganda	**4 m.**	**36%**
U.K.	**1.5 m.**	**2.7%**
U.S.S.R.	**60 m.**	**20%**
U.S.A.	**3.2 m.**	**1.5%**
Yugoslavia	**5 m.**	**20%**
Zaire	**2.4 m.**	**10%**
Zambia	**.7 m.**	**15%**

Total Population : Independent Muslim countries 749 m. (approx.)
Muslim minority countries 308 m. (approx.)

1057 m.*

*The latest population of Muslims all over the world might nearly be 1,100 million. Most population estimates are based on the 1971 census.

Source : 1 World Muslim Gazetteer, Umma Publication, 1975, Karachi.
2 Embassies of different countries in London.
3 Muslim News International, Vol. IV : 10, April 1966, Karachi.

Notes for Teachers and Parents

Teaching Islam to young people requires careful planning and skill. Teachers and parents need to be clear about the aims of providing such teaching. The objective is to educate young people in Islam, to make them conscious and practising Muslims.

The Muslims of the U.K. do not yet have a well organised system of Islamic teaching, although sincere and dedicated efforts are being made in different parts of the country to provide basic Islamic education for our young generation.

The Muslim Educational Trust has started to make Islamic teaching organised and systematic. The Trust published in 1980 a syllabus and guidelines for Islamic teaching. The first edition of this text book, "Islam : Beliefs and Teachings" was published in October 1980, based on the syllabus.

In this second edition, we have incorporated some suggestions for teachers and parents on how to use the book.

A This book is for 11-plus secondary school pupils : it covers briefly the essential aspects of Islam. Some of the topics may not be easily understood by younger pupils at secondary school. At the moment, we are not in a position to publish five or six separate books on Islam to cater for the needs of the pupils of all age groups. The topics covered in this book have been arranged so that they can be studied progressively as the young people move up the school.

B Books on their own cannot work miracles. Dedicated Islamic teachers are needed to guide the pupils and to explain to them the topics given in the book. Without clarification and explanation, some of the material in the book may not be clear to some pupils. Teachers and parents need to be conscious of this.

C Teachers and parents should consult other books for more detailed treatment of different topics and guide the pupils accordingly. The select bibliography at the end of this book may be of help.

D Correct pronunciation of Arabic words needs care and attention. We must take as much care as possible to see that the pupils pronounce Arabic words correctly. The transliteration guide given at the beginning of the book will be useful. We would request Islamic teachers and parents to avoid different spellings of Arabic words.

Given care and attention, young people will be able to pronounce and spell Arabic words correctly. A few examples of varying spellings and pronunciations should make this point clear :

Standard	**Other commonly-used spellings**
i Muḥammad	Mohammed, Muhammed, Mohammad, Mohamad
ii Ramaḍān	Ramadhan, Ramazan
iii Dīn	Deen
iv Mūsā	Mosa, Moosa
v 'Ā'ishah	Ayesha, Aisha
vi 'Uthmān	Usman, Osman
vii Ḥadīth	Hadis, Hadees,
viii Lūṭ	Loot.

It is strongly recommended that the standard spellings should be followed

E The use of charts, maps, posters, slides and films whenever possible will help to make the teaching interesting and effective. Islamic teachers should do their best to use them whenever possible.

F At the end of each topic, we have included exercises for different age groups. The use of the exercises will help to deepen the impact of the teaching, and pupils will grasp lessons better this way. The exercises also indicate to the teacher how well the lessons have been understood.

G With first year pupils, you may find the use of the book ''Islam for Younger People'' more useful, especially for the stories given in it.

H In the second and third years, you should arrange your lessons to incorporate some stories of the prophets.

I In the fourth, fifth and sixth years, the pupils should be encouraged to do projects, and not be limited to the book. These should cover the following topics :

i Ṣalāh and its importance in our life.
ii The role of the Mosque in Islam.
iii Al-Ka'bah.
iv Masjīdun Nabī.
v Ḥajj.
vi Festivals : 'Īdul Fiṭr and 'Īdul Aḍḥā.
vii Qur'ān.
viii Muslim countries and their resources.

Suggested arrangement of study topics according to age group

First Year Pupils

Total No. of lessons for a year : 25

1 Islam : two lessons :
- i Meaning and way of life
- ii Everything in nature is obeying the law of Allah

2 Purpose of creation : one lesson

3 Basic Beliefs : one lesson

4 Al-Īmānul Mufaṣṣal : one lesson

5 Tawḥīd : two lessons :
- i Meaning and Sūratul Ikhlāṣ
- ii Powers of Allah

6 Risālah : two lessons :
- i Meaning of Risālah and its importance
- ii Names of prominent prophets

7 Ākhirah : two lessons :
- i Meaning and Death
- ii Day of Judgment

8 Shahādah : one lesson : Meaning word by word

9 Ṣalāh : one lesson : Names and timings

10 Wuḍū' : three lessons :
- i Importance, Niyyah
- ii How to make Wuḍū'
- iii What makes Wuḍū' invalid?

11 Fard Ṣalāh : one lesson : Raka'hs in each Ṣalāh

12 How to perform Ṣalāh : seven lessons :
- i Niyyah and Subḥanaka
- ii Ta'awwudh, Tasmiyah and Sūratul Fātiḥah (recitation)
- iii Meaning of Sūratul Fātiḥah
- iv Sūratul Ikhlāṣ (Meaning and recitation)
- v Ruku', Qiyām, Tasbīḥ, and Sajdah
- vi Tashahhud
- vii Darūd and Du'ā'

14 Lessons of Ṣalāh : one lesson

Second and Third Year

Total No. of Lessons for a year : 25

1 Islam (introduction) : one lesson
2 Purpose of Creation : one lesson
3 Mohemmedanism is a misnomer : one lesson
4 Basic Beliefs : one lesson : Seven Beliefs and Al-Īmānul Mufaṣṣal
5 Grouping of Basic Beliefs : one lesson :
Tawḥīd, Risālah, Ākhirah
6 Tawḥīd : two lessons :
 i Sūratul Ikhlāṣ
 ii Powers and attributes of Allah
7 Risālah : two lessons :
 i Meaning of Risālah and its significance
 ii Names of 25 prophets mentioned in the Qur'ān
8 Ākhirah : two lessons :
 i Effect of this belief on human life
 ii Death and Day of Judgment (explanation)
9 Basic Duties : six lessons :
 i Names of Duties and the meaning and significance of Shahādah
 ii Ṣalāh — Names, times, importance
 iii Ṣawm — meaning and explanation
 iv Zakāh — meaning and significance with rate
 v Ḥajj — meaning and important rituals
 vi Jihād — meaning and explanation
10 Life of Muḥammad (pbuh) : eight lessons :
 i Explanation of verses (33:21) and (21:107) of the Qur'ān
 ii Birth and childhood and business trip to Syria
 iii Marriage and prophethood
 iv First Revelation (5 verses of Sūratul 'Alaq)
 v 'Alī's acceptance of Islam, 'Alī and the Dinner
 vi The Prophet on Mount Ṣafā
 vii Hostility of the Quraish
 viii 'Umar accepts Islam

Fourth and Fifth Year

Total No. of lessons for a year : 25

1 Islam (introduction) : one lesson :

Explanation of the complete code of life

2 Purpose of Creation : one lesson :
Explanation of 'Ibādah and the verse 51:56 of the Qur'ān

3 Three Basic Concepts : three lessons :
- i Tawḥīd and Al-Qadr
- ii Effect of Tawḥīd on human life
- iii Risālah and Ākhirah

4 Basic Duties : four lessons :
- i Shahādah and its significance
- ii Ṣalāh and its teachings
- iii Ṣawm and Zakāh
- iv Ḥajj and Jihād

5 Life of Muḥammad : twelve lessons :
- i The best example for mankind and the last prophet
- ii Birth, Childhood, Teenager and the battle of Fujjār and Ḥilful Fuḍūl
- iii Marriage and Search for the Truth, receiving the Truth
- iv Islamic Movement begins 'Alī's acceptance of Islam. 'Alī and the Dinner
- v The Prophet on Mount Ṣafā
  Hostility begins
  Emigration to Abyssinia
- vi 'Umar accepts Islam,
  Boycott and confinement,
  Year of sorrow
- vii Al-Mi'rāj and Hijrah
- viii Battle of Badr
- ix Battle of Uḥud
- x Battle of Aḥzāb
- xi Conquest of Makkah
- xii Farewell Address and Death

6 Islamic Personalities : two lessons :
- i Abū Bakr and 'Umar
- ii 'Uthmān and 'Alī

7 Economic and Political System of Islam : two lessons :
- i Economic System

ii Political System

Sixth Form

Total No. of lessons : 25

1 Islamic Way of Life : two lessons :
   i Islam is a complete code of life. The verse no. 3:19 of the Qur'ān and explanation
   ii Excellence and practicality of Islamic way of life for all ages
2 Basic Duties of Islam : three lessons :
   i Basic Beliefs of Tawḥīd, Risālah and Ākhirah and Shahādah
   ii 'Ibādah — the purpose of life — Ṣalāh, Ṣawm, Zakāh and Ḥajj
   iii Jihād, the end result of 'Ibādah
3 Prophet Muḥammad's (pbuh) Life : seven lessons :
   i a) The mission of the Prophet (61:9)
     b) The last Prophet
     c) The best example for mankind
   ii a) The beginning of Islamic Movement
     b) Hostility
     c) Hijrah
   iii a) First Islamic State at Madīnah
     b) Battle of Badr
   iv a) Battle of Uḥud
     b) Battle of Aḥzāb
   v Conquest of Makkah
   vi Farewell address
   vii a) Mission Accomplished
     b) Ideal way of life has been exemplified
4 Sharī'ah : two lessons :
   i a) Sharī'ah and its meaning
     b) Sources of Sharī'ah
   ii a) Six authentic Books of Aḥādīth
     b) Fiqh
5 Family Life in Islam : three lessons :
   i a) Basis of Social Life
     b) Marriage — Basis of Family

ii Rights of Women
iii Polygamy and Islam

6 Economic System of Life : two lessons :
i Islam and Economic System
ii Basic Features of Islamic Economic System

7 Political System of Islam : two lessons :
i Islam and Politics
ii Features of Islamic Political System

8 Quranic Quotations : two lessons :
i Basic Virtues of Life
ii Forbidden Matters

9 Selected Aḥādīth : two lessons :
i Basic Duties
ii Forbidden Matters

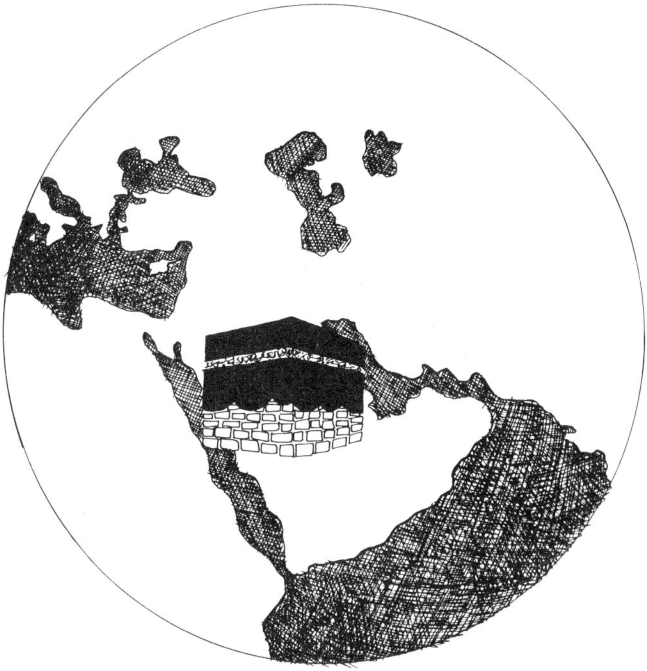

Select Bibliography

The Qur'ān

The Glorious Qur'ān	M. Marmaduke Pickthall, Karachi, 1973
Tafhīmul Qur'ān (Urdu)	Abul A'lā Mawdūdī, Lahore, 1976
In the Shade of the Qur'ān, Vol. 30	Sayyid Quṭb, Trans. A. Ṣalāḥī, A.A. Shamis, London, 1979
The Qur'ān : Basic Teachings	T.B. Irving, Khurshīd Aḥmad, Manazir, Aḥsan, Leicester, 1979
The Qur'ān and You	Muḥammad Manẓūr Nu'mānī, Lucknow, 1971
The Study of Al-Qur'ān	Al-Qur'ān Society, London, 1980-82
Qur'ān in the Classroom	A.D. Ajijola, Lahore, 1977
Glimpses of the Holy Qur'ān	Muḥammad Azīzullah, Maryland, 1963
The Message of the Qur'ān	S. Aṭhar Ḥusain, Lucknow, 1975
Lessons from the Stories of the Qur'ān	A.M. Rāja Muhājir, Lahore, 1973
The Qur'ān : Translation & Study	Jamilun Nisa Bint Rafai, London, 1984

Ḥadīth

Ṣaḥīḥ Al-Bukhāri	Muḥammad bin Ismā'īl al-Bukhāri, Trans. M. Muḥsin Khan, Madīnah, 1973
Saḥīḥ Muslim	Muslim bin al-Ḥajjāj, Trans. in Urdu : A. Raḥmān Ṣiddīqī, Karachi
Mishkāt Al-Maṣabīḥ	Ibn al-Farrā' al-Baghawī, Eng. Trans. : James Robson, Lahore, 1972
Forty Ḥadīth	Imām Nawawī, Damascus, 1976
The Book of Thousand Lights	S. Aṭhar Ḥusain, Lucknow, 1975
A Manual of Ḥadīth	Muḥammad 'Alī, Lahore
Introduction to Ḥadīth	A. Raḥmān I. Doi, Lagos, 1976
A Day with the Prophet	Aḥmad Von Denffer, Leicester, 1979

Sīrah

Ṭabqāt, Vol. I, V, VI (Urdu)	Muḥammad ibn Sa'd, Karachi, 1972
As-Sīratun Nabawiyyah (Arabic)	Ibn Hishām, Beirut, 1975
Tārikh, Vol. I (Urdu)	A. Raḥmān Ibn Khaldūn, Trans. Aḥmad Ḥusain Alahabadi, Karachi, 1972
The life of Muḥammad	Muḥammad Ḥusayn Haykal, Trans. Ismā'īl Al-Farūqī, Indiana, 1976
Muḥammad Rasūlullāh	Ḥamīdullāh, Hyderabad, 1974
The Benefactor of Humanity	Na'īm Ṣiddīqī, Trans. R.A. Hashmi, Lahore, 1974
The Life of Muḥammad	A. Ḥamīd Ṣiddīqī, Lahore, 1969
Sīratun Nabī, Vol. I (Urdu)	Shiblī Nu'mānī, Lahore
Qasasul 'Anbiā' (Arabic)	'Abdul Wahhāb Najjār, Cairo, 1966
Muḥammad : Aspects of his Biography	Ziauddīn Sardār, Leicester, 1978
Al-Fārūq	Shiblī Nu'mānī, Trans. Zafar 'Alī Khān, Lahore, 1970
Abū Bakr	Bahādur Yār Jang, Trans. Moinul Ḥaq, Lahore, 1975
The Glorious Caliphate	S. Aṭhar Ḥusain, Lucknow, 1974
Abū Bakr, 'Umar, 'Uthmān,	Fazal Aḥmad, Lahore, 1971-73
Muḥammad	Martin Lings, Cambridge, 1983.

'Alī, 'Ā'ishah — Fazal Aḥmad, Lahore, 1971-73
Introducing the Prophets — S. Shamīm Rāja, Lahore, 1975
Tales of the Prophets — A.H. 'Alī Nadwī, Trans. E.H. Nadwī, Lucknow, 1976
Maxims of 'Alī — J.A. Chapman, Lahore, 1973
Stories of Some of the Prophets, Vol. I & II — A.S. Hāshim, Maryland, 1976
Jesus : The Prophet of Islam — M. 'Aṭāur Raḥīm, London, 1979

Islam : General

Towards Understanding Islam — Abul A'lā Mawdūdī, Lahore, 1972
Introduction to Islam — Ḥamīdullāh, London, 1979
Islam in Focus — Hammūdah 'Abdal 'Aṭī, Kuwait, 1977
Islam : Its Meaning and Message — Edited by Khurshīd Aḥmad, London, 1976
Ideals and Realities of Islam — S.H. Naṣr, London, 1975
Islam : Belief, Legislation and Morals — Aḥmad Shalaby, Cairo, 1970
The Religion of Islam, Vol. I — Aḥmad A. Galwash, Doha, 1973
Ḥajj — 'Alī Shari'atī, Ohio, 1977
Fundamentals of Islam — Abul A'lā Mawdūdī, Lahore, 1978
Islamic Religious Knowledge, Vol. I & III — 'Abdur Rauf, Maryland, 1968
Islam : Faith and Practice — M.M. Aḥsan, Leicester, 1977
Islam at a glance — S.D. Iṣlāḥī, Lahore

Status of Women

Women in Islam — 'Ā'ishah Lemu, Fāṭimah Heeren, London, 1976
Family Life in Islam — Khurshīd Aḥmad, Leicester, 1974
Purdah and the Status of Women in Islam — Abul A'lā Mawdūdī, Trans. Al-Ash'ārī, Lahore,
Status of Women in Islam — Gamal A. Badawī, Indiana, 1976
Polygamy in Islam — Gamal A. Badawī, Indiana, 1976
The Family Structure in Islam — Hammūdah 'abd al 'aṭī, Philadelphia, 1977
Marriage in Islam — Dr. A. Rauf, New York, 1972

Islamic Law

Islamic Law and Constitution — Abul A'lā Mawdūdī, Lahore, 1969
Fiqhuz Zakāh — Yūsuf Qarḍāwī, Beirut, 1977
Islamic Law — Sa'īd Ramaḍān, London, 1970
Islamic Jurisprudence (Shafi'i's Risālah) — Majīd Khadduri, Baltimore, 1961
Usule Fiqh (Urdu) — Ḥabībur Raḥmān Ṣiddīqī, Karachi
Sharī'ah, the Way of Justice — Khurram Murād, Leicester, 1981
Sharī'ah, the Way to God — Khurram Murād, Leicester, 1981

Islamic Economics

Economic Problems of Man and Its Islamic Solution — Abul A'lā Mawdūdī, Lahore, 1970
Some Aspects of Islamic Economy — Nejātullāh Ṣiddīqī, Lahore, 1970
Islam and the Theory of Interest — Anwār Iqbāl Qureshī, Lahore, 1974
Social Justice in Islam — Sayyid Quṭb, New York, 1970
Insurance and Islamic Law — Muṣleḥuddīn, Lahore, 1969
Islamic Economics — M.A. Mannān, Lahore, 1975

Contemporary Aspects of Economic Thinking in Islam	N. American Trust Publications, 1976
Objectives of the Islamic Economic Order	M. 'Umar Chapra, Leicester, 1979
The Islamic Welfare State and Its Role in the Economy	M. 'Umar Chapra, Leicester, 1979
Economic Development in an Islamic Framework	Khurshīd Aḥmad, Leicester, 1979
Outlines of Islamic Economics	AMSS, Indiana, 1977
Islamic Economy	Dr. M. Kahf, Indiana, 1978
Studies in Islamic Economics	Edited by K. Aḥmad, Leicester, 1980
Muslim Economic Thinking	Nejātullāh Ṣiddīqī, Leicester, 1981

Books for Children and Young People

Islam for Younger People	Ghulam Sarwar, London, 1981
Third Primer of Islam	Muslim Educational Trust, London, 1978
Islam for Children	Aḥmad Von Denffer, Leicester, 1981
Children Book of Islam, Part I & II	Islamic Foundation, Leicester, 1979
Marvellous Stories from the Prophets Life	M.A. Tarantino, Leicester, 1982
A Great Friend of Children	Islamic Foundation, Leicester, 1981
Muslim Nursery Rhymes	M.Y. McDermott, Leicester, 1981
Love All Creatures	Islamic Foundation, Leicester, 1981
Islamic Quiz No. I-II	Dr. J.N. Ṣiddīqī, London, 1981
Muslim Cross Word Puzzles	Islamic Foundation, Leicester, 1981
The Prophets	S.A. Ashrāf, London, 1980
Elementary teachings of Islam	'Abdul 'Alīm Ṣiddīqī, London
The First Man on earth	Muslim Welfare House, London, 1979
Dawn of Islam	Muslim Welfare House, London, 1976

Miscellaneous

The Challenge of Islam	Edited by Alṭāf Gauhar, London, 1978
Islam and Alcoholism	Dr. M.B. Badrī, Indiana, 1978
The Bible, The Qur'ān and Science	Maurice Bucaille, Indiana, 1978
Adh-Dhabḥ	Dr. G.M. Khān, London, 1982
Muslims in Europe	S.M. Darsh, London, 1980
Islam in Britain	Zakī Badawī, London, 1981
Young Muslims in a Multi-Cultural Society	Muḥammad Anwār, Leicester, 1982
The Muslim Guide	M.Y. McDermott and M.M. Aḥsan, Leicester, 1980.

Reference

Encyclopaedia Britannica — Vol. XIX (Status of Women), 1979

The Encyclopaedia of Islam — London, 1927

Urdu Da'irah Ma'arifi Islamiyyah — Vol. VIII (Khadījah), Lahore, 1973
Vol. XV (Fāṭimah), Lahore, 1975
Vol. XI (Sharī'ah), Lahore, 1975

Muslim World Gazetteer — Karachi, 1975

Dictionary of Islam — T.P. Hughes, Lahore

Hidayah — Trans. Charles Hamilton, Lahore, 1963

Index

A

B

C

D

E

F

G

H

I

K

L

N

Q

R

S

T

U